ARMY at HOME

CIVIL WAR AMERICA

Gary W. Gallagher, editor

JUDITH GIESBERG

ARMY
at
HOME

WOMEN AND
THE CIVIL WAR
ON THE
NORTHERN
HOME FRONT

THE UNIVERSITY OF NORTH

CAROLINA PRESS

CHAPEL HILL

© 2009

The University of North Carolina Press

All rights reserved

Set in Bell

Manufactured in the United States of America

The paper in this book meets the guidelines for
permanence and durability of the Committee on
Production Guidelines for Book Longevity of the
Council on Library Resources.

The University of North Carolina Press has been a member
of the Green Press Initiative since 2003.

Library of Congress Cataloging-in-Publication Data

Giesberg, Judith Ann, 1966–

Army at home : women and the Civil War on the
northern home front / Judith Giesberg.

p. cm. — (Civil war America)

Includes bibliographical references and index.

ISBN 978-0-8078-3307-0 (cloth : alk. paper)

1. United States—History—Civil War, 1861–1865—
Women. 2. United States—History—Civil War, 1861–1865—
Social aspects. 3. Working class women—Northeastern States—
History—19th century. 4. Working class women—Northeastern
States—Social conditions—19th century. I. Title.

E628.G538 2009

973.7082—dc22

2009002898

13 12 11 10 09   5 4 3 2 1

CONTENTS

ILLUSTRATIONS

ACKNOWLEDGMENTS

Diego deserves more credit for helping me finish this book than he knows. "Are you done your book yet?" he asked when I met him and his brother, Pablo, after school each day. (In the Philadelphia suburbs, no self-respecting eleven-year-old—or nine-year-old, for that matter—says "done *with*.") And each morning, "Mom, finish your book today." The time between the morning directive and the afternoon inquiry seemed long enough to *him* that it just didn't make sense that it was taking *me* so long. But as any parent of young children will tell you, on a good day you will swear that the hours before three o'clock yielded only about ninety minutes worth of work, leaving you little choice but to work at night and just about every weekend. Even so, the two people who showed the least patience with this project—and who did their best to distract, interrupt, and derail—deserve thanks, at the very least for making me determined to answer, "Yes, I'm done my book." Thanks, Diego and Pablo, for making the school day seem so short and for filling the other days with snow tubing, boogie boarding, and all the other things that take me far away from my laptop.

I am fortunate to have generous colleagues—present and past. Charlene Mires and Paul Rosier read most of this book at the "chapter chats" we have had over the past two years. They pushed me to make the book more than the sum of its parts and are largely responsible for any progress I have made in that regard. Dora Dumont read the entire manuscript, helping me with big questions and small ones, and doing more than any friend should have been asked to do. Sanjay Joshi, Paul Steege, Jeffrey Johnson, and Marc Gallicchio read pieces and offered excellent advice. Advice that Adele Lindenmeyr and Seth Koven offered on my grant applications helped me focus my thinking early on in the project. I received generous help from Amy Spare and Bernadette DiPasquale at Villanova's Law School Library, and Nicole Garafano, who is a part-time graduate student and full-time events coordinator at the law school, provided well-timed assistance. I would also like to thank Villanova Law School colleagues Catherine Lanctot and David Bogen, whose interests parallel mine and whose support for this project was welcome. I owe a debt of gratitude to Joanne Quinn at Villanova's Falvey Library Interlibrary Loan Department for leaving no stone unturned. History Department graduate students Colleen Rafferty and Karen Sause helped track down references and organize them. Dana Kellogg Repash and Chris Filiberti provided critical support at the end. Thank you to Jennifer Pohlhaus of Villanova's UNIT and Michael Foight of Falvey Library for help with the images.

Welcome financial support came from the National Endowment for the Humanities, the Huntington Library, the Massachusetts Historical Society, the Pennsylvania Historical and Museum Commission, a Villanova University Summer Research Grant, and the Department of History. Villanova's Subventions Committee—Charles Zech, Catherine Kerrison, and John Johannes—came through with support for copyrights and image reproductions.

Thanks to Elizabeth (Liz) Varon, Andy Waskie (aka General George Meade), Nilgun Okur, Stephanie McCurry, and John Rumm for welcoming me into the scholarly Civil War community in Philadelphia. I hope Liz and Stephanie enjoy our coffee klatches as much as I do, even if we never get around to talking about our research. Matt Gallman read the manuscript, offered advice and encouragement, and continues to be more generous with his time and friendship than seems possible. Gabor Boritt's generosity, too, is legendary, and I have happily benefited from it these past few years. For sharing their knowledge of Philadelphia's streetcar battle, thank you to Dan Biddle and Murray Dubin, whose much-awaited biography of Octavius Cato will be an excellent addition to the history of the Civil War in Philadelphia. Thank you to James Wudarczyk for giving me a memorable tour of the former grounds of the Allegheny Arsenal. If it were not for his tireless work, this important site would have been forgotten long ago. I would like to thank Gary Gallagher for expressing an early interest in the manuscript and encouraging me to submit it to UNC Press for consideration. Thank you to David Perry and the anonymous readers for providing advice and criticism.

The Pennsylvania Historical and Museum Commission (PHMC) Archives are a treasure trove for any historian interested in learning about the Civil War on the northern home front. I would like to extend my deepest gratitude to Jonathan Stayer, Linda Ries, and Richard Saylor, who helped me to find many of the commission's hidden treasures. All three were— and continue to be—patient with my frequent questions and are always cheerfully ready to help me to cross-check my facts, in person and via the Internet. It was Linda who came to me one day and said, "Someday, someone needs to do something with these letters to Governor Curtin asking for money to retrieve bodies." That collection opened up a whole world for me as I tried to understand what it was like for women dealing with the loss of a soldier-relation. Linda Shopes at the PHMC and Rhonda Newton at the Pennsylvania Heritage Commission deserve thanks for helping me to think clearly about the questions I was asking early on. With cuts in state spending, everyone at the PHMC is doing the work of at least two people, yet they are always willing to help someone to whom they really owe nothing and who generally asks too many questions.

I would like to thank James Mundy, Tom Moran, Bruce Haynes, and the other members of the Union League of Philadelphia's Civil War Round Table for sharing their vast knowledge of the war and their enthusiasm for all related topics—along with scotch and cigars. Although I still haven't taken to the latter enthusiasms, I have benefited enormously from their good humor and hard questions. If I knew half as much about the Civil War as these guys do, this would have been a better book.

Beyond Pennsylvania, I received welcome assistance from the following archivists: Kristin Swett at Boston City Archives; Donna Wells at Boston Police Archives; Daniel Hogan, Elizabeth Bouvier, and Michael Haire at the Massachusetts Judicial Archives; Jim Owens at the National Archives and Records Administration, New England Branch, in Waltham, Massachusetts; Jimbo Burgess at Norfolk (Mass.) County Jail; Karen Abrahamson at Massachusetts Statehouse Special Collections; M'Lissa Kesterman at the Cincinnati Historical Society Library; Genevieve Troka at the California State Archives; and Miranda Schwartz at the New York Public Library.

Thanks to my sister-in-law Karen Fierros, who sometimes doubles as a research assistant and is always willing to pitch in with child care. Thank you, too, to my friend Lynn Parrucci for making a well-timed trip to Pittsburgh and taking along her digital camera. Kathy and Eric Pitochelli and Florence and Alan Reinerman put me up in their guest rooms and fed me on a number of research trips. My friends Dora Dumont, Sanjam Ahluwalia, and Jennifer Denetdale provided support and distraction and never fail to remind me of the importance of the work we all do.

And thanks to Ed, for being a friend and a partner in all things.

ARMY
at
HOME

A TRUE-HEARTED UNION WOMAN
Lydia Bixby's Civil War

If you go searching for Lydia Bixby, you will find very little. She left no diary, memoirs, or photographs. She filed a pension application once, and she sometimes appeared in city directories and in the census. Bixby died as a free patient at the Massachusetts General Hospital in October 1878 and was buried in a largely forgotten section of the Mt. Hope Cemetery in the Mattapan neighborhood of Boston.[1] In the cemetery office a large leather-bound register lists her name and the number of her grave. With some effort—and help from the groundskeeper—you can find where Lydia Bixby was buried. Her headstone is marked with the number 423. There are few other records of her existence, nothing to rescue her from what appears to have been a rather anonymous life and death. Except, of course, for that one famous letter.

It has been called the "most famous condolence letter," but mystery has shrouded many things about the letter President Lincoln wrote to Lydia Bixby during the U.S. Civil War. Scholars have argued about the authorship of the letter and its ultimate fate, but no one doubts that the emotions expressed in it are Lincoln's own.[2] Having heard that Lydia Bixby had lost five sons, Lincoln wrote to her to tender his sympathies and to offer her "the thanks of the Republic they died to save." In a few short words, the letter captured Lincoln's own experience of loss and his deeply troubled conscience over mounting battlefield casualties. Lincoln's words of comfort proved timeless. Historians revisited the letter in the aftermath of World Wars I and II. William Barton dedicated *A Beautiful Blunder*, his 1926 study of the Bixby letter, to "those who suffer most in war: the Wives and Mothers," and F. Lauriston Bullard turned to the letter during World War II.[3] Director Stephen Spielberg resurrected the letter again in his 1998 film *Saving Private Ryan*. Spielberg dedicated *Saving Private Ryan* to the aging survivors of "the last great war"; in the film, General George C. Marshall retrieves a copy of the letter from his desk and then recites it from memory as he prepares to issue orders sending a squad of young soldiers to rescue the last remaining son — the other three having been killed in action — of Mrs. Margaret Ryan. The original might have disappeared, but Lincoln's letter to the Widow Bixby lives on in the national memory. We turn to it to when we need to understand how military families cope with absence and loss and when we try to imagine how to repay them their sacrifices. At various times, Lydia Bixby's loss has stood as a surrogate for the nation's.

Like the famous letter, Lydia Bixby also disappeared. The widow and recipient of Lincoln's condolences does not appear in the Boston city directory in 1865, reappears in 1866, and then disappears again in 1868. Bixby lived in at least five different residences — mostly boardinghouses — from 1861 to 1865.[4] Her frequent moves reflected the reality of Bixby's marginalization — she moved from place to place to get better situations for herself and her younger children, but perhaps also to avoid landlords and bill collectors. As she slipped in and out of detection, she traced a route similar to many women during the war who pieced together a livelihood in the absence of soldier relations. We know very little about how working-class women like Bixby experienced the Civil War, the work they did, the adjustments they made to enlistment, and how they coped with the loss of husbands, sons, brothers. We know even less about marginal rural women and African American women whose experiences paralleled Bixby's. In the Civil War, there were few provisions made for soldiers' families, and what there was in the way of support emerged during the war and in the years afterward — first from private sources and then from state and finally federal programs. Without the support we have come to expect for the wives, parents, and children — and, now, husbands — of soldiers, family members pieced together a living from various sources and applied for private and public sources of aid to sustain themselves during the war.

Few women who applied for help during the Civil War had a story like Lydia Bixby's. That explains why Massachusetts state officials responded with such interest when she came to them with the names of her five dead sons. The state adjutant general, William Schouler, interviewed Bixby and then addressed a letter to Governor John Andrew, describing Bixby as "the best specimen of a true-hearted Union woman I have seen." Andrew immediately wrote a letter to Secretary of War Edwin Stanton, requesting a condolence letter from Lincoln, which the president wrote on November 21, 1864.[5] In his letter, President Lincoln famously apologized for addressing Lydia Bixby with his "weak and fruitless" words, and then

Lydia Bixby's grave, Mt. Hope Cemetery, Boston, Massachusetts. (Photo by Karen Fierros.)

he shared some very powerful words of sympathy. Lincoln prayed "that our Heavenly Father may assuage the anguish of your bereavement, and leave you only the cherished memory of the loved and lost, and the solemn pride that must be yours, to have laid so costly a sacrifice upon the altar of Freedom." With an eye to its significance, Schouler delivered the letter to Bixby in person, but first he gave copies to Boston newspapers. Appropriately, the papers published the letter the day after Thanksgiving. Having been visited personally by Adjutant General Schouler and received condolences from the president himself, Lydia Bixby enjoyed a brief period of celebrity when she was held up as a model of "true-hearted Union" womanhood and received donations of coal and food from local soldiers' aid societies. Then she fell out of public favor and disappeared. Thanks to Schouler, the letter—or at least the text of the original letter—did not.

Skepticism about Lydia Bixby began almost immediately and intensified in the aftermath of Lincoln's death. Perhaps it was the extent of her loss that raised suspicions, or simply the fact that she had asked for help. In response to an inquiry from Governor Andrew, Schouler asked Bixby to produce papers proving her sons' enlistments and provide him with the numbers of their regiments and companies.[6] These she produced, and Schouler sent them to Stanton. Yet even after Bixby was examined by state officials and the U.S. War Department, the elite women of Boston's soldiers' aid societies remained skeptical. Among those who initially came to Bixby's assistance, Sarah Wheelwright later remembered her as "a stout woman, more or less motherly looking, but with shifty eyes." Another one rumored that Bixby ran a brothel. After scrutinizing the widow carefully, these women judged her unworthy and expressed disbelief that the War Department allowed Lincoln's "precious words [to be] sent to this worthless woman."[7] In a memoir written after Lincoln's death, Wheelwright remembered that she and her peers had concluded that Bixby concocted a "convenient" story. Bixby's elite contemporaries found the widow's respectability lacking and questioned the magnanimity of the state in responding to a woman's public display of grief. Having decided that Lydia Bixby was a fake, they worked to sabotage her public image and shape the way Bixby was remembered.

Lydia Bixby's dubious contemporaries were followed by scholars who passionately defended the authenticity of Lincoln's sentiments even as they subjected Lydia Bixby to dispassionate inspection. Several generations of scholars have counted and recounted Bixby's sons to confirm how many actually died—versus those who may have deserted or were discharged—often repeating the disparaging rumors that circulated about Bixby's reputation.[8] In *A Beautiful Blunder*, Barton generously concluded that Bixby "may have found it to her advantage not to relate too small a story when soliciting aid from 'the churches and Christian women of Boston.' Widows were common, and women who had lost one son or two sons were not infrequent."[9] Although he confirmed that at least two—and quite possibly three—of Lydia Bixby's sons died on Civil War battlefields, Bullard was much less generous and decided that Bixby was simply a fraud.[10] More recently, in a 2006 *American Heritage* article entitled "As Bad as She Could Be," Lincoln scholar Harold Holzer repeated many of the rumors that Bixby's contemporaries told about the widow's reputation. But to Holzer, Bixby's greatest offense was not that she exaggerated her loss or misrepresented herself, or even that she may have been a Confederate sympathizer; it was "that she failed to preserve and profit from the one item that would have brought her fame and fortune—the priceless original copy in Lincoln's hand of the most famous condolence letter of the nineteenth century."[11] According to her granddaughter's recollections, Lydia Bixby destroyed the letter soon after Schouler delivered it.

Forgetting for a moment that in 1864 Lydia Bixby could not have known what the outcome of the war would be, nor could she have predicted Lincoln's death and subsequent martyrdom, scholarly treatments of Bixby continue to assume the worst about her, and by implication, any woman who would seek a public platform on which to enact private grief. If we assume, based on her subsequent treatment of the letter, that Lydia Bixby was not in search of condolences when she sought an interview with the adjutant general in November 1864, then we must begin by inquiring about her intentions. Why did Lydia Bixby, a widow some sixty years old, walk several miles from her home in a working-class, largely Irish neighborhood of Boston, up Beacon Hill past the homes of the city's elite, to the State House to call on the adjutant general with the names of five dead (she believed) sons in the first place? She, like so many other women she would have passed along the way, may have gone in search of state aid money or perhaps for help in retrieving the bodies of her dead sons. In addition to herself, Lydia Bixby was supporting a young son, perhaps one of her three daughters, and a grandson—the child of her son Oliver, who died at Petersburg. According to Massachusetts state law, Bixby qualified for twelve dollars a month in relief money earmarked for wives, children, or parents of soldiers.[12] Although inadequate to support herself and one or two dependents, state relief money helped fill the void left by absentee male wage earners, supplemented the money women earned working as domestics or by sewing uniforms, and helped women like Bixby pay for food, fuel, and rent. Before the war, her sons worked as shoemakers and helped their mother support their younger sibling(s). When the war began, Lydia Bixby's sons—Charles, Henry, Edward, Oliver, and George—enlisted and perhaps sent her part of their pay, but when they died or deserted, that money stopped arriving.

In the midst of her grief about the loss of her sons, Bixby faced pressing questions about her own survival and that of her remaining dependents. Tearing up Abraham Lincoln's letter of condolence might have been an expression of Lydia Bixby's politics—she may have resented the president, the war, emancipation—or it may have been symptomatic of her grief at the loss of her sons. Lincoln understood what modern scholars have forgotten: the inability of words to "assuage the anguish of bereavement" felt by widows, mothers, and fathers. If Bixby expressed her grief in part as anger when she tore up the letter, perhaps it was because she had hoped for a more tangible expression of the state's gratitude, in the form of a body to bury, money for a funeral, or an increase in state aid.

Although little else is known about her, Lydia Bixby's Civil War is a story about a woman making a living in the absence of men, her mobility and perhaps displacement, and it is about a woman engaging in the politics of everyday life. Whether intentionally or not, Lydia Bixby's interactions with the adjutant general contributed to an ongoing a conversation about a number of politically significant topics—the soundness of a northern war strategy that relied on a competition *between* states for military bragging rights, for Schouler surely had that in mind when he submitted Lincoln's letter to the papers; enlistment practices that lured away men who were their families' only support; and the increasing anonymity of U.S. Army soldiers, who could desert and be mistaken for dead, or vice versa, to name a few.

At various times and places—rural courthouses, city streets, wartime arsenals, and the public platforms and private spaces in which they grieved—women's movements intersected with those of public officials and gave them opportunities to register their thoughts about these topics and others relating to the administration of the war. Sometimes women intentionally chose sites in which to enact everyday politics—what I will call infrapolitics—such as when Carrie LeCount boarded a segregated Philadelphia streetcar; other times the opportunities came to them, when, for example, Lydia Bixby opened her door to find the state adjutant general on her doorstep holding a letter from the president. Women sometimes adopted disguises that made it possible for them to trespass into the high politics of war. Elizabeth Douglas explained her wartime prostitution by adopting a well-worn narrative of seduction and abandonment; Charlotte Brown wore a veil when she violated a segregation order on a San Francisco streetcar; Martha Yeager posed as a loyal seamstress when she met the president to talk about wages; Lydia Bixby "exaggerated" her loss in order to be heard by state authorities. Disguises may have helped African American, working-class, and marginal women in the North shield themselves from attacks on their respectability, credibility, and femininity, but this camouflage has made it difficult to recover their wartime stories in a narrative that has favored the war stories of middle-class white women—women who returned home from nursing or teaching to write extraordinary memoirs of uncommon adventures. *Army at Home* seeks to begin this recovery process by telling the stories of women like Lydia

Bixby who moved in and out of private and public spaces and who left few records along the way—women whose Civil Wars were no less extraordinary though they were more common. Few of these women interacted with the president—or anyone else in the Lincoln administration, for that matter—but as the war spilled over into the spaces of everyday life, they too found themselves caught up in it and tried to make meaning of it.

INTRODUCTION

In July 1862, facing a string of military setbacks, President Lincoln issued a call for 300,000 three-year volunteers to fill the depleted ranks of
the Union army. The call inspired Quaker abolitionist James S. Gibbons
to write "We are Coming Father Abraham," which became a popular recruiting song.[1] On the eve of a busy harvest season, Gibbons described
patriotic northern communities alive with activity, as men left ripe fields
and workshops and joined the ranks:

> If you look across the hilltops that meet the northern sky,
> Long moving lines of rising dust your vision may descry;
> And bayonets in the sunlight gleam, and bands brave music pour.

Written one year into the war, with the worst bloodshed ahead, Gibbons's
song expressed naïve notions about a genteel and treacherous South facing down a massive citizen army of willing and loyal northern men. The
orderly mustering of men in long lines with glistening bayonets ignored
the more coercive measures Lincoln was taking to fill the army ranks,
such as state-level quotas and the militia draft, and disguised the confusion and chaos many men found in regiments of new recruits. "You have
called us, and we're coming by Richmond's bloody tide, / To lay us down
for freedom's sake, our brothers' bones beside." Emphasizing patriotism
on the part of men, and stoicism on the part of their families, the poem
underplayed the fears recruits had about their own safety and the well-
being of their families:

> If you look up all our valleys where the growing harvests shine,
> You may see our sturdy farmer boys fast forming into line;
> And children from their mother's knees are pulling at the weeds,
> And learning how to reap and sow against their country's needs;
> And a farewell group stands weeping at every cottage door,
> We are coming, Father Abr'am, three hundred thousand more![2]

The manly willingness to die played well as patriotic gore, but it did not reflect soldiers' experiences. In wooden prose, "We Are Coming" portrayed soldiers and civilians united in purpose and young men engaged in synchronized and deliberate movement.

Nor did the poem's portrait of stoic mothers sacrificing their sons to the state attempt to capture the mixed emotions with which women responded to enlistment. In contrast to the striking movement of men, hundreds of thousands of them, in long orderly lines raising clouds of dust in their wake, women stand solemnly in abandoned fields or weeping in "cottage doors." Children crouch behind stationary mothers, where they are prevented from joining the marching men by the fixed knees that shelter them. Stuck behind their mothers—their attempts to join older brothers frustrated—young boys gamely do their part for the war and help with the harvest. Like the trees that line the hilltops or the winding stream, women are at the center of an image of home, frozen in time and place in a way that must have been comforting to those who left it behind. When the boys return, they hope all will be as they left it—their siblings a little older and still impatient, their mothers still standing bravely in the doorways, and themselves grown up but still their mothers' sons.

This book unsettles the wartime imagery of women standing still in anticipation of their sons' and husbands' return. It examines the ways in which working-class and marginal rural northern women moved in response to the nation's call for men—how they picked up the plows in the fields and the tools in the workshop, left home to find work or apply for aid, and traveled to urban hospitals and southern battlefields to retrieve loved ones. To do whatever was necessary to care for their families and for themselves, women—black, white, and immigrant—often with children in tow, moved in and out of focus, liminal bodies in an unsettled wartime landscape. Women altered the urban and rural landscapes of the wartime North when they showed up in small groups or in a steady stream in harvest fields, relief offices, and arsenal buildings and in the streets, streetcars, and railroad depots of cities. Women moved with reticence or with purpose into these spaces; once there they challenged the ways in which the war marked gender in both time and space. Though popular images sought to create a sense of distance between home and the war, women exposed that separation as largely imaginary when they fought with state officials over resources, engaged in war-making activities at arsenals, and turned rural communities and city streets into everyday sites of politics. With the war disrupting traditional politics and siphoning off state resources, women's activities on behalf of their families and themselves created alternative and unorthodox sites for political engagement.

As men mustered out, leaving for the Civil War battlefield, their marching steps marked the distance between home and war, between women and men, creating two distinct wartime geographies in the popular imagination. Marked as noncombatants, northern women (and children and elderly parents) stood at the center of an imaginary domestic geography safe from politics and protected from the ravages of war. Men inhabited the terrain of the battlefield, their whereabouts changing to reflect new threats and opportunities. The strangeness and itinerancy of the soldier's life convinced many young soldier-correspondents of the values of stability and domesticity. As the war dragged on and drew an ever-widening circle around men, however, these parameters were undermined when war pulled women into its business, enlisting them as protectors of home and makers of war. The departure of men sent women into motion, driving them from home to support their families or find husbands and sons that the war had taken. The demands of providing for families required women to range far and wide across the wartime landscape. Lydia Bixby registered a new address every year of the war and likely had more residences than the census reflects. By the end of the war, five of Bixby's sons had enlisted, two of them had died, and Lydia was still in motion, trying to sustain the rest of her family—and theirs—in their absence. As they moved into new spaces, or expanded to fill the void left in old ones, women redrew the lines that separated home from war and mapped an alternate wartime geography dictated by the material conditions of war rather than the ideological constraints of gender or the limitations of the middle-class imagination. This book examines this alternate wartime geography by considering the strategies women used to weather the war years and focusing on women facing different wartime challenges—managing their farms, working in munitions, collecting state aid money, adjusting to changes in their sewing work, locating and caring for injured or dead soldiers.

IN 1884, Elizabeth Cady Stanton declared that the Civil War had "created a revolution in woman herself, as important in its results as the changed condition of former slaves"; and, she added, "this silent influence is still busy."[3] A number of scholars followed Stanton's lead, producing studies that firmly established women's roles as nurses, supply agents, spies, and in some cases soldiers in the war and raised questions about how

Victorian understandings of gender underwent adjustment or redefinition, either temporarily or permanently.[4] Writing in the midst of postwar reaction to women's expanded roles, Stanton refused to admit that her middle-class white contemporaries were in retreat when she insisted that the war's influence was "still busy." Accordingly, recent scholarship has tied middle-class women's war work with their postwar leadership in the temperance movement, labor activism, and suffrage.[5] Other studies have rejected Stanton's sanguine conclusions, pointing to lackluster postwar interest in suffrage campaigning and the willingness of postwar women's groups to accept male leadership and support male prerogatives.[6] Because of this work, the Civil War is no longer off-limits to women's historians, and Dorothea Dix, Clara Barton, Mary Livermore, and Elizabeth Blackwell have now become part of that history.

While scholars of northern women have established that war was also women's work, their continued (almost exclusive) focus on the experiences of middle-class white women has offered them few opportunities to make comparisons with work done on southern women. Trapped in the narrative of northern victory, historians have struggled to define what women "won." Working-class, immigrant, and African American women are noticeably absent from this work, except as beneficiaries of middle-class white women's benevolence. Inasmuch as they linger outside history, these women remain the war's silent victims; conversely, there remains no appropriate place for "unruly women"—as Victoria Bynum has called southern women who disrupted the administration of the war—in a narrative that stresses unanimity of purpose among the northern public and assumes that the goal of all political expression was the same.

Southern historians were quicker to give up the debate about whether the war was liberating for women and to move on to questions about how the war was waged—and lost—on the home front. Drew Faust has shown how elite southern white women withdrew support for the war, aggravated already sagging military morale, and accelerated the internal collapse of the Confederacy when the collapse of slavery threatened to capsize southern gender relations.[7] Poor white women contributed to internal chaos in the Confederacy, Victoria Bynum found, when they hid and protected draft resisters, rioted for bread, and attacked businesses that withheld food and textile material from the needy wives of soldiers. In response, local officials came to recognize that the needs of the Confederate army clashed with the needs of southern families, and, in some cases, they decided that sacrificing the latter for the former came at too high a political and human cost.[8] Catherine Clinton, Leslie Schwalm, and Laura Edwards showed how enslaved women contributed to Confederate defeat when they escaped, committed acts of sabotage, and assisted Union troops.[9] Released from the compulsion to connect the war to an overall narrative of women's liberation, southern historians have found multiple origins and legacies of southern women's wartime politics.[10] For some time now, southern historians have offered models for historians interested in recreating the lives of working women in the North. Even so, the field remains, as Thavolia Glymph has described it, "the most racially gendered and regionally segregated historiographical space in U.S. history."[11]

One might assume from the literature that political behavior was the purview of white middle-class women in the North and that the politics of the streets—disruptive behavior and wartime protest—was unique to southern women, both black and white. This book challenges that assumption as it reaches deeper into northern society to uncover the lives of a broader spectrum of women and understand how they engaged in wartime politics. Though in most cases women were far removed from the seat of war, shortages of labor and of supplies, stagnant wages, and the high price of necessities brought the war home to the northern public. Taking their demands to government offices and to the streets, women revealed that the currents of war had not only carried off the men but brought politics into the various spaces of everyday life. The war would determine the success or failure of the Republican experiment in free labor nationalism, a belief in male economic independence and female dependence. Enlisted in that war in a number of ways, women forced their contemporaries to confront some of free labor's unanswered questions.

The boundaries between home and war were eroded as women made war and protested it. Local and federal officials responded in an ad hoc and irregular manner, but they ignored women's demands at their own peril. Civilians on the southern home front recorded the effects of this erosion early, and some tried, with little effect, to get state and federal officials to respond to new home-front realities. Observing the effects of food shortages, government contracting, and high prices on women and children in southern Mississippi in 1862, W. H. Hardy warned the governor of Mississippi that "another army besides that in the field must be supported—*the army at home*. . . . Their preservation and their comfort are as essential to our success as that of our Soldiers in the field."[12] It is a commonplace to link Confederate defeat, in part, to the South's inability to make adequate provision for its army at home—or in the field. But what of the North? To what extent were the federal government and state governments willing to provision this army? Or was it not so much the *will* but the words and movements of women that gave them little choice?

Methodology and Sources

This book explores the fragile barriers separating battlefield from home front, soldier from civilian. Historians resist comparisons between the Civil War and twentieth-century wars, but they generally agree that the seeds of modern warfare were sown in the mid-nineteenth century.[13] One of the hallmarks of modern or total war is the obliteration of the lines separating civilian from soldier. In his essay "Was the Civil War a Total War?" Mark Neely argues convincingly against the total war comparison, yet he characterizes as "fragile" the "barriers separating soldiers from civilians."[14] And even as Neely insists that both sides agreed to the rules, he admits that they both also violated them. As the war entered into its second, third, and fourth years, rules of engagement changed, and the lines separating soldier from civilian shifted. These shifts may indeed have been more tentative than they would be in later wars, but to ignore them as anomalous is to fail to understand how a generation of Americans made sense of them. By the end, the Civil War had moved into the spaces of everyday life, challenging the ways people experienced that space and moved about within it; the acceleration of new methods of mass production and transportation—and the expansion of the state apparatus necessary to support these changes—revised contemporary expectations for personal liberty and bodily integrity. Some of these changes were abrupt, violent even, others were imperceptible; many were temporary; and all produced new ground on which to reevaluate and reconstruct relations of gender and power.

This book examines the Civil War as a moment when antebellum experiences of space collapsed, and women produced spaces where they ceased being the object of war and became its subjects. These spaces where women lived and worked were both old and new, and in them women now came into more regular contact with the state, in the body of relief agents, draft officials, policemen. Reflecting on the thinking of the generation that came of age after World War I, French theorist Henri Lefebvre remarked that "around 1910 a certain space was shattered. It was the space of common sense, of knowledge, of social practice, of political power." According to Lefebvre, the "crucial moment" came in World War I, when the modern state emerged triumphant but also permanently disabled, for after a half century of imposing order through violence, the postwar state was forced to accept the permanence of disorder and transgression. Marginalized groups (for Lefebvre, the working class) resist by appropriating space—what Lefebvre refers to as "the production of space"—and using it to create new social relations.[15] *Army at Home* proceeds from the assumption that the U.S. Civil War was another such "crucial moment."

Seeking to claim these spaces, women wrote letters, signed petitions, and filed suit, or they expressed themselves nonverbally, by showing up, trading insults, throwing bricks, moving or refusing to move. In addition to the work of Lefebvre, the work of anthropologists Mary Douglas and James Scott is useful for understanding these kinds of expressions and for overcoming the limitations of sources that privilege written expression and male experience. Women found themselves in *new* spaces during the war, where their appearances did not go unnoticed or unremarked. Nonetheless, men's remarks often had less to do with the real dangers—and, as we shall see, there were real dangers—of allowing women into spaces inhabited solely by men than with expressing what Douglas described as societies' tendencies to condemn "any object or idea likely to confuse or contradict cherished classifications."[16] Women's bodies were seen as threatening because they signified rapid changes underway. In this case, when women came to work, refused to be laid off, or showed up at military camps, they initiated conversations that reflected—and reflected on —the larger economic and political context of the war. But women also engaged in politics in traditional spaces, such as in their homes or in the streets of their communities—technically *old* spaces. To analyze these confrontations, I rely on the work of James Scott, who argues that disfranchised groups commonly resort to everyday acts of resistance in order to survive, and that in these acts we can trace the outlines of an informal political culture, what Scott calls "infrapolitics."[17] The stage for this interaction was the urban street, where in overcrowded working-class and ethnic neighborhoods, women were a significant presence: watching over their children, visiting with relatives, and conducting the affairs of the household and the extended family. Here women confronted city officials, police officers, soldiers, and others in positions of authority; encoded in these regular confrontations with authority are what Scott calls "hidden transcripts" recording the interactions—sometimes peaceful, sometimes violent—between urban residents who wielded very little power and those who were powerful, between infrapolitics and mainstream politics.

Primary source materials for this project tend to be extensive rather than intensive, like those documenting the lives of middle-class women.[18] We still need many good local histories of the wartime North, a study of the effects of the transition to mechanized farming in the Midwest, a comprehensive history of industrial work, and many more histories that describe postwar recovery, family reconstruction, and adjusted expectations. While this book fills none of these voids, it attempts to move the research in these directions. The representativeness of the conclusions I draw, based on my consideration of women in rural and urban areas—primarily in Massachusetts and Pennsylvania but also in New York, San Francisco, and Washington, D.C.—is a question that I hope will elicit many more comparable studies.

Chapter Outline

The northern public—through words, music, and popular images—imagined women's wartime lives within particular spaces. Like the lives of the largely working-class and marginal women it analyzes, *Army at Home* does not move neatly through time or space. Instead each chapter considers a group of women out of those imagined spaces—rural women, munitions workers, displaced women, female protestors, and mourning widows. In each case I seek to understand how women—in their words and actions—experienced the war, how they cared for themselves and their families, and how they sought to give the war meaning.

Chapter 1 begins where Gibbons's poem leaves off—in the fields, where sturdy farmer boys left their plows, mothers, and younger siblings. By examining letters and relief applications from hundreds of rural Pennsylvania women and claims filed for the loss of property in the 1862 and 1863 Confederate invasions, Chapter 1 describes how women managed farms and rural families on their own and shows how they withdrew their support for the war when the integrity of their families was threatened by their husbands' continued service.

Examining case histories of over 1,000 women seeking shelter in two Massachusetts institutions, Chapter 2 shows how men's enlistment could displace their dependents, initiating dramatic patterns of wartime movement in which women and children left home to locate adequate means of support. In the process, displaced women came into conflict with city officials who tried to keep order and who believed—and, in some cases, rightly so—that women were simply working the system.

The movement of women described in Chapters 1 and 2 eroded the separation between home and war imagined in the popular songs of the era; in Chapter 3 women engage in the business of war making, traversing that border and erasing differences entirely. This chapter follows controversies surrounding the employment of women in the all-male space of munitions factory work. Despite care taken to prevent the destruction of wartime illusions of home, attempts to reimagine the separation between home and war were imperfect and incomplete, as women sought to tell their side of the story.

Chapter 4 considers how African American women made use of the opportunity of the war to move into segregated spaces and to begin conversations about civil rights on the northern home front. This chapter focuses on two campaigns to end streetcar segregation in which women played key roles: those in San Francisco and Philadelphia. White working-class and immigrant women also engaged in politics when they sought to protect the spaces of their communities and workplaces from change—in particular, enlistment, emancipation, and integration. These women are the subject of Chapter 5.

And finally, Chapter 6 follows women as they left their plows, workshops, and cottage doors to retrieve the bodies of dead soldier husbands and sons and to accompany them home for burial. To make these trips to southern battlefields, widows commanded state and federal resources and took their grief into public spaces, where their appearance stood as a sharp critique of the ways the war had objectified male bodies, as so many "bones beside."

The southern "army at home" has been well-memorialized. Northern women were not well commemorated and were memorialized almost exclusively as nurses. For a vast army of northern women, the war became part of their everyday lives; it entered the spaces where they lived and worked, where most made their peace with it but some did not. The Conclusion revisits some of the spaces in which women experienced this war and where they have been, like Lydia Bixby's grave number 423, for the most part, forgotten. The line separating battlefield from home front that had eroded during the war was redrawn in monuments remembering northern soldiers and resolute southern white women who managed to survive war's many disruptions of home and family. This book finds resolve and resistance among northern women—black and white, working-class and rural—for whom the war was also (mostly) an unwelcome guest but who nonetheless tried to shape the experience of it in their lives.

ONE

FROM HARVEST FIELD TO BATTLEFIELD
Rural Women and the War

Despite the withdrawal of a significant part of the agricultural labor force in the northern states during the Civil War, agricultural output remained high and employment in agriculture constant, suggesting that with men gone, women assumed more of the responsibility of running farms.[1] Isaac Newton, Lincoln's commissioner of agriculture, made special mention of the consistent productivity of American farms in his 1863 report. "Although the year just closed has been a year of war on the part of the republic over a wider field and on a grander scale than any recorded in history," Newton began his second annual report, "yet strange as it may appear, the great interests of agriculture have not materially suffered in the loyal States."[2] Attributing this great feat to "machinery and maturing youth at home and the increased influx of immigration from abroad," Newton made no reference to the part women had played in increasing the annual output of wheat, oats, and other products for which the Lincoln administration gathered statistics.[3] The report noted approvingly that some women had taken to raising bees—a work that Lincoln administration officials believed was particularly well suited for women and for disabled soldiers because the physical demands were light.[4] Otherwise, Lincoln's expert on agricultural affairs remained silent about women's farm work.

Traveling the countryside in a parallel path to Isaac Newton during the war, Mary Livermore, chair of the Chicago Branch of the United States Sanitary Commission, was also impressed with the work of the nation's farms, though so many men were gone. But unlike Newton, Livermore was not confused by this "strange" observation; she attributed U.S. agricultural productivity to the hard work of women in the nation's harvest fields. She welcomed women's farm work as evidence of a transformation underway in the lives of her fellow countrywomen. The war had opened up opportunities for women to do great work—for the soldiers and for their country. In her travels across the Midwest, Livermore remarked on what she believed to be "a great increase of women engaged in outdoor work, and especially during the times of planting, cultivating, and harvesting."[5] Livermore noted that, "women were in the field everywhere, driving the reapers, binding and shocking, and loading grain." Raised on Victorian virtues of domesticity, Livermore was shocked when she first saw women engaged in such strenuous work. Nonetheless, once she "observed how skillfully they drove the horses round and round the wheat-field," Livermore admitted that "they are worthy women, and deserve praise; their husbands are probably too poor to hire help, and, like the 'helpmeets' God designed them to be, they have girt themselves to this work." Intrigued by stout and sunburned Wisconsin farm women effortlessly guiding reapers as they cut swaths into the grain and stooped to gather the stalks into sheaves, Livermore stopped to talk with them about their work. The women spoke of the men off fighting the war and those who had died. "It came very hard to us to let the boys go, but we felt we'd no right to hinder 'em," Livermore recalled them saying. When asked about the physical demands of the work, the women and young girls provided an answer that Livermore found most satisfactory. "As long as the country can't get along without grain, nor the army fight without food" the women declared, with more than a little flourish, "we're serving the country just as much here in the harvest-field as our boys on the battle-field."[6]

Between the Lincoln administration's unwillingness to see women in the agricultural labor force and Mary Livermore's celebration of women's labor are the stories of women who experienced the war from rural communities throughout the North. Women like Elizabeth Schwalm, whom Livermore likely never met and who seems to have had very little in the way of "machinery" to lighten the labor at her Schuylkill County, Pennsylvania, farm—although she did have access to "youth," though hardly mature. Elizabeth interrupted a letter to her soldier husband, Samuel, detailing a long list of her work planting corn, oats, wheat, and many other crops intended for the family's consumption and for sale, with a plea for her husband's safe return. "I hope dat god is with youse and kepe yous alife dat you can [re]torn onst home," Elizabeth exclaimed.[7] Both working and overseeing the work of her children on her family's seventy-five-acre farm, Elizabeth Schwalm likely captured the wartime sentiments of many women on farms throughout the North. The daily press of the work left her little time to think about how her labor made possible the work of the nation, nor was she in a position to remark on what Isaac Newton saw as the industrialization of the harvest fields. Even with good health, productive land, and a family to help, the war strained Elizabeth Schwalm's resolve and her ability to keep up the farm while raising four young children on her own.

The extra work stretched Esther Jane Campman of Clearfield County, Pennsylvania, to her limits, too. "I have worked night and Day and ceep mi children together and I have touck sick and am on able to Do enething," Campman began a letter addressed to Pennsylvania governor Andrew Curtin late in April 1865. Facing a dire financial situation, Campman joined a chorus of wives of U.S. soldiers who addressed state officials requesting money to help support themselves and their families. Though the Campmans had anticipated that Esther's husband's U.S. Army wages would sustain his family in his absence, she had "not received a sent yet to ceep mi family on and he never has had eney pay yet." With Frederick Campman drafted and his labor abruptly withdrawn from the family's rural home, Esther worked to make up the difference. In the winter of 1865, after Frederick had been absent for eight months, Esther became ill and was forced to ask for help. "I truly hope you will Do something four me," she asked Governor Curtin.[8]

Having no family or friends to turn to, Campman applied to the county for relief money offered to the families of soldiers. Perhaps because the application came so late in the war or because it came from the wife of a drafted man, Campman's application for aid was denied. "I went to the commisherns and the[y] said the[y] woud not give me eney," Campman explained. To make matters worse, in April 1865, a time when many Americans were celebrating the end of the war and the imminent return of the soldiers, Esther Campman received a dated letter from her husband who was hospitalized at a military hospital at City Point, Virginia. With no recent word from Frederick, Esther feared the worst, "I have begun to think he is cilled but I dount [k]now." Having sustained herself and her children for eight months without her husband's labor or his wages, Esther could do so no longer. As long as she could work and her husband's return seemed imminent, Esther Campman had managed in Frederick's absence. But with his return home delayed indefinitely and with her own health failing, Campman became desperate.

Historians estimate that half of all soldiers in the U.S. Army were farmers or farm laborers and an estimated 30 percent of all soldiers were married.[9] A number of northern women experienced the war as a withdrawal of labor from their farms and their rural communities. The enlistment or drafting of a husband necessitated that rural soldiers' wives like Elizabeth

Schwalm and Esther Campman do more than offer support for a husband's decision to enlist or his willingness to go when called up. When a husband left for the war, women faced an altered set of domestic circumstances. With or without the help of new machinery or immigrant labor, woman's work on the farm expanded to fill the void. Their letters suggest that women in rural communities were in constant motion, doubling up the work of caring for children with taking over work on the farm. Seeking to cover the space left by men, women seemed to accelerate, as if by doing so they might also hurry the men home. Middle-class observers such as Mary Livermore suspected that the war opened up a space in which gender would be renegotiated and family relations reconstituted, for she saw women's farm labor as the beginning of the end of domesticity. Livermore suspected that a deep-seated patriotism informed women's decisions to take up the "unusual" work of the harvest and concluded that "each brown, hard-handed, toiling woman was a heroine."[10]

Livermore's conclusion was consistent with that of other middle-class northern women who saw in the war multiple opportunities to expand their reform work and become engaged in the great political and social debates of the day. After the war, some parlayed their wartime work as relief agents, nurses, and teachers of the freedwomen and men into postwar careers in temperance, suffrage, and urban reform. As they did, middle-class war workers like Livermore created new spaces for women, subtly renegotiating lines of authority within their households and working to do so in the society at large. With the collapse of slavery and the withdrawal of men, southern women renegotiated lines of domestic authority during the war, as well. After the war, southern families had to be reconstructed to account for the loss of husbands and sons and property. Elite slaveholding women rose to the occasion brought on by the war and worked in place of white men and slaves on southern plantations—experiences that left more than a few women questioning the infallibility of men. But whereas the war challenged assumptions about women's dependence, elite white women, as Drew Faust has argued, "came to regard the rehabilitation of patriarchy as a bargain they were compelled to accept" in order to retain their class and racial superiority.[11] Freedwomen and -men weathered the war's disruptions by making use of "a wide range of flexible and fluid household structures," as Nancy Bercaw found in communities in the Mississippi Delta.[12] To make ends meet, African American women and men negotiated a variety of domestic relationships—some patriarchal, others not—based on a recognition of their mutual dependency.[13]

But what of the domestic adjustments required of rural northern women? This chapter extends the analyses of freedwomen and southern white women to the North, examining how Pennsylvania farm women with absentee husbands, fathers, and brothers took care of their families and managed farms; the strategies they deployed to make up for the temporary loss of farm labor; and the consequences to families of an extended or permanent loss of landowners and male labor. Despite the social distance that separated her from Esther Jane Campman and Elizabeth Schwalm, Mary Livermore's observations raise several questions about rural women's wartime work. How were work allocations within rural families renegotiated when men enlisted or were drafted? What happened when the work became too much, the harvest too little, or when family and neighbors would not help? Were relations between rural women and men changed by the war? How were families reconstituted in the postwar era, and which, if any, of these experiences cut across regional lines? Evidence documenting the lives of rural women during the Civil War is fragmentary, but these fragments offer a glimpse at the spaces rural women inhabited during the war — the wheat fields where Livermore caught up with them and the homes where women waited but rarely stood still.

While not short on enthusiasm for a war to suppress rebellion, rural women and women living closer to the margins of antebellum northern society experienced the absence of male labor as a family crisis. Farm families hoped to keep one adult male at home to help with the heavy work of running the farm. Samuel Schwalm, for example, arranged to have his brother, Peter, help Elizabeth manage the farm. The U.S. Army allowed no occupational exemptions to the draft, and the lure of bounties and salaries worked against families trying to keep young men at home. Without the option of taking furloughs to coincide with harvests and other seasonally heavy work, soldiers left farm labor to their wives, children, extended family, and elderly parents. With news and money from their soldier husbands not forthcoming, women worked, inquired about their husbands' bounty money, and applied for local relief to soldiers' families. Wherever possible, women sought help from family and friends while they awaited their husbands' wages or their return. Some managed disrupted family life with considerable success, like Elizabeth Schwalm, who managed to plant, harvest, and send to market the family's crops. Many others waged a home-front war of survival that was common in the wartime South, where state officials were forced to respond to women and families on the brink of destruction. In the North, when sources of support failed them, women and families applied for outdoor relief or went in search of temporary shelter at a number of institutions—a fate that Esther Jane Campman feared and many other women experienced. Theirs is a different perspective of life on the northern home front during the war—one not as stable and stoic as Livermore would have liked nor as mechanized and male as Newton imagined. Livermore saw a rural wartime landscape alive with women's movement—women were driving, binding, loading—and indeed it was; but as women moved, they rarely traced paths that were as predictable or uninterrupted as the rows of wheat and corn in their fields.

"Brown-handed heroines": Women's Farm Labor

Mary Livermore's celebration of the central place women's agricultural labor played in the Union war effort was influenced by her own personal transformation. Before the war, Livermore lived a life of conventional domesticity; as a wife and mother of three children, she had had no public career. Working for the United States Sanitary Commission during the war, Livermore discovered her affinity for a life of public activism, began a long career of suffrage and labor activism, and learned that she could support herself and her family in the process. Livermore's story is parallel to those of other middle-class contemporaries who found in the absence of men an opportunity to create new spaces for women in public life, although few would stay there permanently, as Livermore did. Many found the experience to be invigorating and sought ways to turn their wartime work into a blueprint for women's greater independence and for a collective rethinking of women's political passivity and domestic seclusion.[14] Livermore recognized in the unusual image of women working on the large, commercial farms of the Midwest proof of the transformative moment of war and the potential for women's work. For Mary Livermore, farm women were not just harvesting the crops necessary to feed the massive army in the field, they were planting the seeds of women's equality.

With family money and a husband's wages to rely on, Mary Livermore's wartime experiences were far removed from the women on whom she heaped such praise and placed such high expectations. Nonetheless, Livermore's relief work put her in regular contact with women who struggled in their husbands' absence, for many of these women turned up at her Chicago relief society office with stories not unlike Campman's or Schwalm's. The women described here lived in a variety of rural communities—some on family-run farms located some distance from their closest neighbors; some in closer settled communities, like the women living in and around Gettysburg, Pennsylvania; still others seem to have been newcomers in less-settled communities in which they worked and rented land but had no close ties. It seems unlikely that many of these correspondents lived on the large commercial farms that Mary Livermore observed in the Midwest. With seventy-five acres of property, the Schwalms produced crops for consumption and for sale, but a farm of this size depended on a family's ability to hire seasonal laborers. With the U.S. Army promising bounty money and a regular salary, however, farmers had difficulty finding men to hire. Indeed, Elizabeth Schwalm was unable to find a man to help her work on the family's farm when Samuel enlisted and worried that she could not afford one in any case. Judging by remarks made in their letters about back taxes and rents, some women lived on land that they rented, and others were only nominal owners of their property and the equipment they used to work it. Some men were farm laborers who worked on neighboring farms for wages; others worked as shoemakers, coal miners, in iron making, and at other skilled, semiskilled, and unskilled trades. Wives of farmers and tradesmen worked both in and outside their homes at a variety of paid and unpaid positions to supplement seasonal work on the farm or the wages of laborers.

Pennsylvania women were part of families engaged in a variety of occupations. While Pennsylvania boasted strong manufacturing output—particularly textiles, leather, iron, and coal—the state was predominantly rural in 1860.[15] Large pockets of Irish immigrants lived and worked in the mining regions of central Pennsylvania—Carbon, Schuylkill, and Luzerne Counties—and German, Scots-Irish, and free black farmers working land in southeastern counties such as Chester and Lancaster. Farm families produced a variety of products for consumption and for transportation to Philadelphia and cities south of the Mason-Dixon line, including a variety of grains, flax, and dairy products.[16] Women were extensively engaged in what historians refer to as "household commodity production," in which they sold agricultural products for cash, allowing farm families to pay mortgages and taxes, invest in new farm tools, and purchase livestock.[17] Not particularly bound by urban bourgeois notions of domesticity, Pennsylvania farm women did not likely welcome the war as an opportunity to transcend them. More likely, the war threatened to upset a careful domestic balance that allowed rural women both to meet their families' needs and to engage in commodity production.

Samuel and Elizabeth Schwalm before the war. (From Johannes Schwalm Historical Association, *Johannes Schwalm, the Hessian,* courtesy of the Johannes Schwalm Historical Association, Inc.)

"I am to[o] long from home": Working Farms without Men

Letters rural women exchanged with their husbands at the front paint a different picture of women's wartime agricultural labor. Women reported on the status of crops and the purchase and sale of farm animals and complained about the difficulty of finding and keeping adequate hired help. They spoke of the extensive and physically demanding work they performed. And, rather than finding the work rejuvenating or heroically linking it to the objectives of the war, women filled their letters with evidence of the emotional and physical stress resulting from the prolonged absence of their soldier husbands. Women sought advice from their husbands on planting and harvesting, but, when responses were misdirected or delayed, women often resorted to seeking approval for the decisions they had already made.

Before the war, work allocations in the Schwalm household were probably similar to those found in other rural homes, where there was no absolute division of labor and a considerable degree of flexibility. With greater flexibility in their roles, rural women rejected domesticity and enjoyed more egalitarian marriages and greater autonomy, historians such as Nancy Grey Osterud and Joan Jenson have argued.[18] Whereas men were largely responsible for plowing and planting the fields and women processed and preserved the products for the family's consumption and for sale, women's outdoor labor was essential during the harvest season. Like most rural women, Elizabeth Schwalm was no stranger to field labor, but when her husband left, planting and tending the fields, caring for the livestock, and harvesting the crops required that Elizabeth take considerable time away from her other tasks — such as childcare and commodity production — and here she could not turn to Samuel for guidance. Early in the war, Elizabeth attempted to follow Samuel's advice on planting the next season's crops because she had worked those fields before and understood which plots of land were best for planting potatoes, corn, and wheat. Occasionally, Elizabeth sought Samuel's advice on the uses of oxen, horses, and cows, but she also seems to have relied on her own judgment about caring for and disposing of farm animals.

When her husband enlisted on August 19, 1861, Elizabeth Schwalm had four children at home under the age of five, and three weeks after Samuel left, she gave birth to a third son. With four toddlers at home and a newborn to care for, surely Elizabeth was relieved when Samuel arranged to have his brother, Peter, come to stay with her and the children. Peter's help was essential for Elizabeth in those first few months, for Samuel left home in the middle of the busy harvest. By January, in fact, several Schwalm relatives and friends were helping Elizabeth, for Samuel addressed his planting instructions to all of them. "My dear wife and children and Brothers and Sisters," he began.[19] Well before the first spring planting season arrived, Samuel provided a list of instructions that assumed Elizabeth's past participation in spring planting and her knowledge of many aspects of running the farm. "Further you ask me where you Shall put the Lime," Samuel began, and continued: "I want that field behind the Barn for potatoes and that field where we (illeg.) that Little Strip potatoes Last year for Corn and there I want the Lime and if you hall any more ten you Shall put it were we had Corn Last year and try to Sprt the Lime were yous put the Corn before you plough the field and if you can hal Lime after the potatoes is planted So you Shall put it on the potatoes."[20] What looks like a jumbled list of instructions probably made perfect sense to Elizabeth, who had lived and worked the farm alongside Samuel for more than five years. By March of 1862, Samuel's arrangement with his brother was breaking down, and that summer Peter left. Though Samuel's relatives living nearby surely continued to help out, Elizabeth largely assumed responsibility for running the farm. "I wasent pleased when I have heard that youse juden [you'd] agree," Samuel commented on his brother's departure. But he agreed with his wife when she assured him that she was better off on her own. "I hop you can take good care of it," he offered.[21]

To manage the farm, Elizabeth relied on a number of different sources of labor, but chiefly her own and that of her children. The children helped their mother clean out the stables, care for the livestock, and bring in the grain harvest. Whereas Samuel expected that Elizabeth was capable of doing heavy work, he did not approve of his children engaging in such labor. "Take good care of the Childrens and don't Let them do hard work," he chastened his wife, for "I Sooner like to hear that you sent them every day in school[.] I don't like to have them Cripeld up by hard working."[22] On these occasions and on others, Elizabeth and Samuel disagreed over the family's finances. Elizabeth was very careful not to spend, and Samuel always encouraged her to hire a "girl" to take care of the children and to buy the children things. Samuel wanted Elizabeth to dress his children well and send them to school, but Elizabeth insisted that she could not spare them on the farm and that there would be time for school later. It was difficult to hire a "farmer," a term that Elizabeth reserved for hired help, but when she could, she did. When Elizabeth managed to do so in August 1864, she was at pains to justify his pay of "14 Dolers fur a munth." "I thinke noboty cant do it lore by dis time fur to worke on the state rote a man get 2 Dolers fur a day," Elizabeth explained to her husband fighting at the front.[23] With prices so high during the war, Elizabeth asked Samuel repeatedly for money, and on one occasion, Samuel became frustrated and replied, "I have Sant you all the money I posable can Spair I don't think that you want me to Sant my Clothsing and go naced."[24] Elizabeth stretched the family's budget to pay the taxes and buy what was necessary for the family, but even with all her care, the sheriff came to the Schwalm home and threatened to sell off some of the family's property when she fell behind in her payments.[25]

Nearly three years after Samuel's enlistment, Elizabeth asked fewer questions of her husband but continued to report dutifully to him about her work on the family's farm. In April 1864, Elizabeth reported that she had successfully planted oats and had sowed more corn and fewer potatoes than the year before, based on her experience the previous summer. In addition to completing the spring planting, Elizabeth weaned the couple's youngest child, Reilly, now twenty-eight months. "He was to druble-som or els I hat live him drink til you hat bean at home," she explained.[26] Elizabeth offered her husband an explanation for her decision to wean their son, but she made the decision based on what she had determined served the best interests of both the household and the family farm. One of Mary Livermore's "brown-handed heroines" had proudly reported that she could reap as much as any man, even though she had a three-year-old son "toddling beside her, tumbling among the sheaves, getting into mischief every five minutes, and 'causing more plague than profit.'"[27] Weaning Reilly allowed Elizabeth Schwalm to leave him to the care of his older sisters and brothers and freed her to more easily complete the work on the farm without a toddler getting under foot. And at the end of a long day of work, Elizabeth could look forward to a full night of sleep, rather than one interrupted by breastfeeding.

Adjusting the outlay of the farm, the planting and harvesting of crops, and the family's childrearing expectations were all decisions Elizabeth made on her own. She continued to seek her husband's approval, and Samuel responded in the only way he could—by deferring to her judgment. "You shall do as you think right," he wrote, often adding in the last months of his absence, "I cant say much I am to long from home."[28] Three years into the war, Elizabeth sought very little advice, and Samuel, having been absent from the farm for several years, was reluctant to offer her any—even abandoning his persistent pleading with Elizabeth about sending the children to school and sparing them of work. Instead, Samuel encouraged Elizabeth to "just do how you think."

In the absence of alternative sources of labor, women's flexibility allowed farms to remain productive during the war, but not all rural soldiers' wives welcomed these reallocations of work. Perhaps Elizabeth sold milk, eggs, or butter to help pay for clothes for the children and household supplies, but once Samuel, and then Peter, left, she surely found less time for this commodity production—leaving her little money to buy shoes for the older children to attend school and to pay taxes and other bills. Despite adjusting to her husband's absence, the strains of the work and responsibility took their toll on Elizabeth. She accused her husband of failing to write and expressed concern about unpaid tax bills and other financial matters. Schwalm never imagined she would be on her own this long, and she wanted her husband home. In August 1864, Elizabeth wrote to Samuel, "I never had saut dat we wot be so a lange launge time a parte form enoter."[29] Samuel agreed, hinting that Elizabeth might assist him in seeking his discharge. "I don't Like to Stay any longer then I have to," he wrote.[30]

While she understood that her husband was serving the country by putting down the rebellion, Elizabeth, unlike Livermore's Wisconsin farm women, never described *her* work in those terms. Though Elizabeth was privy to information about the Confederate invasions of south-central Pennsylvania in the fall of 1862 and the summer of 1863, she did not discuss these matters in her correspondence. She seems to have scanned her husband's descriptions of battles and conditions in camp quickly, in search of information about his return. For Elizabeth Schwalm the war began when Samuel left the family farm, and she experienced the years of his absence in a deeply personal way. Raising her young children in rural Pennsylvania without her husband's company and without his help, Elizabeth managed the many demands placed on her time and her emotions by expanding to fill the empty spaces created in his absence. Women made adjustments within their families and on their farms when men enlisted, hoping that extended family would help with the work or that wages sent home from soldiers would allow them to hire replacement help. But informal agreements within families to make up for the loss of a soldier husband's or son's labor broke down, leaving women to pick up where the men left off.[31] As for Esther Jane Campman, the war had meant greater work and worry for Elizabeth Schwalm, and the sooner the men returned and reassumed their share of the work, the better.

More than necessitate that Elizabeth acquire new skills or new knowledge about the farm, Samuel's departure meant that Elizabeth had more work than usual and required her to rethink how she allocated her time and energy. In rural families that depended on women's ability to produce goods for the market, the war disrupted the balance that women like Elizabeth Schwalm had struck between commodity production, childcare, and fieldwork. Women shifted their daily work allotments, perhaps moving children into work sooner or leaving some things undone. Elizabeth clung to antebellum patterns of mutual dependency as long as she could—until her husband's extended absence necessitated that she restructure the lines of authority and economy within the household. Whereas Pennsylvania law did not recognize her as capable of making decisions about the couple's property, for more than three years, Elizabeth made uncontested decisions about which bills to pay and which to accumulate. But if Elizabeth's ability to move in and out of domesticity translated into greater autonomy in her marriage with Samuel, she did not relish his wartime absence as an opportunity to exercise it.

Women and Kinship Ties

We cannot know how much Elizabeth Schwalm continued to rely on her family for support in the three years after her brother-in-law left and before her husband returned. Schwalm's letters suggest that when the war took away male relatives, rural women relied heavily on kinship networks and on neighborly relations for help in the fields and with the livestock. Women living in close-knit rural communities were not entirely alone when their husbands enlisted. Anecdotal evidence in depositions taken after the Confederate army's invasion of Gettysburg, Pennsylvania, in June–July 1863 confirms what historian Mary Grey Osterud found for the women of Nanticoke Valley, New York.[32] In stable rural communities such as those in south central Pennsylvania, women benefited from close connections to and intermarriage among neighbors. Women could rely on neighbors for help and labor when husbands enlisted or were drafted because of the strong relationships of mutuality they developed. Kinship connections ran deep in south central Pennsylvania, with married children living close to their parents.[33] Overlapping community connections assured that women did not experience the absence of soldier husbands as an immediate threat to their families' survival.

When the Confederate army descended upon the rich York Valley of Pennsylvania in June 1863, soldiers were overwhelmed by the lush pastures they saw and what seemed to be never-ending fields of ripe corn, wheat, and oats.[34] Hungry southern soldiers helped themselves to the bounty.[35] Among those who suffered losses at the hands of the foraging soldiers were women tending to farms while their husbands and sons served in the army. With the withdrawal of male labor from the community, the women of Gettysburg and the surrounding countryside looked to densely overlapping kinship networks and neighborly cooperation to fill the void. In depositions gathered in Adams County documenting individual losses incurred during the invasion, women described the informal network of cooperation that had evolved during the war. Women fending off marauding soldiers called on the help of brothers, sisters, parents, and in-laws living nearby—family and friends who cared for their horses, looked over their livestock, and took an interest in the status of the crops in their fields. While John Musselman was off exercising the horses belonging to his neighbor, Elizabeth Musser, he was overtaken by rebel cavalry who intercepted him on the way to the mill and took Musser's horses. When Eliza Hill's cow turned up missing, James Bowling confirmed that

Confederate soldiers were responsible. In support of her damages claim, Bowling explained, "I went down twice a day to see after the cattle." But when he came to Hill's place on July 5, the place was overrun by soldiers and the cow was gone.[36]

Disaster struck these women twice—once when their husbands enlisted or were drafted, leaving them to manage farms and households, and once when Confederate soldiers trampled their crops, seized their cows, and forced them out of their homes. Whereas women relied on neighbors for help managing the everyday work involved with caring for livestock and horses and perhaps helping with the harvest, recovering from an invasion of this magnitude placed unusual strains on those relations of reciprocity. Plowing and planting a trampled field, repairing damaged fences, and redigging a spoiled well was heavy and involved work requiring a considerable commitment of time and the labor of experienced farmhands. Replacing lost livestock or missing farm tools required a significant outlay of cash. For these reasons, York Valley women continued to rely on nearby kin and long-established networks of neighborly cooperation to sustain them until the extra work could be done.

But they also sought damages from the state. On at least two occasions —in 1868 and again in 1870—Adams County widows filed claims against the property they lost—fields of grain trampled and livestock stolen. Unlike Elizabeth Schwalm, Pennsylvania's war widows were left with a number of postwar challenges to their livelihood.

Rural Women and Wartime Isolation

Not all rural women could count on family, friends, or neighbors to help when the Civil War took away their husbands and left them to work small farms on their own. Rural women living more marginal existences and in less-settled communities were particularly vulnerable to illness and deprivation when their husbands enlisted or were drafted. Like Esther Jane Campman, they worked hard to support their families and to keep them together, but without the safety net provided by a sizable and productive farm or neighborly cooperation a husband's absence could have tragic consequences. Living lives marked by rural isolation, these women appear in the record of the war when they had exhausted all sources of work and when their health or that of their children gave out. Then women applied to local wartime relief societies for small sums of money offered to the wives and mothers of soldiers.

State and local relief varied widely throughout the North during the war. States such as Massachusetts and New Hampshire encouraged enlistment by offering advance payments on bounties and aid to soldiers' families. In contrast, Pennsylvania left the sustenance of wives and families of soldiers to local relief agencies or to overseers of the poor. City and county relief societies offering support to families of soldiers were privately funded and run by middle-class relief board members. Not all local societies extended aid to the families of drafted soldiers. Women applying for relief had to provide proof of their marriage to a soldier and that the county in question had received credit for his service. In Bucks County, Pennsylvania, the Relief Board ruled on the applications of more than 300 women each month who sought payments of $0.50 to $2.50 per week to help support themselves and their children while their husbands and sons were away. To qualify for relief, women had to be residents and their husbands taxpayers.[37] In both Bucks and Mifflin Counties, suspicious relief board members demanded that needy wives of Pennsylvania soldiers take an oath swearing that they had no other means of support before receiving aid, and members regularly denied relief to women who failed to live up to their standards of respectability.[38]

Once a soldier's wife qualified for relief payments, her behavior was carefully scrutinized by the board. Women were summarily cut from the rolls when their husbands deserted, were discharged, or died; when they claimed more children than they had; or when, as in the case of Mary Kinsey, wife of William, and Elmira Pfrender, wife of Joseph, the Bucks County Relief Board found a woman to be "not acting as a virtuous wife should do."[39] Marginal women living a hardscrabble existence in rural Pennsylvania surely found it difficult to provide proof of their marriages and to live up to relief board members' standards of propriety. Arrangements made for a family's survival—hiring children out to work or taking in boarders—raised the suspicions of neighbors and middle-class relief board members. As in the wartime South, rural Pennsylvania women made use of fluid family structures in the absence of men—combining residences, living with kin, or hiring themselves and their children out to neighbors to make ends meet. While these households allowed women to maximize their meager financial resources, such practices clashed with the bourgeois expectations of relief board agents.

Rural women who relied on the wages provided by their husbands' seasonal farm labor had to live off of small plots of land and to find whatever work there might be available in their communities. Women took in laundry, boarders, or sewing; collected debts and favors from friends and employers; and performed tasks for neighbors. Despite their efforts, rural women's letters and their applications for relief tell the stories of women whose meager resources were stretched to their limits in the absence of male support and whose efforts to support their families failed. When Maria Thomas's husband, Henry, a coal miner in Blair County, Pennsylvania, was drafted in December 1864, Maria's situation quickly deteriorated. Without Henry, Maria Thomas applied for relief from a local aid society, but she only received a few dollars to support herself and her children over the winter. When she wrote the governor in April 1865, she sought additional relief. "My little Children is naked and I am very near naked," Thomas explained.[40] On January 3, 1865, Rebecca Snook applied for relief in Mifflin County after her husband was drafted.[41] With children ages fifteen, eleven, nine, seven, five, three, and one, Snook explained to relief board members that she would have to buy her own bread because, she admitted, the couple's "crops the past season were a failure." Lavina Rheam was awarded a pension from Mifflin County when her husband was drafted, leaving her with three children under the age of six living on a ten-acre farm that the couple did not own. For Rheam and for others, falling behind on rent could result in eviction.[42] Elizabeth Schwalm had fallen behind on her taxes and suffered a humiliating visit from the sheriff, but she never expressed the worry that she and her children would be turned out of their home as a result of Samuel's enlistment. Mifflin County board members awarded pensions to Sarah Kile and Martha Ann Beacer when their husbands were drafted, leaving each with two small children to feed on farms that relief agents described as "unproductive."[43]

Unlike Schwalm, whose husband left her with an extensive and working farm and extended family to turn to if she needed them, women like Thomas, Snook, Rheam, Kile, and Beacer had few resources at their disposal when their husband's labor and his wages were abruptly withdrawn. Sometimes, adhering to the middle-class expectations of the relief boards came at a tragically high cost, as in the case of Rachel Darsak, wife of Moses. In the process of applying for aid in Bucks County, Rachel and the younger of her two small children died. In their mercy, the board voted to award the remaining Darsak child a weekly pension of $0.50.[44] Board members ordered Martha Murray, wife of Mahlor, struck from the rolls when her husband deserted. With no soldier salary to count on and no local relief forthcoming, Martha and her children checked themselves into the Bucks County Almshouse.[45]

When women sought aid from state officials, they came in search of money they felt rightly theirs. Despite their desperate situations, women understood relief as a debt that was owed to them when they were denied their husband's support. And when fickle local relief boards failed to pay the debt, rural soldiers' wives took their grievances to the state. Nearly four years after her husband's enlistment, and one year after he was taken captive at Fort Wagner, Sarah Heffner of York Borough addressed a letter to Governor Curtin when town officials denied her the local pay offered to the wives of soldiers. "The captain come to my self in York market house and said I would draw that releaf every weak for me and my children," Heffner remembered of the day her husband enlisted.[46] "All the other women is a [drawing money] for there husbands and suns," Heffner explained, "and I thing my husband is gone to fight for the union as well as the rest."[47] When she was denied relief from Huntington County officials, Mrs. M. H. Roberts directed a complaint to Governor Curtin. With five children to support and bad health, Roberts was angry when the county denied her relief. "If I have no wright to live of the goverment," Roberts directed at Curtin, then "plese sur to give my husbent his discharge."[48] Roberts's demanding aid money as a "wright" suggests that marginal women believed that, through their husbands' war service, they had proven their loyalty to and established a relationship with the state. As soldiers' wives, Heffner and Roberts had assumed their share of the obligations required of citizens in wartime, and they believed they should be extended certain rights in return—in this case, the right to the support of a husband, or if not, from the state.[49]

Women worked hard to make up for the void left by absentee men, but when they were not successful, they wrote to bring men home. In the winter of 1865, rural women who had managed to do the work of husbands and sons for some time addressed themselves to soldiers and state officials when they faced another season without the men in their families. Early in March, Anne Sloan directed a letter to Governor Curtin from Somerset County, Pennsylvania, requesting a furlough for her only son, Joseph, to come home and help her see to the work around her house. As Sloan explained it, "I have no one to get a stick of wood or to feed or to take a bushel of grain to mill for me . . . and I hant able to doe any thing out in the wet with out geting pretty sick." "It is actually necessary that I could get a furlough for him for 30 or 40 days to come home and help me to get a lot of wood," Sloan added.[50] Less specific about the work that she was unable to do in her husband's absence but no less insistent with her request, H. B. Whiteman of New Columbus, Lucerne County, Pennsylvania, wrote to Curtin late in January 1865, after her husband reenlisted for a second three-year term, to request a furlough. "I humbly pray," Whiteman began, "that you will grant or cause to be granted him a furlow of twenty days to come north to provide proper means for his family for the rest of the winter."[51] Like Elizabeth Schwalm, who reported on her planting and harvesting of crops, seeing to the livestock, and caring for her children, correspondents who requested aid from the county and furloughs and discharges for their husbands also registered the work they did for their families and for their communities. When these efforts failed, women expected the state to help make up the difference. Like the work rural women exchanged with their neighbors, a husband's war service created the expectation of a mutual exchange.

In addressing themselves to state officials, women carefully catalogued the work they did in their husbands' absence, and, unlike Elizabeth Schwalm, who may never have addressed a relief agent or a state official, they were careful to characterize their work as patriotic. Supporting their families in the absence of their soldier husbands was — like military service — war work and deserved to be recognized and compensated as such. While perhaps not all women articulated a sense of entitlement as directly as did Mrs. Roberts, the war drew women into public, encouraging them to frame their work within the larger political contest underway, distinguish their own political beliefs from those of their neighbors, and seek support from agents of the state. In the letters they addressed to Governor Curtin and other officials, Pennsylvania women acted from a set of expectations similar to those that historian Stephanie McCurry describes among southern soldiers' wives. "In commanding their loyalty, their allegiance, and their support," McCurry argues, the "individual state and Confederate governments had acquired a new and undesired constituency."[52] Some marginal rural wives saw their husbands' soldiering as a household's collective service to the state — service that guaranteed wives certain rights and that they could withdraw when these rights were disregarded.

Postwar Family Structures

After more than three years of service, Samuel Schwalm returned home in September 1864. Frederick Campman was mustered out late in June 1865, two months after his wife, Esther, wrote to Governor Curtin asking for help supporting herself and her children. Elizabeth Schwalm's war ended several months before the fighting was over; Esther Campman's ended a couple of months afterward. An absence of documentation prevents our knowing whether Schwalm and Campman—preoccupied with sustaining their families in their husbands' absence—believed that their work had transformed them or helped win the war. Surely both women were relieved to have their husbands home again, and both anticipated the men's return would bring financial security. Though she had proved herself capable of running the farm in her husband's absence, Elizabeth had struggled to negotiate the needs of her children and the demands of her husband's family while assuming much of the work Samuel had done before he enlisted. Keeping the family's farm operational and her children contented had required all of her time, leaving her none to prepare and sell goods to help pay the family's bills or to write to her husband about her thoughts on the war and the larger significance of the work she did every day. Samuel Schwalm returned to a working farm and intact family, and in the postwar years, he added considerably to the farm's size and output. We can only speculate how power between the two had been subtly adjusted by Elizabeth's wartime experience of running the farm and raising the children on her own. After Samuel returned, perhaps Elizabeth asserted herself more often into daily decision making about the purchase and sale of property or the use of farm animals. With no evidence to the contrary, we might suppose that Elizabeth Schwalm was willing to once again share the responsibilities of farm management and family sustenance with her veteran husband and that she was relieved to have him organize the labor on the family's farm.

Through no fault of his own, a husband's absence could have catastrophic consequences for his wife and children; when his wages were delayed or when they failed to reach home at all, no amount of resourcefulness could keep a woman living a marginal rural existence from indigence. With Esther Campman's health compromised and the family nearly destitute, the Campmans' postwar recovery perhaps was more extended than was the Schwalms'. If Frederick Campman was able to collect the remainder of his bounty money and his back pay in a timely manner, Frederick, Esther, and their two young children might have found the relief in Frederick's return that Esther had sought in his absence. Again, we can only speculate about the long-term consequences of Frederick's absence from his family's rural home. As hard as Esther had worked, she had been unable to support herself and her children without Frederick. And, when she had turned to her community for help, she was refused. Neither Frederick nor Esther Campman appear in either the 1860 census for Clearfield County, suggesting that the family was new to the county when Frederick was drafted, and they seemed to have moved again when the war was over.[53] Perhaps the family's postwar relocation reflected an attempt to improve the Campmans' financial situation or Esther's desire to distance herself from a community that had failed her and her children in Frederick's absence.

As Esther Campman's experience suggests, the war exposed deep political and social divisions in Pennsylvania's rural communities, and women negotiated an explosive terrain of class prejudice and divided loyalties. In some Pennsylvania communities, the wives of soldiers who had enlisted were treated with more empathy than wives of draftees. In others, women whose husbands enlisted became lightning rods for criticism of Lincoln and Curtin. In January 1865, a group of women from Gallitzin in Cambria County, Pennsylvania, addressed Governor Curtin requesting money to support themselves and their families. Speaking for the group, Sedesa Cochran explained that their husbands were fighting in "generl Sherman army" and had not been paid for some time, leaving "there familys [in] g[r]ate nead of sum a sist enc[.] we have neither food ner fu[e]l ner the means to get it." With families to feed and without the benefit of their husbands' wages, the women sought relief money from the county. Sedesa Cochran explained how county officials rejected the women's plea, adding that "we cold not be more a bused in richmon amoung the rebles then we are her with the copperheads and conscrips."[54] Unable to rely on the political loyalties of their neighbors, Sedesa Cochran and her friends appealed to the state they were serving by lending their husbands to the cause. Cochran insisted that as wives of enlisted men the women had a legitimate claim to the state's support. Making their case to Governor Curtin, it was no accident that Cochran and the others drew parallels between their own condition—Union loyalists among "copperheads and conscrips"—to the condition of soldiers held prisoner of war in Richmond, "amoung the rebles." Sedesa Cochran counted on the governor to sympathize and to agree that abandoning soldiers' wives to the whims of a community of copperheads, northerners who sympathized with the South, was no way to repay their wartime loyalty.

Rural women living rather marginal existences relied on neighborly cooperation and reciprocity, but in many cases, the war brought disillusionment. The meager financial support offered by local aid societies could stand in for neighborly reciprocity and kinship ties, or the administration of this relief could accentuate a woman's wartime isolation from adequate means of support. The war years stretched the resources of these families to their limits, enlisted women as heads of households, and pitted the wives of soldiers against neighbors who might have provided support. Though we do not know what their thoughts were about the war and the administration, Campman and Cochran became conscripts—and their communities held them responsible for their husbands' war service. In the postwar years, these families struggled with difficult decisions about the future, and women's wartime experiences—facing down starvation, exposure, incarceration, and hostile neighbors—figured into these postwar plans. Women like Mrs. Roberts, Sarah Heffner, and Sedesa Cochran claimed their husbands' support as a right, but their letters to state officials stop when the war ends, making it difficult to know how this attitude shaped postwar ideas about work and family. When husbands returned, perhaps women were content to give up their claim to the recognition of the state. When veteran husbands were unable—because of illness or injury—to adequately support their dependents, this compounded their families' economic fragility and perhaps strained the emotions between women who had become politicized in the process of providing for their families and soliciting the state for support and men who continued to believe that they should provide it. And for rural women whose husbands did not return, the system of pensions—initiated in 1862 and expanded several times during the war and in the decades that followed—indicates the federal government's growing assumption of responsibility for this "undesired constituency," perhaps in part in response to the outpouring of letters demanding support as a "wright."

Rural Widows and Property Ownership

Although it is difficult to know the subtle ways that relations between women and men—Elizabeth and Samuel, Esther and Frederick—were renegotiated and whether wartime shifts of responsibilities and power lingered into the postwar years, the death of male property owners turned soldiers' wives into widows and resulted in a decisive reordering of family relations. The war left widowed women permanently in charge of farms they had worked with their husbands. During the war and in its immediate aftermath women whose husbands died in the war or afterward from their injuries or illnesses became property owners. Thirty percent of the

Adams County women who filed claims for damaged property in 1868, for example, had become property owners since the war began, indicating that the war had precipitated a transfer of property to the county's female population.[55] Unlike Elizabeth Schwalm, war widows who had assumed responsibility for running their farms—and, in the case of Adams County, protected their property from invading troops—now faced a number of postwar challenges alone. Whereas extended family members and neighbors might have helped women make up the labor shortage temporarily, more permanent arrangements became necessary when farmer husbands died on the battlefield or returned home disabled. By the time they filed claims in 1868, some Adams County women would have adjusted to what had become a permanent change in their rural homes and in the rhythm of their lives and devised long-term strategies for family survival.

Women inheriting property during the war had to navigate confusing and contradictory state legislation that treated female property owners as anomalies and was designed to keep women dependent. In 1848 Pennsylvania, like most states, guaranteed married women control over the property they brought into marriage, and in 1851 the state granted widows whose husbands died without a will $300 of their husband's estate.[56] However, an 1865 amendment to the 1851 law restricted Pennsylvania widows' claims to intestate inheritances that exceeded $300. In the amendment, widows inheriting estates assessed at more than $300 were expected to turn over their rights to the excess.[57] The significance of an amendment restricting widows' claims to property could not have been lost on women whose husbands' premature death had left them with an excess of property. In her claim for the loss of nearly $300 worth of damaged real estate and stolen farm animals and blacksmith tools, Louisa Wistler was keenly aware of state laws limiting her access to her husband's property. Ephraim Wistler died in 1863, presumably without a will, and Louisa filed her 1868 claim in the joint interests of herself and her children. But she carefully noted on her deposition that much of the property in question was hers, not her husband's, suggesting that Louisa was bracing herself for a contest over possession of the family's Adams County property. Similarly, Lydia McElroy was concerned about what agents would make of her claim for lost property when her husband, John, who died in the U.S. Army in 1863, left neither a will nor instructions for administering his estate. As Lydia explained, when John died, "he was not possessed of more property than is allowed to widows by the laws of Pennsylvania." When rebel soldiers entered Gettysburg in July 1863, Lydia and her daughter, Julia, left their home, and in their absence soldiers entered and seized their personal items.[58] When she filed her claim, McElroy, like Wistler and other women in her predicament, had unexpectedly become the owner of property that exceeded the state limit for intestate widow inheritance and was left to herself to defend her claim to that property.

Though the war had demanded that women act independently and collaboratively to work their farms and protect their property, once the immediate crisis of the war was over, state laws worked powerfully to reinscribe their dependence.[59] As long as her sons were unmarried and not yet acceded to the property, a widow might continue to act as head of the household, as she had while her husband had been away fighting the war. But her claims to that property became tenuous when her sons matured and within an overall postwar climate that sought to limit women's property rights. Nonetheless, a number of Adams County women inheriting property through the premature death of their soldier husbands continued to head their own households or to live alone—sometimes even with grown male children living nearby.[60] Whereas historian Nancy Osterud found that rural widows rarely lived independently once their children were grown, the experiences of women who lost property in the Confederate invasion of south-central Pennsylvania suggest that the war created an unusual situation for inheriting widows. The median age of the Adams County women was sixty years old when they filed their postwar claim for lost property, suggesting that they may have counted on the occasional labor of grown children living nearby. Nonetheless, middle-aged Adams County women seem to have preferred to live independently, on the land they had worked with their husbands and which they were not ready to turn over to their children.

Here too the experiences of rural Pennsylvania women offer us an opportunity to draw parallels to the postwar South. In her work on Petersburg, Virginia, historian Suzanne Lebsock has argued that despite conservative legislators' disinterest in women's rights, southern women stood to gain a measure of independence from antebellum and postwar measures taken to protect married women's property.[61] Whereas the war opened opportunities for women to exercise control over their and their husbands' property—a right that northern women enjoyed before it was granted to their southern counterparts—it remains unclear how women's control over their property weathered the postwar era. Indeed, Stacy Lorraine Braukman and Michael Ross found that, after the war, antebellum married women's property laws were largely dismantled and replaced with generous guarantees to lenders and business interests.[62] Further work on postwar landownership will help us understand if the experiences of the war generation of women who inherited property were anomalous or whether they represented an adjustment to antebellum expectations of landownership.

Conclusion

Mary Livermore, the Sanitary Commission agent who toured midwestern harvest fields, was correct when she assumed that the war devolved greater responsibility on the shoulders of farm women. Women took the place of male farmers and farm laborers during the war—either temporarily or permanently, and either alone or alongside family, friends, and neighbors. Yet in scores of postwar collections celebrating women's wartime contributions, women who worked on farms were consistently overlooked. Postwar accounts celebrate the daring nurses, aid society members, and freedmen's teachers whose largely middle-class status relieved them of the worries brought on by a temporary loss of household income and for whom the war offered relief from domesticity and the opportunity to pursue exciting careers in public activism. After the war, middle-class women like Livermore became part of a revitalized suffrage movement and sought to claim their share of the credit for saving the nation. It is appropriate, then, that Livermore included a colorful description of Wisconsin farm women in her postwar memoirs, entitled *My Story of the War*. The sight of women harvesting grain proved useful grist for Livermore's mill—hardy farm women became part of her story of feminist awakening, and farm women's thoughts about the war were filtered through Livermore's own. Livermore may have underestimated the extent to which the war disrupted life in rural households, but she sensed it had blurred the line separating harvest field from battlefield and destabilized gendered notions of service to the nation.

President Lincoln's secretary of war, Edwin Stanton, credited the North's victory in the Civil War to farmers' keeping the soldiers supplied with bread. Like Commissioner of Agriculture Isaac Newton, Stanton was convinced that machines had made northern victory possible by releasing young men from the fields and insuring that the harvest was gathered though there were fewer hands to go around.[63] Stanton's gendered picture of the victory gave credit to manmade machines and young boys and was consistent with the Lincoln administration's determination to deliver on

Widow Thompson's house, Gettysburg, Pennsylvania. The house pictured belonged to Mary Thompson, a widow living outside of Gettysburg in 1863. During the battle, General Robert E. Lee used Thompson's house as his headquarters. The image was taken in 1886, more than ten years after Thompson's death. No information is available about the woman and child pictured, though the woman may be one of Thompson's daughters or daughters-in-law. (Massachusetts MOLLUS Photo Collection, vol. 87, p. 4363#1—Lee's Headquarters, U.S. Army Military History Institute, Carlisle Barracks, Pennsylvania.)

one of the promises of free labor—independent yeoman farmers working the land, unencumbered by debt and free of unfair competition from un-free labor.[64] As the ideological corollary to free labor, the Lincoln admin-istration's embrace of domesticity allowed Stanton and others to ignore the extent to which yeoman farmers depended on the work of women and other household dependents. Like Livermore, who saw women's farm work as heroic and an appropriate alternative to domesticity, Stanton based his reflections on the war on a limited understanding of the antebellum rural household, in which women (and children) moved in and out of field labor and brought essential income to the family through commodity production. Unlike Livermore, Stanton failed to recognize how women's visible and essential work for their families, rural communities, and nation offered a challenge to the gendered prescriptions of free labor.

Fitting uncomfortably into postwar eulogies on domesticity or paeans to male independence, rural women living on the periphery of northern society were written out of the history of the war with the same alacrity in which they were at times overlooked by their communities and shunned by their neighbors. Pennsylvania women compensated for the loss of labor by marshalling all the resources available to them in their communities: calling in favors from their neighbors, taking their husbands' place in the fields, finding work in the community, and applying for local aid. Their experiences challenge us to consider how women's work insured the continuance of family farms and maintained antebellum agricultural productivity. On farms and in rural communities, women's work freed men to fight, put bread in the hands of U.S. Army soldiers, and sustained families and rural communities.

Pennsylvania women's letters reveal that the absence of alternatives to male labor strained communities and stretched women to their limits. In rural communities that relied on the productive labor of all members of the household, the war had taken a heavy toll. Women and families paid dearly when a husband's U.S. Army service left them without adequate resources or when it raised the resentment and hostility of neighbors. Political and ethnic identities fractured northern communities in ways that we are only beginning to understand, and we have not yet explored the gendered consequences of these wartime tensions. For women living in rural communities with no kinship ties and with little institutional support, the war brought great hardship, accentuated their marginality, and isolated them further from their communities. Letters describing homefront hardships caused soldiers to question their continued commitment to serve. Samuel Schwalm must have had some doubts, for in January 1862 he explained to Elizabeth, in a tone that was meant to convince himself, perhaps, as much as his wife, "I know that yous need me at home but I must Say for my part it is right for to go and destroy the rebelion and fight for union."[65] That as stalwart a unionist as Samuel Schwalm questioned his continued service to the U.S. Army in response to his wife's concerns reminds us that we cannot take women's loyalty for granted. Women began to question a war that took away men and threw their families onto the goodwill of their communities. As Sarah Heffner explained in a letter requesting her husband's discharge, "I think it is very hard wen a sholder goes to fight for his country and they put his family out on the street."[66]

Rural women did not draw upon bottomless wells of feminine patriotism or filial loyalty when they sent their husbands and sons to fight. Like their southern counterparts, women drew limits on their own war service. In Grahamton Township, Pennsylvania, Hannah C. Main fed, clothed, and provided shelter for her two small children and her husband's aged parents, "bed fast with the rhumitism," until May 1865, when she addressed Governor Curtin with a letter that marked the outer limits of her tolerance for a war that had gone on far too long. "O now for god sake send them home as sune as you get this," Main pleaded, "fore years is long a nought to live a widow."[67] Hundreds of Pennsylvania women wrote state officials requesting money, furloughs, and discharges, stepping briefly into the public spaces of state government, where their letters were read and their claims assessed in the office of the state's adjutant general or at the governor's desk. Like Main, most sought no formal recognition for their work but they withdrew their support for the war when the integrity of their families was threatened by their husbands' continued service. Others came to believe that working in place of soldier husbands had earned them special recognition from the state; Mrs. M. H. Roberts believed it was her "wright" to address the governor. Some Pennsylvania widows refused to accept dependence as postwar pay-off for defending their farms and sacrificing their husbands to the nation. Seeking to hold on to land they had worked with soldier husbands, rural women attempted to give their own meanings to the defense of free labor that had exacted such a heavy price on their households. Holding on to their land worked against powerful postwar trends that eroded women's control over their property.

That historians continue to search for evidence that women's war work propelled them into postwar suffrage activism speaks to our contemporary needs, but it may not help us understand how the war challenged women and men to rethink relations within rural households. Whether in politicized language directed to state officials, damage claims filed at county courthouses, or in the subtle renegotiations that occurred in postwar households, rural women adjusted to wartime changes in their households—changes that had allowed them to see when their interests corresponded to or differed from those of the state. In what was surely her first contact with a state official, Esther Jane Campman, wife of a drafted Pennsylvania soldier, addressed the governor as she might have an old friend. "Hit is with the graitst of pleasher I have seatied mi self to Drop aline to you to in fourm you i have had a leter from mi husbund," Camp-man began. Though broken down from work and worry and in bad health, Campman anticipated a response from Curtin, whom she referred to as "our gouverner."[68] Whereas the gap between the wartime experiences of a marginal rural woman like Esther Jane Campman, who worked to feed her family, and a middle-class urban woman like Mary Livermore, who imagined the implications of that work, is considerable, perhaps the differ-ence in their responses is less apparent. For Livermore the war opened up the opportunity for women to demand political rights. For Campman the war demanded that she act as if she already had them.

Rural women did their best to cover the ground left vacant by the de-parture of soldier husbands and sons. The added work and worry left them little time to stand in the doorway, like the woman pictured above in postwar Gettysburg. Like Mary Livermore, we can catch glimpses of these women moving in and out of neat rows of corn and wheat—or per-haps beating a path from their front doors to rural courthouses to lay claim to lost property. To locate displaced women, to understand their wartime geography, we have to look beyond the fields to the almshouses and temporary shelters of wartime cities.

TWO

RUMORS OF RELIEF,
STORIES OF DISPLACEMENT

In July 1862, Susan Hinckley of Greenfield, Maine, penned a letter to Massachusetts governor John Andrew seeking information about relief money promised to the families of soldiers. Hinckley's husband, John, had enlisted with the 9th Massachusetts Regiment the previous year. "I have a husbon whitch inlisted in that regt," Hinckley explained to Andrew, "and I stand in need of some of his pay whitch I have not rec eny." By word of mouth, Hinckley learned that men enlisting in Maine in July 1862 qualified for an advance on their bonus and that the state paid aid money to soldiers' wives and families. Now, Hinckley wanted to know what money she was entitled to as the wife of a Massachusetts soldier. "Hear in this state thear is provisions made for solgers familys and if thear is eny provisions maid in mass by law you would oblige me by writing me," wrote Hinckley.[1]

Nearly three years later, in April 1865, Sarah Heffner wrote a similar letter from Norristown, Pennsylvania, to Governor Andrew Curtin. Enlisted with the 76th Pennsylvania Regiment, Daniel Heffner was taken prisoner at Fort Wagner, and Sarah had learned nothing of his whereabouts since hearing rumors that he was held at Belle Isle Prison outside Richmond. Denied relief money from town officials, Sarah Heffner and her four children—Mary (thirteen years old), Daniel (ten), Christiana (eight), and Abraham (four)—faced eviction from their home. "I have bin sick nerley all the winter," Heffner explained, "and the members of the church have bin keeping me and my children and I am [some] rent back and I ant got no muny to haf it with and they are a going to put me out on the street there are no one but me to work for 4 children." Worried that her husband might be among the Union dead at the Confederate prison, yet determined to keep her family together, Heffner drew a stark picture for Curtin of the mounting costs of her husband's enlistment: "I think it is very hard wen a sholder goes to fight for his country and they put his family out on the street."[2]

Though one woman hailed from New England and one from Pennsylvania, one account described a soldier's short tour of duty and one an extended one, Susan Hinckley's and Sarah Heffner's letters highlight two common but unexplored aspects of the home-front experiences of working-class, immigrant, and freedwomen—the circulation of rumors and the experience of displacement. Most of Susan Hinckley's and Sarah Heffner's information—about their husbands and about state and local aid to soldiers' families—seems to have come from informal sources, neighborhood gossip and rumor. Heffner appeared unaware that Pennsylvania did not offer statewide aid money to soldiers' families—or perhaps she hoped Curtin could prevail on Norristown relief agents on her behalf—but she knew that women in her neighborhood were receiving money and she believed that she had some coming to her. As she put it to the governor, "all the other wimin is a dra[win]g it [money] for there husbands and suns and i thing my husband is gone to fight for the union as well as the rest."[3] Hinckley or one of her Maine neighbors might have read of the Massachusetts relief program in recruitment ads, but if she did, Hinckley did not mention it.

In both cases, the women relied on informally transmitted information about the status of soldier husbands and the availability of relief money, and each followed a similar course in her attempt to locate and secure aid—addressing the highest-ranking state official, listing as much information about her husband's enlistment as possible, and describing the home-front deprivations that she and her family faced. Acting on information gleaned from talk and neighborhood observation, Susan Hinckley and Sarah Heffner revealed how rumors swirled around the homes, churches, and streets of wartime northern communities, filling the void left by missing letters from the front and the absence of official communication—raising expectations or anxiety. Based on a reading of hundreds of case histories of women seeking relief payments and temporary shelter in Massachusetts and Pennsylvania, this chapter highlights some of the recurrent themes in the narratives of northern women's wartime displacement and interprets evidence of rumor as suggestive of women's aspirations for a state that went beyond free labor platitudes to support soldiers' families.

Hinckley and Heffner's letters catalogue the consequences to fragile family economies of the temporary (or permanent) loss of male wage earners, including poverty, separation, and displacement. Heffner pointed out that she had managed to keep a roof over the heads of her four children for more than three years without applying for relief in Pennsylvania. But now, in straitened circumstances, Heffner wished she had more than a vague recollection of having been promised support by her husband's recruiter. Remembering the day Daniel Heffner enlisted, Sarah explained that "the captain come to my self in York market house and said I would draw that releaf ev[e]ry weak for me and my children."[4] Having exhausted the resources of her community as well as her own, Heffner would have to face down a landlord or face eviction. Depending on her circumstances, it is likely that Hinckley experienced similar uncertainty, as she would have been denied Massachusetts state aid because she was not a resident. Susan Hinckley could stay on in Maine, where she might rely on neighbors or extended family to sustain her, but without the aid offered to the families of Maine soldiers. Or, like Heffner, she might leave her home and come to Massachusetts, where, though displaced, she could rightfully draw money earmarked to help the families of soldiers.[5]

Enlistment could have catastrophic effects on marginal families, uprooting those who did not qualify for local or state relief and driving women, often with young children in tow, to the doorsteps of private charities — or, worse, to the doors of the almshouse. When soldiers left home, their absence set into motion a series of adjustments within their families. Women who managed to stay on farms or those who found remunerative work handled these wartime adjustments with some measure of success. Rumors and community news could sustain women with few resources at their disposal, helping them to locate relief funds and keeping them in their homes and connected to their communities.

Women who became disconnected from their communities showed up at a variety of urban institutions — hospitals, asylums, jails, and temporary homes. But women's displacement is not a story of personal failure. Rather, it is a record of the limitations of free-labor nationalism based on a static and middle-class notion of domesticity. The ideology of free labor celebrated women's dependence with paeans to domesticity and low wages for women's work — but with no federal commitment to support the wives (and dependent children) of soldiers. The story of women's displacement highlights one of a number of wartime contests over space as women who left home to apply for outdoor relief or to demand shelter collided with officials attempting to keep order. Like farming women, displaced women found themselves navigating an altered wartime landscape. Strangers in new towns and without friends or family, women confronted city and state officials with demands for support and shelter and exposed the limitations of free-labor nationalism, which divided home and war in two separate spaces.

As they moved in and out of institutions, the vast majority of these women left no record of their wartime experiences of enlistment and displacement, having neither the literacy nor the resources to write letters to politicians, relief agents, or soldier husbands. Those who did write left the faintest of trails. But even these reveal that women were not cast afloat in a sea of neglect and misinformation — they contain evidence of women's attempts to keep families together by patching together fragments of indoor and outdoor relief, the sustaining power of rumor, and women's efforts to use the fluidity and anonymity of wartime to reinvent themselves.

Rumors, a number of studies have suggested, become particularly important in wartime, when there is a great desire for information but none — or only ambiguous information — is available.[6] "Under such circumstances," James Scott suggests, "one would expect people to keep their ears close to the ground and to repeat avidly whatever news there was."[7] During the Civil War, rumors carried "news" between the battlefield and the home front, sustained hopes that men were coming home alive, and fed fears that they were dead. Whereas women looked to civilian and military authorities for "information," they relied on home-front rumors they gathered from neighbors and on the streets for their daily sustenance. From an almshouse in Lancaster, Pennsylvania, Rachel Culbert wrote to Andrew Curtin for "infermation" about her sixteen-year-old son, John. Culbert hoped to find out "wat ridgement he inlisted in." She recognized that civilian and military men had information that was important to her, but she hoped that home-front hearsay — she had heard that John had fought at Fredericksburg (in December 1862) — would give her access to that information.[8]

Within their communities, rumor shaped women's demands for aid. When aid failed them, women followed advice and rumor in addressing letters to state officials, demanding what they believed was theirs — despite experience to the contrary. And, finally, displaced women followed each other into cities where, it was rumored, friends, work, or aid might be found. Susan Hinckley's and Sarah Heffner's wartime experiences were shared by many other working-class and immigrant women who survived the domestic disruption of enlistment; in most cases, the evidence of their effort was in the (mostly) intact families that greeted soldiers upon their return. The nature of wartime emancipation and black enlistment produced similar—if often more dramatic—disruption to African American families.

If we could look across the landscape of the Civil War South, we would see a scene alive with the movement of soldiers and civilian refugees of all sorts—elite white women fleeing to the homes of relatives, indigent whites forced out of their homes by hunger or foraging soldiers, and slaves who, in the fog of war, freed themselves.[9] If we keep this perspective as we turn our eyes northward, we will discover a similarly dynamic process of remapping underway.

The Geography of Enlistment and Relief

On July 2, 1862, President Lincoln launched an ambitious enlistment campaign intended to fill the ranks of the Union army with 300,000 three-year volunteers. Growing lists of casualties had largely dispelled dreams of a quick and glorious war that had attracted men in great numbers the previous spring.[10] To speed the process, Secretary of War Stanton authorized advance payment on bounty money ($25 of the $100 paid upon discharge) as compensation to a volunteer and his family for the loss of income.[11] When incentives proved inadequate, Stanton issued a quasi draft, requiring states to mobilize militias or risk intervention by the U.S. War Department. The mixture of incentives and ultimatums was successful. By the end of the year, nearly 500,000 men had enlisted as volunteers or militiamen.[12]

The 1862 recruiting drive produced a confusing and contradictory set of federal, state, and town incentives. In an effort to fill the ranks, cities and states engaged in a competitive bidding war, offering their own bounties to would-be soldiers and promising state or city aid money to their wives and children. New York, for example, offered additional bounty money to recruits, and city elites offered special incentives—including extra bounty money and aid to soldier dependents—to Philadelphia recruits.[13] In Massachusetts, Governor Andrew initiated a generous program of aid for families, and additional money was made available through a myriad of private relief agencies located in Boston and other cities.[14] State bounties in Connecticut and New Hampshire were competitive with town bounties in Massachusetts, but the statewide guarantee of aid to soldiers' families made enlistment in a Massachusetts regiment a better fiscal choice in the long run.[15] And whereas aid to soldiers' families was aimed at encouraging recruitment, once a man enlisted there was little incentive to continue to support his wife and children. The result of this bidding war was a chaotic patchwork of incentives to soldiers and their families, who found themselves weighing the benefits of one-time bounty payoffs versus long-term support for their dependent wives, children, and parents. Rumors of enlistment bonanzas and generous aid packages spread.

Once enlisted, soldiers left wives and dependent parents to navigate an overlapping and even more confusing terrain of state and town relief. Responding to the most attractive bounty offers, soldiers did not always enlist in their town or state of residence, yet even the most generous relief programs were dependent on continuous residence in the place of enlistment. Bounties were intended as a way to sustain the families of new recruits until their regular pay began to arrive, but wives relied on aid money to support themselves and their children when soldier pay failed to arrive or proved inadequate. Women like Susan Hinckley often discovered that a husband's decision to enlist left wives with little to support themselves beyond what they and their children could earn and the little they received from soldier husbands. These resources might prove adequate for a few months or possibly a year or two, but stretched to their limits, marginal family economies snapped with the least provocation—the illness or injury of a remaining wage earner, the loss of a job, a spike in prices, or a delay in soldier wages. When this happened, women went in search of relief they had heard about from recruiters or neighbors. Searching for money they believed they had coming required women to gather information about those receiving aid and to formulate their own wartime narratives. This entailed turning hints or rumors of relief into expectations and demands. Women likely rehearsed their requests for aid inside their community before they presented their cases outside.[16]

Aid to soldiers' families was administered by local relief boards; in many cases, the same people who administered town poor relief were charged with receiving applications from soldiers' wives and other dependents. The widespread stigmatization of poor relief surely meant that many women who were legitimately eligible for aid to soldiers' families did not apply.[17] Despite her obvious needs, Sarah Heffner tried to avoid that stigma by defensively declaring: "I dident draw none of that releaf since the first time they was hard of." Middle-class administrators of wartime charities were charged with discerning between worthy and unworthy soldiers' wives and were often of the opinion that providing relief to families of servicemen was "injurious."[18] Frank Sanborn, secretary of the

Massachusetts Board of State Charities, was skeptical about the social benefits of aid to the wives and daughters of soldiers, and he suspected that women with too much money at their disposal were likely to lead a life of crime. "The possession of more money than usual makes these women idle and exposes them to temptation," Sanborn concluded in an 1865 report on prisons, reformatories, and almshouses.[19]

The intimate nature of locally dispensed soldiers' aid left applicants vulnerable to being unfairly judged by middle-class neighbors or employers or those, like Sanborn, who little understood their situation. Like Sarah Heffner, Catherine Purelle addressed a letter to Pennsylvania governor Andrew Curtin when she could not get aid from her local relief board. "My self an my 2 little children are just starving for want of some reliefe. I am [tired] of speaking to the gentlmen of Pittsburgh and my helth is very poor," Purelle explained.[20] Unable to stand up to the scrutiny of her social superiors, Purelle hoped the governor could give her some information about her soldier husband, taken prisoner at Andersonville. As wives of POWs, Catherine Purelle and Sarah Heffner saw their delicately balanced family finances spiral out of control with the abrupt halt of money from the front.[21] Only then did women resign themselves to applying for relief, for doing so opened them up not only to the scrutiny of relief agents but to the interest of gossips. Indeed gossip, rumor, and other sorts of anonymous information could cut both ways.[22] When a neighbor reported that Sarah Cosgrove celebrated Lincoln's death by "danc[ing] for joy" at her home in Philadelphia, she stood to lose her aid.[23] Elizabeth Tucker was cut from the relief rolls when "unfavorable information in relation to her chastity" was reported to the relief board in Doylestown, Pennsylvania.[24] Rumor spread word received from the battlefield and from the home front. Sarah Myers worried that people at home in Philadelphia were gossiping about her to her soldier husband; she wrote, "I think thay are people riting to you a bout me."[25] Talk and informal information gathering could help a woman or sink her.

When women failed to pass muster with local relief agents, they looked carefully around them to see who was receiving aid and who was not. Failing to convince local agents, women addressed letters to civilian and military authorities, choosing their words with care and painting carefully crafted self-portraits of themselves to men who did not know them. It was no accident that Heffner referred to the support she received from her church, as ministers were entrusted with passing judgment on women's credibility and morality. No matter their desperation, women were careful to include details in their letters that would cast their character in a favorable light; including a minister's recommendation, for example, helped a woman find a job or served as proof of marriage. When she sent a letter to Governor Curtin, Mrs. Mary A. Sanno of Adams County, Pennsylvania, remembered her soldier husband, who died on the battlefield at age "33 years 3 months and 5 days." Having received no money in aid from her town, Sanno described the poverty she faced in widowhood, explaining, "I have nothing to live on I have nothing hardly to ware I cant go to church or any place for I have no clothes to go in."[26] Like Heffner and others, Sanno drew a heart-wrenching picture of her poverty, but she also took care to include details that she believed would reflect favorably on her character—the fact that she knew her husband's exact age, her wish that she could still attend church—and that she hoped would yield a positive response from men who were unfamiliar with her.

Indeed, Sarah Heffner most certainly talked with Sophia Rucstool before she wrote her own letter requesting help with recalcitrant Norristown, Pennsylvania, relief agents. Heffner's letter of April 11 included many of the same details as Rucstool's April 10 letter, though the circumstances they described were different. In addition to the opening salutation (both letters started with "I take my pen in my hand"), Heffner and Rucstool referred to knowledge about neighbors who were receiving aid money, inquired about why their applications were rejected, and communicated a shared sense that the state owed them money. In place of Heffner's POW husband and the pressing needs of feeding four children, Rucstool described her "2 suns in the army" who were her only support, "one ofe them had his arm taken of and the other was shot throu the hed and he was sent on duty before his wond was well and put him on the front."[27] It takes little to imagine the neighbors rehearsing their requests and agreeing on the details they believed were important to include—perhaps even deciding that, with two men in the army, Rucstool ought to go first.

In addition to a shared strategy, Sarah Heffner and Sophia Rucstool both measured their sacrifice against that of others, and both worded their requests for aid as the fulfillment of a contract. Heffner's comment that "my husband is gone to fight for the union as well as the rest" echoed Rucstool's words: "I think my suns are as go[o]d as others and there are a fighting for the unin as well as the others."[28] When applying for relief in their communities or appealing their cases to higher authorities, women relied on each other for sharing information about neighbors and confirming rumors, identifying the proper officials and locating relief offices, and settling on what they collectively believed were the important details to include in a letter addressed to a state official. A letter may have been the first expression of the rumor outside of the community, but it was likely only the tip of the iceberg of the hidden transcript it represented.

Failing to receive money from local relief boards left soldiers' wives like Sarah Heffner and Susan Hinckley particularly vulnerable to displacement. Women who had no kinship ties in their local communities had few options when their money ran out. As noted in the previous chapter, many rural women could relocate to a neighboring town to live with extended family, but immigrant, working-class, and freedwomen often had no such safety net. Forced out of their homes because of unpaid bills, displaced women gathered their children and whatever belongings they could carry and went in search of support. Some working-class women followed their husbands to the front, where they supported themselves and their children working as laundresses, cooks, and nurses.[29] One soldier observed the seasonal appearance of women with children at the army camp, explaining that "such cases are not rare I know of many Irish women that have shared the privations and hardships of a winter in a camp with their husbands."[30] The rigors of camp life were preferable, perhaps, to scraping together enough to survive on at home. These experiences carried women and children far from home, and their presence at camps was subject to the whim of army men. Ann Shield and her two young daughters, Mary and Ann, came to Boston in search of shelter in July 1862 when Peter Shield's regiment, the 36th New York Volunteers, was ordered away from Fort Monroe in Virginia, where the family had been living for eight months.[31] Ann and her daughters had traveled from Buffalo, New York, to join Peter's regiment in Virginia, had managed the trip from Fort Monroe to Boston, and now were looking for a way to get back to Buffalo.

Other women traveled to cities in search of more sympathetic relief agents or at least anonymity. Major cities were overrun by soldiers traveling to and from the front, invalid and ill veterans making their way back home, and family members rushing to military hospitals to care for wounded loved ones—creating fertile ground for the transmission of rumors. To the contemporary observer, it was probably difficult to discern between soldiers simply passing through the city and indigent wartime refugees. Indeed, in the early months of the war, urban residents complained of rough-mannered soldiers—for whom the U.S. Army had made little provision—sleeping in the streets and other public places and seeking handouts from local residents. Recognizing that state and federal of-

Woman and children at camp. This family picture suggests that this soldier's wife supported herself and children by doing laundry for her husband's regiment. Working-class and immigrant women might have preferred the rigors of camp life to facing the uncertainty of the home front. (American Memory Digital Library, Library of Congress, LC-USZC4-7983.)

ficials were overwhelmed by the sudden increase in human traffic and alarmed by the spread of misinformation, private organizations such as the United States Sanitary Commission opened city offices that acted as clearinghouses for information about the whereabouts of soldiers and at times provided food or train fare for the wives and children of soldiers who traveled great distances and then found themselves without a place to stay.[32] The attempt to control rumor speaks to its power to disrupt.

With city and state governments slow to realize the needs of soldiers' families, existing institutions such as hospitals, jails, asylums, and poorhouses served as way stations for wartime refugees—and as spaces for exchanging information of all sorts. Statistics on wartime crime suggest that cities used incarceration as a means of dealing with a transient and unruly wartime population. Boston, New York, and Philadelphia all re-

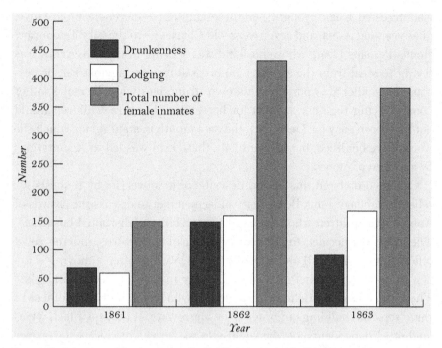

Rates of lodging versus incarceration for female inmates in the Boston watch house, 1861–1863. Women who needed a place to stay — or those who needed to sleep off a drinking binge — could board at police station houses or watch houses. In Boston, the watch house offered breakfast to indigent or displaced men but would not board them. Women could stay the night and get breakfast in the morning before being released. Numbers are based on the entry data for the 963 women documented as having stayed at the watch house for the years in which records were available. Total number of men and women seeking aid was as follows: 840 in 1861, 2,012 in 1862, and 1,588 in 1863. Source: Boston Watch House Records, September 1861–January 1863, Boston Police Department Central Supply, Boston, Massachusetts.

ported increases in female incarceration.[33] Institutional records from this period indicate that little effort was made to distinguish between war refugees and criminals, with one identity blending easily into the other. Police stations or watch houses, for example, incarcerated women and men charged with petty crimes, and these institutions doubled as temporary shelters for displaced women. In Boston, one such watch house primarily provided lodging for displaced women in 1861; two years later, the same beds were occupied by women incarcerated for public drunkenness.

Surely some crimes were a result of the day-to-day imperatives of living. The circumstances surrounding Mary Dean's September 1862 arrest for "shaking a soldier down" in Boston are unclear. The police officer who arrested Dean brought her three children—eleven-year-old Olive, nine-year-old Anna, and seven-year-old Charles—to the City Temporary Home. Perhaps Dean, whose husband was serving in the U.S. Army, was trying to steal from the soldier who pressed charges against her, or perhaps the soldier was pursuing his own ill motives when he came to her home. Piecing together support for herself and her three children would not have been easy for Dean with the $4 a month in state aid for which she would have qualified, but it is unlikely that Dean was led to "temptation" by an *excess* of money.

City records from this period describe offices overrun by requests for relief. In January 1862, Boston city aldermen met to discuss the crowds of women and children who "thronged" City Hall and disrupted business.[34] The aldermen decided to completely overhaul the process, moving relief offices out of City Hall and shifting the "heavy and often annoying" burden of dispensing relief on to hired clerks instead of elected officials.[35] These changes did little to help applicants who had to visit three offices in three separate buildings in order to be approved.[36] If they qualified, wives (and other dependents) of Massachusetts soldiers had to locate the proper ward office on the correct day of each month in which payments were dispensed.[37] The multilayered system was baffling not only to women who dragged their young children from office to office to file papers but at times even to overwhelmed clerks who made mistakes. The aldermen suspected that there were a number of women applying for relief in more than one city ward.[38] Perhaps women shared information about careless clerks, making it possible for some to double dip, or maybe the aldermen were responding to rumors about women living well off the few dollars a month they stood to get for their trouble.

In Boston, city aldermen also fought a losing battle against periodic influxes of wartime refugees, in particular in the winter months, who registered with the overseers of the poor for relief money and free coal to heat their homes.[39] City officials repeatedly tried to refuse relief to nonresident soldier dependents, but gave up in the end. By 1865, Boston had little choice but to extend aid to the wives, widows, and children—legitimate or illegitimate—of any soldier filling the quota of a city or town in Massachusetts. In what was probably an idle threat, Boston's overseers threatened to sue neighboring towns for sending dependents of Massachusetts soldiers to the almshouse.[40] These measures were at once an acceptance of responsibility for displaced women and children and an attempt to staunch the flow of refugees into the city.

The War's Displaced People

The North's economy was strong during the war and grew considerably in the postwar years. Male unemployment virtually disappeared, and workers in some industries benefited from wartime production. We might conclude, then, that economic displacement and institutionalization were anomalies in an overall story of economic prosperity, but we would be doing so based on data collected on male workers. In fact, historians have recently cast some doubt on this sanguine portrait of the North's wartime economy, suggesting that social mobility was uneven, manufacturing output rather flat, and real wages declining.[41] In any case, poverty might have been the short-term consequence of economic expansion, and women with small children to feed were particularly vulnerable to rising prices and other wartime economic fluctuations. A slight spike in prices here or there, one month without pay, or one illness could turn working-class soldiers' wives into refugees.

City officials might have agreed that a bed at the almshouse was a poor reward for the wives and dependents of soldiers, but these aging and overcrowded institutions served as collection points for women and children who had filtered through wartime relief agencies and city offices. The registries of almshouses record brief case histories of wives, children, and dependent parents of U.S. soldiers who, like Sarah Heffner, ran out of options and resources while waiting for support to arrive from soldier relatives or for husbands, fathers, and sons to return from the war. Almshouse registries expose the limits of the state's allocations on behalf of soldiers' families, but they also serve as important sources for following women's efforts on behalf of their families, mapping how homeless women and children moved through time and space, and understanding how women controlled access to the personal details of displacement.

If Sarah Heffner was evicted from her home in Norristown, she and her four children might have sought shelter at the almshouse in York County or perhaps in Philadelphia, where she would have shared the crowded space with the indigent insane, chronically ill, and incorrigibly drunk. But she would have also found many young mothers, mothers-to-be, and young children who, like her, were at the almshouse for the first—and, they hoped, the last—time. Letters from and interviews taken at almshouses confirm contemporary concerns that enlistment would come at considerable cost to families, in particular those with young children. The withdrawal of men from the home front disrupted the process of child bearing for many young mothers, but, with limited ability to control their fertility, women continued to bear children in men's absence.[42] Indeed, when Daniel Heffner followed a recruiter into the U.S. Army in 1861, Sarah had two children. By the time Sarah Heffner faced eviction in 1865, the Heffners had four children. In Daniel's absence, Sarah had given birth once or twice—presumably in the home that she now stood to lose amidst rumors of his death. At midcentury, working-class and immigrant women continued to face childbirth with trepidation; contemplating widowhood and displacement would have added to Sarah's anxiety. Traditionally, women's confinement was just that—toward the end of pregnancy, women's movement became circumscribed and remained limited for some time after giving birth. Limitations on women's movement and the demands of caring for newborns made it difficult to work, file papers at ward offices, or pursue leads on sources of relief. Facing confinement without the luxury to stay put, women with limited means and several young mouths to feed sought shelter; surely most women hoped to leave the almshouse as soon as they and their newborns were well enough to travel.

The records of the Massachusetts State Almshouse at Tewksbury give us a sense of wartime family displacement and the connections between displacement and motherhood.[43] The almshouse had 300 beds, but by 1861, the aging institution regularly served the needs of more than 500 men, women, and children, leaving it hardly prepared for the onslaught of wartime refugees. Convalescent soldiers, injured and out-of-work mill workers, and freedmen and -women all sought shelter at the almshouse during the war. The majority of inmates, however, were immigrant and working-class women with young children. Women represented 47 percent of more than 1,000 entries I sampled for the entire eight-year period, and children represented 23 percent of the total sample. In particular, women with multiple children sought shelter when one or more of these children were three years of age or younger. Tewksbury admissions data suggest that, in Massachusetts, displacement of women with young children may have peaked in the last year of the war.[44]

Brief case histories recorded in almshouse registries allowed indigent women to explain the circumstances that brought them to the poorhouse. The women who came to the almshouse during the war were mostly young white women with young children. (The median age of women listing the absence of a husband as the circumstance of their incarceration was twenty-seven, whereas the median age for all entrants was twenty-nine.)[45] Forty-four percent of women and fifty-four percent of children for which

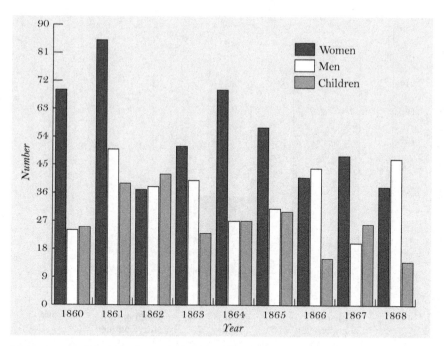

Massachusetts State Almshouse inmates, 1860–1868. Almshouses served as temporary shelter for women and children during the Civil War. Legible entries were selected at random, with at least one hundred for each year and with care to keep family groups together. Of 1,057 entries, women represented 47 percent and children 23 percent of the total inmates at the Massachusetts State Almshouse in Tewksbury from 1860 to 1868. Annual totals included in the sample are as follows, beginning with 1860: 118, 174, 117, 114, 123, 118, 100, 94, and 99. Source: Inmate Case Histories Microfilm, Massachusetts State Almshouse Records, Tewksbury State Hospital, Massachusetts State Archives, Dorchester, Massachusetts.

the circumstances of their incarceration could be determined named the enlistment of or abandonment by a husband or father as the determining factor for their displacement. Besides enlistment or abandonment, illness or childbirth brought women to the almshouse in Massachusetts. Women with no extended families to turn to (28 percent of the women for whom the circumstances of incarceration could be determined listed the absence of extended family support as a reason for incarceration) sought temporary or permanent shelter when they were ill (19 percent) or when they were about to give or had recently given birth (12 percent).

Individual case histories help us to understand how women avoided station houses or almshouses by seeking help from family members and churches and by combining their resources. Women traveled from city

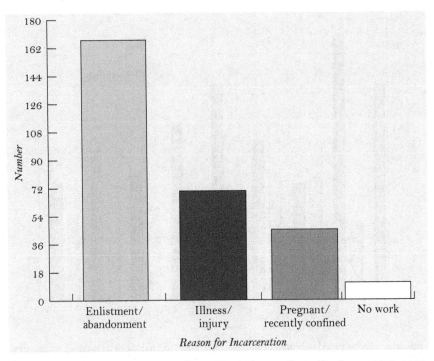

Circumstances of women's incarceration at Massachusetts State Almshouse, 1860–1868. During the war, people came to the almshouse for a variety of reasons. The most common circumstances that brought women to the almshouse were enlistment of or abandonment by their husbands, illness/injury, and childbirth/confinement—with considerable overlap in the last two categories. This figure illustrates the four most frequent circumstances for the 501 cases that could be coded in the inmate sample cited in the preceding figure (the three just mentioned, plus having no work), excluding the category of "no relatives," which overlapped significantly with the other categories listed above. Source: Inmate Case Histories Microfilm, Massachusetts State Almshouse Records, Tewksbury State Hospital, Massachusetts State Archives, Dorchester, Massachusetts.

to city looking for work, appealed to family members for support, wrote to civilian and military officials, and took whatever work was available to them. The war and the limitations of public and private relief moneys forced working-class women and their children out of their homes and onto the doorsteps of the northern public. Among the many people who sought shelter at this state-run almshouse during the war are four women whose brief case histories illuminate the high costs to families of an extended war. In each case, a woman with children used the almshouse as a temporary solution to wartime displacement.[46]

Thirty-six-year old Julia Fitzgerald checked in to the Massachusetts State Almshouse at Tewksbury on January 25, 1865, with her four children: nine-year-old Kate, seven-year-old John, six-year-old James, and three-year-old David. Fitzgerald's husband was serving in the 31st Massachusetts Regiment. As the wife of a soldier, Fitzgerald drew state aid for her family, but the state stipend proved inadequate to pay for food and shelter. The Fitzgeralds had emigrated from Ireland and settled in Boston seven years before the war began. Perhaps enlistment offered Julia's husband financial security or a chance to prove himself a worthy citizen; it left Julia with a great deal of responsibility and few resources. As a last resort, Fitzgerald checked in to the almshouse with her children and stayed there until October 11, 1865, when her husband was discharged and came for his family. For Julia Fitzgerald, the almshouse served as temporary shelter until her husband returned from the army. Perhaps Fitzgerald's access to state aid allowed her to keep the family together as long as she did, having to use the almshouse only in the last few months of her husband's enlistment.

Margaret Malloy's search for aid was more convoluted—and less successful than Julia Fitzgerald's. Like Susan Hinckley's story, elements of Malloy's case history were common to many immigrant and working-class women who were displaced by their husbands' enlistment. Margaret's husband, Dennis, enlisted in Portsmouth, New Hampshire, while the family was living in Framingham, Massachusetts; the two cities are more than seventy miles away from each other. Dennis Malloy's decision to enlist out of state left his wife and young children without access to the aid money offered to families of Massachusetts soldiers. Margaret Malloy managed to support herself and her four children—eleven-year-old Thomas, nine-year-old Mary, four-year-old Julia, and two-year-old Margaret—in Framingham for one year in Dennis's absence, but when she applied for state aid to soldiers' families, Massachusetts authorities sent her and her four children to New Hampshire. New Hampshire relief officials were equally unhelpful when they "refused to pay for the 12 months she was in Framingham." Unable to maintain her family in Massachusetts or to receive adequate aid in New Hampshire, Malloy sought admission to the Tewksbury Almshouse north of Boston. Upon admission, Malloy requested that she be provided with adequate funds to return to Portsmouth to await her husband's discharge. As it had for Julia Fitzgerald and Susan Hinckley, enlistment required Margaret Malloy to plot a course for herself and her children, traveling back and forth between Massachusetts and New Hampshire and across an unfamiliar wartime landscape.

When Sarah Lee was admitted to the almshouse she had traveled an even greater distance. The Massachusetts state employee who admitted Lee and her five-month-old son, Henry, in 1864 described them alternately as "colored" and "contraband," terminology that accentuated the fluidity of wartime identity. Lee arrived in Massachusetts from Arkansas early in 1863. The term "contraband" implies that Sarah and her husband, also named Henry, likely were two of the thousands of slaves who left their masters and came over to Union lines. Henry Sr.'s wartime fate is unclear; perhaps upon arrival in Massachusetts he enlisted or perhaps he was seized by Confederate soldiers as the couple made their way north from Arkansas. The Massachusetts aid program did not extend to the wives and children of out-of-state soldiers, leaving Lee and other wives of black soldiers — the vast majority of whom enlisted from out of state — out in the cold. By 1863, private relief agencies operating in the South provided support and instruction to former slaves. Seeking entry to the almshouse indicates that Sarah and little Henry's wartime situation in the North was precarious, but it is safe to assume that Sarah took this long and dangerous trip by choice, seeking to bring herself and her child up in a free state. To the almshouse employee taking down her account, Sarah was careful to refer to Henry Sr. as her husband, though in all likelihood, as slaves, Sarah and Henry were not legally married. Sarah began her new life facing considerable wartime obstacles, but she did so by presenting herself and her son as the legitimate recipients of state aid.

Like Lee, twenty-three-year old Sarah Hogan considered carefully the story she would relay to almshouse agents when she sought admission when she was about to go into labor. Like so many single, pregnant, young women who wanted the help of local and state officials, Hogan painted a defensive portrait of herself as the victim of seduction and betrayal. She explained how John Day had seduced her with a promise of marriage then abandoned her to enlist in the army. By now, stories such as Hogan's were hardly shocking for almshouse employees. Indeed, a flip through the pages of the registry would have turned up similar stories of seduction, enlistment, and abandonment relayed by Elizabeth Connors (pregnant by Jason McCarty), Mary Burns (pregnant by Joel Levine), Abby Morrison (pregnant by Daniel Morrison), Julia Boyle (pregnant by Grove Nichols), and Mary Lee (pregnant by Henry Sullivan). Fortunately for women hoping to garner the sympathy of almshouse attendants, the widespread nature of wartime dislocation lent stories like these an air of legitimacy, even if they were repetitive and formulaic.

Traditionally, attendants at an almshouse delivery demanded that an unmarried mother divulge the father's name during labor, convinced that in this compromised position, even fallen women would tell the truth. During the war, women added additional details to their confessions, including references to the enlistment of the child's father. In most cases, the information was sketchy and seemingly based on hearsay or rumor —noted in the entries as "thinks he enlisted"—but if the expectant mother could name his regiment, she stood to gain the sympathy of the almshouse attendant and perhaps some help securing the father's support. Hogan's ability to recall the specific details about Day's enlistment—according to Hogan, Day enlisted with Captain Curtis in Company B of the 2nd Massachusetts Regiment—impressed almshouse administrators, for her interviewer added "look out for him" at the end of Hogan's entry in the registry.[47] The wartime disruption of the home front left young women vulnerable to the kind of deception that Sarah Hogan claimed she was a victim of, but women might also have consciously tapped reservoirs of civilian concern about men's immorality and the temptations of army life.

As dependent women with children moved in and out of cities and pressed on private and public institutions seeking aid, shelter, or permanent support, their wartime narratives revealed the limitations of local arrangements to support the families of U.S. soldiers. Displaced from their homes, women found themselves navigating new territory in the wake of enlistment. In new cities and to new officials, women could craft—or at least embellish—their self-portraits based on information gleaned from other young women facing motherhood alone during the war. Revealing that a woman's seducer was a U.S. soldier would allow her to gain sympathy from moral reformers and temporary food and shelter, even if the soldier-seducer could not be found or the story corroborated. Some women had a hard time standing behind their stories; Mary Lee, for instance, was willing to name the father of her child, a drafted man, but she refused to swear to the information.[48]

Unattached Women and Wartime Stories

Like Mary Lee, eighteen-year-old Elizabeth Douglas treated her interviewer at the almshouse in Philadelphia to a compelling story of wartime hardship. "There seems to be a [measure] of misfortune or rather calamities, in connection with the History of this unfortunate and wretched child," the interviewer began the unusually long entry in his 1863 log book. "Her father was murdered on Market Street Bridge on Christmas

Eve 1856. In 1857 two of her sisters, decent, Respectable Girls committed Suicide on the same night by taking Laudanum. She says they where [sic] found dead in the same bed, and they were both buried in Potters Field. She had four Brothers and one Uncle in the 'Union Army' one of the brothers a Captain Douglas was killed at the Battle of Fair Oaks under Gen. McClellan. Her uncle wounded at Antietam and the poor child is in the Alms House without anyone to care for her." Elizabeth Douglas's narrative of seduction and abandonment would have been familiar to antebellum moral reformers, such as the one collecting information on the city's prostitutes.[49] Douglas, too, was seduced by the promise of marriage, but her story of abandonment particularly impressed her interviewer because of her brothers' military service. Struck by the string of misfortunes Douglas had survived, he concluded, "I think in Honour of her Loyall Brothers she ought to have a better Home than this."[50]

Douglas had worked as a prostitute for two years, had given birth to one child out of wedlock, and was in the syphilis ward of the Philadelphia almshouse for the third time.[51] Even so, her anonymous interviewer found her story so compelling, that he transcribed it at length. In compiling his "Register of Prostitutes," Douglas's interviewer was following a long line of antebellum moral reformers who had studied the problem of prostitution, most recently William Sanger, who interviewed hundreds of prostitutes in New York City and published his findings in 1858.[52] Although he believed that there were compelling economic reasons for women to become prostitutes, Sanger blamed prostitution on men who preyed on innocent women. Elizabeth Douglas's interviewer was predisposed to see the young woman's prostitution not as resulting from her own moral failing but that of society. Douglas, her interviewer thought, deserved a home. But the young woman had not gone in search of reformation—the interviewer found her in the hospital where she was being treated for syphilis. Perhaps Elizabeth Douglas had suffered all that she described—or perhaps she had told the well-meaning reformer what she thought he wanted to hear.

Throughout the war, city officials worried about the proliferation of prostitution and the spread of disease. Some cities took the unprecedented step of licensing and inspecting prostitutes and treating those who carried a venereal disease.[53] Wartime observers who had worried that women's wages were inadequate to sustain them in the absence of men had predicted that the war would increase the problem of prostitution. A letter addressed to a newspaper in Lowell, Massachusetts, for example, blamed low seamstresses' wages offered by government contractors for driving "the wives and daughters of soldiers" to prostitution.[54] As a relative of three U.S. Army soldiers, Douglas might have found work sewing uniforms on government contract at the Schuylkill Arsenal in Philadelphia, or she might have applied for aid to soldiers' families from any number of private sources in the city, for herself and her mother. It is likely that she too would have found this path littered with bureaucratic obstacles, with little in the way of reward. Elizabeth Douglas did not claim to have been led to prostitution by the wartime withdrawal of male support, but she allowed her interviewer to draw that conclusion.

Some of the concern over what was perceived as a wartime increase in prostitution can likely be explained by women's greater visibility and mobility, in particular in cities where large numbers of soldiers congregated. City officials expressed concerns that were inflected with assumptions about wartime space and the prerogatives of race, class, and gender. A visitor to Camp William Penn where United States Colored Troops soldiers were encamped outside of Philadelphia, for instance, complained about the presence of black women at the camp who came to visit soldier husbands and sons. Thomas Webster counted more than one hundred African American women at the camp when he visited; most of them, he imagined, were "harlots" whose behavior was "blasphemous and obscene."[55] In response to this affront, the soldiers circulated a petition attesting to the women's morality and good behavior. To a white, middle-class observer such as Webster, though, the easy familiarity of the women and men was unseemly and required intervention.

Her interviewer was convinced that what Elizabeth Douglas needed was a home, but the results of his survey suggest that home offered little protection to working-class and marginal women in the Civil War North. Indeed, more of his respondents claimed to have caught a venereal disease from their soldier husbands than admitted to being prostitutes.[56] In Boston, reformers opened up the City Temporary Home based on similar conceptions about home as a space protected from war. Alarmed at the growing "number of young girls from the country and the neighboring states" who made their way into the city during the war, Boston city officials applauded the home as a preventative to the problem of prostitution at a time when many homes had been disrupted.[57] Boston reformers believed that placing young women as domestics would stabilize the domestic disruption brought on by war.[58] That some women returned to the home when employers abused them and that wives of soldiers had to indenture their children out in order to find a position seems not to have disturbed the self-congratulations of city reformers who applauded the home as evidence of the city's benevolence and who were convinced that it was helping to solve the "problem of prostitution."[59]

Neither were reformers dissuaded by their (sometimes recorded) suspicions that the beneficiaries of their benevolence refused to be reformed. In her attempt to save Margaret Duffee from a life of "infamy," for example, a City Temporary Home matron took down two different stories in the logbook. In the first, Duffee presented herself as the wife of a Massachusetts soldier in the war; in the second, the matron revised the entry, describing her charge as sixteen-year-old Louisa Brunt, a "2d comer" and "a bad girl [who] should be at the Reform School, if she is here again."[60]

Conclusion

We can only imagine what the matron discovered about Louisa Brunt—aka Margaret Duffee—that convinced her that the young woman was not a loyal soldier's wife but a "bad girl" in need of reformation. In the fluid geography of the wartime North, working-class, immigrant, and freedwomen moved in and out of cities and, in some cases, transformed themselves in the process. Civilians worried that the trials of the battlefield and the transience of camp life would turn boys too quickly into men, making them unrecognizable to their families when they returned. As the war dragged on, drawing off more men and more resources from the home front, life on the home front, too, became more transient and women's identities more unstable. Under orders and to fill quotas, men found their way to the battlefield in small and large groups, passing by and stopping in cities and towns as they went, mapping out a geography of enlistment that others would follow or modify. As they did, they crossed an overlapping geography of relief that women navigated, sometimes with the help of information but more often guided by rumor. Sometimes their paths intersected, like when soldiers returned to take their wives and children from the almshouse, when women retrieved convalescent soldiers from the front, or when a wife came to blows with a soldier home from the front.

Women passed along news about soldier neighbors and monitored the behavior of soldiers' wives and daughters. Neighbors repeated rumors that states had deep reservoirs of cash to offer the wives of soldiers and factories offered daughters remunerative work. Keeping their ears close to the ground, women showed up at relief offices and army camps, addressed civilian and military authorities, and gathered in the streets of wartime cities, where they attracted the attention and concern of city officials. In some cases, women forced local officials to take note and even to expand the reaches of wartime relief to meet their needs. But, in general, local officials went little beyond hand wringing and stopgap measures to keep displaced women (and dependent children) off the streets. Women's incessant demands for relief, their attempts to double dip and to misrepresent themselves, were strategic choices to get the support they needed without inviting the scrutiny of local or state officials.

Rumors can be read as aspirations; in acting on rumors of relief, marginal northern women imagined a free-labor nationalism that did not merely celebrate women's dependence but sustained soldier dependents. "In this state thear is provisions made for solgers familys," Susan Hinckley explained to Massachusetts governor John Andrew, seeking not only an explanation of her eligibility but also claiming the right to support.[61] Rumors traveled across the wartime landscape, permeating spaces marked as home front and battlefield and creating opportunities of self-creation for women and men who carried them. Almshouses, relief offices, and temporary homes were inadequate "provisions" for soldiers' wives, but they proved to be fertile ground for the transmission of rumors. So, too, were wartime munitions arsenals.

THREE

BODIES OUT OF PLACE
Women War Workers

On September 17, 1862, a series of powerful explosions ripped through the U.S. Army Arsenal at Allegheny, Pennsylvania. At around two o'clock in the afternoon, residents of Allegheny and nearby Pittsburgh were jolted by the noise and the vibrations. Some who had been following the progress of the fighting at Antietam Creek in Maryland braced for what they believed was a Confederate invasion. As news of the explosions spread, residents crowded into the streets and surged toward the arsenal, following the column of smoke that rose from the burning buildings. Arriving at the arsenal, residents found what the *Pittsburgh Gazette* called "an appalling sight."[1] The roof of the building where young women and girls worked assembling cartridges had collapsed and the flames enveloped the remains of the laboratory. The intense blasts caused by exploding barrels of gunpowder blew out windows and doors of surrounding buildings.

Residents arriving after the blasts described the ghastly scene. Girls ran screaming in terror and agony from the building with their clothes on fire and their faces blackened and unrecognizable. As the building burned, women jumped from the windows, and others were trampled underfoot by terrified women trying to escape. Witnesses tried to help fleeing young women who pleaded with onlookers to tear burning clothes from their bodies. Mary Jane Black was just returning to her post after picking up her pay when she heard screams and, turning in the direction of the sound, saw "two girls behind me; they were on fire; their faces were burning and blood running from them. I pulled the clothes off one of them; while I was doing this, the other one ran up and begged me to cover her."[2] Exploding cartridges tore apart women's bodies as they were propelled from the blast, and onlookers discovered female remains riddled with shells, cartridges, and minié balls. Limbs, bones, shards of clothing, and bodies of girls were found hundreds of feet from the explosion, on the streets, in the Allegheny River, and suspended in the trees that lined the arsenal grounds. In a macabre postscript, the *Gazette* noted that "curiosity hunters" carried away human remains as souvenirs of the blast.[3]

With the gruesome scenes of this civilian disaster in their minds—but the plight of survivors who had managed to escape yet unknown—residents of the community arranged for victims to be buried. On September 19, the coroner's office began an inquiry to determine the cause of the explosion and assign blame for this tragic loss of life. The coroner's jury heard testimony from a number of survivors and witnesses and issued a damning verdict on September 27 that found three officers and two civilians in charge of the arsenal responsible for "gross negligence" and demanded that the army take measures "to ensure the safety of the lives and property of our people from a calamity far more destructive and appalling than has yet befallen us."[4]

Reverend Richard Lea, minister of the Presbyterian church located near the arsenal, presided over the burial of the victims of the blast on September 28. Seeking to console grieving residents, Lea entreated those in attendance to forget recent scenes of suffering and loss of life and remember instead how townspeople came together to render aid to the hapless victims, women whom he described as "noble Union girls." Looking into the "large deep pit," Lea described the "thirty-nine coffins side by side, filled by those whom no one could recognize, but whom the whole community adopted."[5] No effort was made to separate the human remains from the materiel of war, bodies were buried with the shells, and women were buried with the few male victims of the blast. Memories, too, remained entangled. On the first anniversary of the blast, townspeople erected a monument at the grave where "female beauty and manhood's vigor commingle."[6] The tablet listed forty-five victims, indicating that further investigation had yielded the names of six more victims.[7] Eventually official counts held the death toll at seventy-eight; not all the victims were buried together and some of the dead were still considered to be missing at the time of the original burial.[8] Despite the haste with which Lea and others sought to forget the images of young girls cut down by the materiel of war, townspeople remembered that the war had, indeed, come home and that death had stalked soldier and civilian alike. As they read the accounts of the bloodshed in Maryland, the people of Pittsburgh could not have missed the similarities between the two landscapes, scarred by unidentified bodies, unmarked graves, and unconsoled families.

Domesticating the War Machine

The indiscriminate burial of the victims of the Allegheny blast was part of a larger effort to disguise the militarization of the home front. The Civil War blurred lines separating battlefield from home, and the effects elicited concern among contemporary observers who saw the war as a distinctly separate experience and a male space. Yet, in many ways, war became part of life at home, as people gathered in the streets to receive news about wartime casualties, children greeted injured and convalescent soldiers at railroad stations, and women walked to and from the factories where they manufactured materiel of war. No one who lingered long at the scene of the arsenal blast could have overlooked the extent to which war had erased the very differences that lay at the heart of the North's self-image. In the streets they found women's beauty blackened; they discovered the dismembered bodies of wives, mothers, and daughters suspended in the trees; and in their pockets, some of them carried home the remains of women and children riddled with shot. The blast revealed that as much as contemporary rhetoric demarcated a careful line between battlefield and home—a line that was redrawn by the minister's soothing words about the purity of noble girls—the war defied those boundaries, invaded women's bodies, and violated sensibilities.

Residents of Pittsburgh avoided difficult questions the war raised about gender and work by burying the memory of the blast. But questions about women as workers vexed Americans for the rest of the war, as arsenals and U.S. Army contractors increasingly relied on female labor and as women negotiated the meaning of this work. The employment of women as munitions workers during the Civil War opened a temporary space in antebellum understandings of war, work, and gender in which women workers and contemporary observers disagreed about the propriety of a domesticated war machine. As women moved into spaces left by men during the war, they created all sorts of unanticipated conversations about national identity and gender. Rumors and gossip swirled around promiscuous workplaces, expressing contemporary fears of women who were out of place. When women war workers prepared petitions—as we shall see in this chapter and again in Chapter 5—they carried on these conversations outside of working-class communities, further collapsing the space separating the experience of war from everyday life. This chapter considers two such conversations as they evolved at federal arsenals in Allegheny (near Pittsburgh), Pennsylvania, and in Watertown (outside Boston), Massachusetts.

Allegheny Arsenal Monument, Allegheny Rural Cemetery, Pittsburgh, Pennsylvania. This plaque was originally commissioned in 1863 and replaced in 1929. The plaque lists forty-five of the seventy-eight victims of the Allegheny Arsenal blast in 1862. In the grave, "female beauty and manhood's vigor commingle." (Photo by author.)

Mary Douglas has argued that discussions of the body are often about society. "The powers and dangers credited to social structure," Douglas explains, often are "reproduced in small on the human body."[9] Women entering into the manufacture of war represented both power and danger. As workers, women were empowered as agents in the national struggle. Arsenal work offered women decent pay, esprit de corps, and patriotic fulfillment. But allowing women to become makers of war introduced the possibility of an unwelcome side effect of the triumph of free labor—a modern industrial society that disregarded antebellum notions of gender and national identity. Women working in these industrial settings triggered dangerous questions about the integrity of male labor, the meaning of war, and the shape of the postwar political economy.

Conversations about these issues centered on women's bodies, suggesting that contemporaries saw women war workers as bodies out of place. "The body is a complex structure. The functions of its different parts and their relation afford a source of symbols for other complex structures,"

Douglas explains. "Its boundaries can represent any boundaries which are threatened or precarious."[10] The language of the war referred to secession and the integrity of the national body. Abraham Lincoln referred to the nation as a patient with a "diseased limb . . . so long as there is a chance of the patient's restoration, the surgeon is solemnly bound to try to save both life and limb."[11] In the case of women war workers, a similar discussion took place as northerners noted—with approval and with approbation—their work helping arm soldiers in the field. Women working in support of the war indicated unanimity of purpose and a willingness to defend the integrity of the country at all costs. But it also raised questions about how northern society would be transformed in the process—about the society they were defending. Like the alarm about wartime female crime and prostitution, we can detect some of this ongoing conversation when northerners expressed shock at or revulsion to women in the strange place of domestic war manufacturing or when they reassured themselves of the necessity of this kind of transgression. Women war workers played key roles in these conversations, using the moment opened by the war to seek collectively to reshape the wartime workplace and to assert themselves into local politics.

Domesticity and the Gendered Prerogatives of Free Labor

The rightness of the northern cause of free labor was brought into question when home and war became fused in the superheated fire of the arsenal explosion. That the people of western Pennsylvania sought to cover their eyes is no surprise. The Republican ideology of free labor was based on protestant notions of discipline and the promise of upward mobility. Free-labor ideologues clung to expectations of male economic independence while they embraced the modernizing national economy that threatened to leave these expectations unfulfilled. In the midst of rapid midcentury economic expansion and intensified capitalist competition, economic independence was elusive as men competed with each other and with women and children for wages in the industrial labor market. But what men were denied in wages they recouped by reaping the benefits of women's paid and unpaid labor, both in and outside the home. Free labor embraced hegemonic notions of domesticity and separate spheres in which women and children existed outside the labor market and were dependent on the work of men for their support. By identifying the workplace outside the home, free labor rendered women's work invisible. And, arguing that the biggest challenge to male economic independence came from chattel slavery, not capitalism, free-labor ideology diverted attention away from a critique of class inequality that would have revealed that low wages and job insecurity required male wage laborers to depend on the work of women.[12]

Working-class men in northern cities such as Pittsburgh held firmly to notions of respectability that, not unlike free labor, considered men's wage labor as a temporary condition and women's wages as secondary to men's. Women kept order in the home and maintained appearances in the neighborhood, helping realize the family's claim to respectability and improving men's employment options. Women policed the family's morality and controlled the household income—oftentimes working against the impulses of men to do so.[13] Women and children might (and often did) work outside of their homes, but skilled labor—like party politics—was the privilege of men. In return, respectable working-class men provided for their families and protected dependent wives and children from the vicissitudes of industrial capitalism. Unlike free-labor ideals that largely ignored women's wage labor, working-class respectability often relied on the added income brought in by wives and dependent daughters.[14]

Employment patterns in wartime munitions factories fit comfortably within the traditions of working-class respectability that anticipated women moving in and out of the workforce at different stages in their lives and when the fiscal needs of the family required it.[15] At the Allegheny arsenal, for instance, employment seems to have been a family affair.[16] Men who held positions at the arsenal arranged positions for their daughters, perhaps to look out for the young women. Alexander McBride lived near and worked at the arsenal beginning in 1846. When Colonel John Symington began hiring women to work as cartridge formers, McBride was well positioned to get a job for his fifteen-year-old daughter, Kate.[17] As the bodies of victims of the blast were identified and pulled out of the rubble, it became clear that some Allegheny families would feel the effects of the blast more than others. The body of a "Mrs. Shepperd" was identified in the remains of the building where she had worked as superintendent with her daughter, whose body was never recovered.[18] Sisters Mary and ten-year-old Kate Dugan, Eliza and Mary Jane Lindsay, and sixteen-year-old Ellen and eighteen-year-old Mary Slatterly died together in the collapsed building.[19] Employment of several family members at the arsenal could help working-class families bring in more collective income when the cost of food, fuel, and other necessities was rising due to inflation and wartime shortages. An arsenal income could sustain a young widow—like "Mrs.

Gabby," whom witnesses believed had died in the arsenal fire, widow of John Gabby of the 102d Pennsylvania Regiment—and her children while she awaited their husband's pension and back pay.[20]

The premature deaths of young wage earners upset notions of respectability as fathers failed to provide for or protect their families. For western Pennsylvania families that had come to rely on the income of a daughter, wife, or mother, the loss of this support compounded the emotional toll. U.S. Army veteran and arsenal superintendent Alexander McBride seems to have never recovered from the loss of his daughter, Kate. When McBride was interviewed by a local newspaper in 1905, he was still haunted by the conclusions of a civilian jury that had found him—along with his U.S. Army superiors—guilty of negligence in the Allegheny fire. During the interview, he never mentioned his daughter's untimely death.[21] McBride must have brought fifteen-year-old Kate to work with him at the arsenal, hoping that he could look after her while she worked. His family's personal losses were aggravated by lingering suspicions about his incompetence and the loss of respect he suffered.

The specter presented at the Allegheny explosion represented the worst fears of free-labor ideologues careful to ignore women's labor in the new industrial workplace. The growth of women's industrial labor during the war confounded middle-class hopes that free labor would bring the working class under its benign influence. Even before the arsenal explosion, free labor was tested when the nation went to war. Drawing off male wage earners, the Civil War exaggerated class differences in the North by stretching already fragile family economies and increasing family reliance on women's earnings. Soldiers' wages were notoriously unreliable and, with wartime inflation, often woefully inadequate to support their families. Without regular contributions from their husbands, sons, and fathers, women fulfilled the needs of their families in a variety of ways. They took jobs vacated by men or sought work in the needle trades. In urban areas, women supplemented domestic work by doing piecework for readymade clothing companies, often on an outwork basis.[22]

Working in family units to make up for an absence of male wages was consistent with working-class respectability, but when family connections and paternalism failed to protect them and their reputations, women working in the war industries defended themselves.[23] Caught up in the enthusiasm of war volunteering, young women saw the work in patriotic terms. Free-labor rhetoric notwithstanding, the success of the Union's war efforts would depend on women supporting their families and working in the domestic war machine stitching uniforms and filling cartridges. Arsenal jobs offered competitive salaries and the opportunity to work in something other than textile manufacturing. At the federal arsenal in Watertown, Massachusetts, cartridge formers earned salaries ranging from $14 to $25 a month, making these positions more desirable than sewing army clothing on an outwork basis or working in any one of a variety of textile manufacturing jobs.[24] Women's arsenal wages helped fill the gap left by inadequate soldier wages and offered women the opportunity to work with other women as well as to feel they were doing their part for the war. The munitions arsenal was an unusual space in the wartime geography, one where women explicitly linked their daily work with the national crisis. But here as elsewhere, women experienced the war as part of their everyday lives and became for a time not merely the object of war but war's subjects.

"A veritable hive of industry": The Separate Spheres of War Production

In July 1861, *Harper's Weekly* featured the Watertown Arsenal in a cover image reassuring readers that there was nothing inappropriate about the workspace nor unusual about women's munitions work. In the top frame, neatly dressed women are seated at long benches in an overcrowded room. With pushed-up sleeves, women lean into the work. The women's coats and hats hang on the wall beside them, suggesting that women have access to this one room, where they come to work every day and are carefully supervised by a stern-looking man in uniform. In the lower frame, men are at work in a far-less-crowded room where they are seated with their hats on, and no supervisor monitors their work. Men are working in a noticeably less-regimented manner, as they appear to be engaged in a variety of jobs in the same room, and the work is more clearly linked to the war, with boxes of cartridges ready to be shipped to the front and rifles crossed over the men's heads. The paper was at pains to preserve gendered notions of war as man's work and women's work as an extension of their domestic nature, for the caption described the arsenal as a "veritable hive of industry." "Abundant life was in evidence," the *Weekly* continued, describing the bucolic setting, "in spite of the dread nature of the task an occasional overflow of animal spirits, light jokes and merry laughter, [could be heard] as the employees approached or departed from their daily duties."[25] By aligning women's arsenal work with popular assumptions about separate spheres, the journal assured readers that the arrival of women on the arsenal grounds did not pose a threat to industrial order or to military discipline. And the women's carefully hung outerwear suggests that home would remain a distinctly marked feminine space; for when the work was done, women put on their coats and hats and returned home.

The picture simultaneously engaged civilian concerns about women's work in wartime factories and dispelled them. Consistent with free-labor ideology, men's arsenal work was portrayed as dignified, skilled, and varied; and women's work was repetitive and separate. Women entered and exited the factory under the watchful eye of a male superior and rarely came in contact with male employees. The only links to the war in the cartridge-formers' room were the neatly stacked cartridges and the uniformed soldier carefully scrutinizing the women's work. Juxtaposing the picture of men so obviously engaged in the work of war helped to distance the women in the upper frame from war making. With curved backs and rolled up sleeves, the women might just as well have been stitching clothing as forming cartridges. War remained a masculine space. Women's bodies are carefully disciplined and protected by the walls of this highly specialized room and, on the arsenal grounds and in city streets, by the coats and hats hanging on pegs. This disarming portrait of separate spheres of work surely allayed contemporary fears of women as makers of war—nothing here would have led readers to imagine the ways in which the Civil War had offered women the opportunity to feel empowered by the patriotic work and had, in so doing, opened up a space in which relations of gender and work might be rethought. Nothing here hinted at the way that the bodies of female munitions workers defied army discipline, blurring the line between soldier and civilian.

"Blushing young virgins": Women Enter the Arsenal

The decision to hire women at arsenals during the U.S. Civil War was based on a matter-of-fact assessment of labor needs. In Indianapolis in June 1861, an observer visiting a state arsenal noted with approval the arrival of "ninety blushing young virgins and elderly matrons [who] are constantly employed, making Colt's revolver cartridges, common musket, rifled musket, Mine, Enfield, ball and buckshot cartridges. It is a beautiful and patriotic sight to see the young and tender happy in the bloody work. They laugh and chat gaily . . . as they roll up the balls and fix the fatal

THE REISSUE OF

HARPER'S WEEKLY.

JOURNAL OF CIVILIZATION.

Vol. V.—No. 238.]   NEW YORK, SATURDAY, JULY 20, 1861.   [SINGLE COPIES SIX CENTS. $2 50 PER YEAR IN ADVANCE.

Entered according to Act of Congress, in the Year 1861, by Harper & Brothers, in the Clerk's Office of the District Court for the Southern District of New York.

FILLING CARTRIDGES AT THE UNITED STATES ARSENAL, AT WATERTOWN, MASSACHUSETTS.—[SEE NEXT PAGE.]

Separate spheres of arsenal work. This portrayal emphasized the separate work of women and men and the close supervision under which women worked filling cartridges at federal arsenals. In the top frame, there is very little to suggest war making, with hats and coats hung neatly on the walls and women bent carefully over their work. ("Filling Cartridges at the United States Arsenal, at Watertown, Massachusetts," *Harper's Weekly*, July 20, 1861, 1.)

charge intended to let daylight through some man's heart."[26] Nothing in the records of the federal arsenals at Watertown or Allegheny suggests that the army resisted introducing women into these settings. Unlike the army's reluctance to hire women as nurses for fear of the disruptive power of introducing women into field hospitals, officers in charge of arsenals employed women early on in the war. And when the army finally consented to employing women as army nurses under the auspices of the United States Sanitary Commission, Dorothea Dix issued strict orders limiting the positions to middle-aged, self-supporting women who dressed plainly and came with testimonials to their moral standing.[27] Women engaged in the production of war materiel were often young, and, unlike the mostly middle-class women who sought nursing appointments, they came to earn a salary. Employment at Allegheny or Watertown was not perceived to be a right reserved for soldier wives or daughters (though this might have worked in favor of some applicants), as were jobs in U.S. Army clothing manufacturing.[28]

Gendered notions of obedience informed the army's decision to open munitions work to women. The work was simple and repetitive, but it required extreme care to avoid catastrophic explosions. Women placed lead balls in paper tubes, filled the tubes with gunpowder, and then tied up the loose ends; Colonel Thomas B. Brown of the Washington (D.C.) Arsenal, where twenty women died in a July 1864 fire, referred to the process as "choking cartridges."[29] Spilled gunpowder was carefully swept from work benches and floors several times a day; operatives wore special slippers or moccasins; and movement in and out of rooms containing gunpowder was severely restricted.[30] Colonel John Symington began replacing teen-aged boys with girls at Allegheny when the boys flouted common-sense safety precautions in the powder rooms. Arsenal employees repeatedly found matches in the powder rooms, and, on at least two separate occasions, matches were discovered packed with cartridges awaiting shipment to the front. Failing to discipline the boys, Symington decided in October 1861, six months into the war, to "supply their places with females."[31] Response to his call for female applicants was brisk, and Symington quickly filled cartridge-former positions with women and girls living in the neighborhood just west of Pittsburgh. Once women were employed in the powder rooms, Colonel Symington reported no additional problems with discipline. Indeed, so effectively did Symington integrate women into the arsenal that women continued to be employed long after Symington himself had been removed for incompetence. Adhering to expectations of women's obedience, Symington hoped to solve problems raised by young boys who failed to follow rules by integrating women into the male space of the arsenal.

Colonel Thomas Rodman, commanding officer of the Watertown Arsenal, began employing women as cartridge formers in October 1861, perhaps with a similar desire to improve discipline by classifying cartridge forming as women's work.[32] Women had worked stitching cartridge bags before the war, making it easier for Rodman to expand their presence in the arsenal to keep up with the U.S. Army's growing demand for materiel.[33] As at Allegheny, women employed at the Watertown Arsenal lived in the neighborhood and worked alongside family members, often to support families in the absence of soldier fathers and brothers.[34] Eighteen-year-old Violet Smith worked with a brother and at least one sister at the Watertown Arsenal; together they helped support their mother when their father died fighting in the war.[35] In addition to their connections with male arsenal employees, nearly half of the more than 300 women employed at the arsenal worked alongside their sisters, mothers, and female cousins in the cylinder rooms. Working-class families sent more than one daughter to work in munitions in hopes that the girls would look after one another.

The expansion of women's work at the Watertown Arsenal may have improved safety in the powder rooms, but it created new and unanticipated challenges for military authorities. Family connections contributed to a strong sense of solidarity among the women at Watertown and a willingness to take chances to improve work conditions. Workplace cohesion was further enhanced by a shared sense of the importance of the work. From their army superiors, women understood the significance of even a short interruption in the work. They, too, followed news reports of battles and kept count of their cartridges, and when they left their posts to address their superiors, they knew what a work stoppage could mean not only to an arsenal's bottom line but to the progress of the war. Watertown cartridge formers petitioned their direct supervisors—and civilian authorities—repeatedly about wages, employment practices, and safety violations.[36]

Choosing to seek redress through petitions, women war workers adopted a well-worn tool of political expression, one that had been used repeatedly by antebellum workers and abolitionists.[37] In the antebellum period, women workers often petitioned employers to protest wage cuts, and antislavery activists energetically turned to the petition, inundating

Congress with their demands.[38] Even so, the petition remained a contested right, as these missives, drawn up in homes, workplaces, and streets populated by the powerless, found their way to the spaces of power, where the powerful would just as soon ignore them. Even in war, petitions begged a response.

Buoyed by early petitioning efforts, female operatives addressed Colonel Rodman with a number of complaints related to a change in command at the Watertown Arsenal. The petition represented operatives' mounting frustration with the appointment of a new supervisor to oversee the women's rooms. In 1863, the third year of the army's experiment employing women in munitions manufacturing, Rodman replaced the operatives' immediate supervisor—Eddy Fields, a teen-aged boy—with Major Frank Hilton. A rather imperious army veteran, Hilton abruptly began reordering work in the cylinder room, carefully monitoring the women's productivity, and singling out some operatives for special attention and privileges. Most alarming was Hilton's abrupt decision to lay off all but a very select group of women from September to November 1863. Though the veteran cartridge formers were employed once again in December, the women returned to their posts determined to hold onto their jobs. Counting on the compliance of obedient female operatives, Hilton and Rodman simply ignored the women's repeated complaints, until the women decided to go over Rodman's head.[39] In November 1864, operatives sent the petition to Congressmen Daniel Gooch of Boston, a member of the Committee on the Conduct of the War, a body of civilian lawmakers armed with the power to investigate military affairs.[40] Thomas Rodman was the darling of the military establishment because of his technical genius. The civilian committee, however, was in the process of investigating the political loyalties of a number of Watertown employees, Rodman included, when they received the operatives' petition.

The letter of protest is evidence of the operatives' sense of themselves as war workers who were willing to assume a reasonable amount of risk in their work for the army in the field but were unwilling to suffer disrespect at the hands of army regulars. Referring to themselves as "American women," the operatives exploited the political situation of the fall elections to strike a blow at their superiors.[41] In an ingenious move, the women approached an elected official (Gooch) whose political future was tied to the Republican Party. Their petition explicitly linked Rodman's and Hilton's neglect for women's safety with the officers' support for Democratic Party candidate George McClellan, tapping civilian concerns about the po-

litical disloyalty of the U.S. Army officer corps. The Watertown operatives linked their fate to that of workers at other U.S. arsenals, those in
Allegheny and Washington, D.C., where a deadly July 1864 fire was still
fresh on the minds of area residents, including members of the Committee
on the Conduct of the War. The petition evoked operatives' solidarity and
defended their respectability, employing the rhetoric of free labor to condemn Frank Hilton as a regular army man who rewarded cronyism over
(female operatives') hard work. "This Hilton has treated us in a manner
which self respect forbids us to endure. He has subjected us to every an-
noyance and petty tyranny which his ingenuity could devise," the petition
began. Operatives reversed the free-labor language of dependence when
they described themselves, as opposed to Hilton and those he favored, in
the following manner: "Many of us have husbands, brothers or sons in the
Army, some of us have sacrificed our nearest and dearest upon the Altar
of our Country; others of us have wounded and maimed relatives returned
from the War *dependent* upon us. We all look to our present employment
for our means of subsistence." [emphasis in the original][42] In the absence of
a response from the U.S. Army, the women employed politically charged
language to point out that the war made men dependent on women not
only as family wage earners but also as makers of war.

Led by a middle-aged and widowed firebrand, Abby Eldridge, it is no
surprise that Watertown operatives came to describe their work in terms
of male dependence. As a widow of some twenty years, Eldridge supported
herself and her son working in a tailor's shop until she landed the arsenal
job. When her son returned from the army disabled and needing care,
she began asking questions about inequalities of pay at the arsenal and
organized a successful petition drive to raise the per-piece rate the women
were paid for completed cartridges. After enjoying the relative autonomy
and solidarity of arsenal work, Eldridge and other Watertown operatives
saw Hilton's tyrannical management style as a violation of their rights as
workers. Among the rights the women lost was an easy familiarity with
their superiors, the ability to keep track of their own cartridge production,
the freedom to open and close the windows to control the temperature in
the room, and the opportunity to talk and move freely through their work
space. Eldridge explained that, after Hilton's appointment, the women felt
"that all our rights are taken away; that we are trampled upon."[43] With an
eye on their output, military employers had entertained earlier complaints
levied by the women. But an army at war could not tolerate an organized
and vocal challenge to military decision making by an undisciplined but

organized group of munitions workers intent on counting their own cartridges and exercising their rights. Led by Eldridge, the operatives came to see military men as dependent on the work of women. The army saw things differently.

The army's decision to employ women as cartridge formers was consistent with expectations of women's obedience and an understanding that women and young girls were an expendable labor force; as in the winter of 1863 layoff at the Watertown Arsenal, women could easily be let go when the army's demand let up. Under the sexual division of labor, male arsenal workers were paid better, held positions of authority, and often remained in the army chain of command.[44] Civilians, veterans, and active military men at the arsenal anticipated enjoying a distinct advantage over women, who would be carefully separated into their own rooms at the arsenal compound and who would easily conform to the demands placed on them. Male arsenal managers and supervisors—many of them returned from the front or biding their time until they could be reassigned—saw arsenal work as a means to an end and expected girls to cooperate.[45]

Abby Eldridge and the forty-three women who appealed their case to the army's civilian authorities felt that war work had earned them certain rights—as women and as workers. Their understanding of gender and work differed from that of both the army men who supervised them and the civilians to whom they appealed their case. For women, the Civil War emergency had opened up the opportunity for meaningful work and delivered the added benefits of esprit de corps and female solidarity. Arsenal work was dangerous, but so was soldiering. Like soldiers, arsenal operatives were willing to put their bodies in harm's way if their assumption of risk was repaid with respect. Talking with one another, in the space of the arsenal and outside, women had come to see their work as essential to the nation and to their families and relied on their collective strength—and, at times, political friends—for protection. The army wanted efficiency and obedience from its wartime workforce and resented civilian meddling. Civilian authorities, jealous of the power and attention lavished on U.S. Army officers, used the opportunity opened by the women's complaint about safety to position themselves as defenders of domesticity—blushing young virgins, laughing and chatting gaily in their female sphere—and appropriate home-front gender relations against an expansive military that threatened to overturn them.

"An occasional overflow of animal spirits":
The Wartime Arsenal as No-man's-land

Despite the domestic portrait of the separate spheres of the wartime arsenal, arsenal work was comparable neither to women's traditional work at home nor to textile manufacturing. Though small numbers of women held antebellum positions, women who manufactured cartridges for Civil War armies entered a male space that was at times openly hostile. Arsenal commanders such as Colonel Thomas Rodman encouraged an environment of competitiveness and experimentation in which men who made improvements to the materiel of war were rewarded with accolade and promotion.[46] The U.S. Army Ordnance Department issued strict rules regarding the safe handling of gunpowder and other explosive materials; nevertheless, unofficial experimentation on arsenal grounds was common. Young officers desirous of military fame found in the arsenal environment a spirit of daring and male bravado.[47] Investigations at both the Allegheny and Watertown arsenals revealed that men were conducting unauthorized gunpowder experiments—in the latter case, the experiments were conducted in close proximity to the cylinder room. With the exception of Symington's removal from Allegheny, in neither case were responsible officers punished for taking unnecessary risks.[48] But at Watertown, military thrill seeking clashed with the emerging consciousness of women workers who saw no benefit in this reckless experimentation.

When women addressed army superiors with their safety concerns, they launched a direct challenge to this culture of experimentation and male prerogative. Petitioners described the situation at Watertown, where Major Frank Hilton had "caused the powders to be removed from a room in the extreme end of the building, to one almost immediately adjoining the cylinder room, in which the undersigned are employed. He has experimented with powder in a most careless and dangerous manner. Twice within a very limited period, terrible explosions resulting from these experiments have been narrowly avoided. These experiments were performed in a part of the building where the same were strictly forbidden."[49] It is no surprise that Hilton moved quickly to squelch the protest, forbidding operatives from passing notes in the cylinder room and from discussing explosions and fires at other arsenals. When the women sent the petition on to the civilians on the Committee on the Conduct of the War, Hilton bullied them into removing their names from the petition or losing their jobs. Despite Hilton's strong-arming, nineteen women refused to remove their names and were discharged. Congressmen, who were intent on discrediting Rodman by exploring his connections to the Democratic Party, latched on to revelations about the colonel's management of the arsenal. Members of the committee saw safety concerns as part of a larger pattern of mismanagement of which Rodman's experiment with employing women was symptomatic. In pursuit of political dirt on Rodman, the committee conducted an investigation of the management of the Watertown Arsenal in 1864; the findings fed civilian suspicions about the military and concerns about women's war making.

Unlike the *Harper's Weekly* cartoon that attempted to disarm readers' concerns about women engaged in making war, civilian investigators examining women's war work in 1864 were interested in exposing prurient details of the promiscuous workplace. Questions focused disproportionately on sexual improprieties—which women had referred to only obliquely in their petition—rather than on the reckless experimentation described in detail. Asking probing and leading questions, congressmen found much to interest and titillate. Witnesses described preferential treatment granted to women who were the regular "playmates" of their male superiors, men circulating pornographic images among the women, and even an episode in which men talked about placing a fan in the powder room to blow women's dresses. Witnesses were asked about unofficial parties on arsenal grounds, after-hour pageants, and all manner of horseplay that occurred in the arsenal. Apparently, the *Weekly* had understated the case when it alluded to "an occasional overflow of animal spirits" at the arsenal. Army men employed in munitions work, like those in the army camp, prided themselves on their individual heroism and their indulgence in what historian Reid Mitchell has referred to as "the thoroughly masculine vices" of "gambling, drinking, and whoring."[50] Men and women called to testify about the culture of the Watertown Arsenal recounted how men "fooled with the girls" in their offices and kept some women secretly employed at the arsenal during slow periods for their own entertainment and pleasure. Despite family employment patterns and other precautions, women working at the arsenal were stripped of gendered protections—the work made them simultaneously objects of male desire and objects of derision.

Soldiers, too, described factory women in highly sexualized terms, seeking to affirm their masculinity among their peers. Lieutenant Lyman of Northampton, Massachusetts, for example, remarked on the influx of women industrial workers in a letter to a soldier friend still at the front. "There are many very pretty girls here now, lots that I don't know, working in some of the Factories I presume," Lyman teased his friend, adding, "hurry up the war and come home and make your selection."[51] Lyman collapsed the distance between home and the war when he described women war workers as available for soldier consumption. Henry Schelling was even more explicit about his desires in letters he wrote to Private William Hertzog of Illinois. Marching with his regiment through Tennessee in November 1863, Schelling described an encounter with southern women working at a local factory who came out on to the road to see the soldiers. Schelling enjoyed being the object of feminine gaze, but he was quick to reverse it by noting, "I seen a few I would like to take on my staff for a few minits away the boys have for taking young ladies on their cocks."[52] The stain of factory work hung on the bodies of war workers. Indeed, promiscuous workplaces involving middle-class women raised similar pollution fears and elicited equally negative reactions, like those that were leveled at the U.S. Treasury Department after its decision to hire women in the printing department.[53] When soldiers at Watertown showed women pornographic pictures, they disregarded women's claims to respectability and dismissed their self-image as patriotic workers. Men who were threatened by the feminization of war work embraced an aggressive masculinity.

Inducing women to describe the sexual culture of the arsenal allowed civilian authorities to measure the distance between the army and polite society. Congressman Gooch and other committee members asked women leading questions and pushed them to describe some of the most embarrassing incidents of harassment; in so doing, the civilian committee reminded petitioning operatives of their need for male protection. One recurring line of questioning, for instance, focused on an order that Major Hilton issued regarding the cleanliness of women's bodies soon after he was assigned to the women's room. When questioned about the order, Margaret Connley, a cartridge former, responded that Hilton "spoke at one time of the girls not being clean, and of their making the air of the room very unpleasant for him and others. He said their underclothes were not clean, and they were unfit to stay there. He sent home six at that time, and said if they didn't come back cleaner, and if those who were there did not keep themselves properly clean, he should discharge them."[54] Once Gooch discovered this order, he doggedly pursued it with each woman he called to testify, holding it up as an example of how women's delicacy had been violated. "Have you any knowledge of an order given by Mr. Hilton in relation to the cleanliness of the girls?" Gooch asked Annie Farnsworth, who insisted that women had made very little of the order.[55] With Mary

Leonard, Gooch pushed the issue again, asking, "Has there been an order given in relation to [the cleanliness of the girls] since Mr. Hilton has been in charge?" When Leonard remembered the order only vaguely, Gooch pushed her repeatedly for details, asking: "Might not the difficulty have been remedied by notifying these persons privately, who were offenders, as well as by giving a general order?" Leonard, like so many others, declined to elaborate, offering only, "Well, it might and might not."[56] Eager to discredit Hilton and the others, Gooch presented himself as a defender of the women's delicacy. His attempt to do so, however, was frustrated by women operatives' reluctance to play along. In their eyes, Gooch had provided them the opportunity to address their concerns in the political sphere—they had sought his political clout, not his paternalism.

Hilton's clean underclothes directive was a feeble attempt to dirty women workers' war record, but Congressmen Gooch's very public display of concern for their modesty was unwelcome and misplaced. Margaret Connley insisted that she "never saw anything particularly unclean about the girls. Of course, they are very poor, some of them but I thought they all looked clean. He may have seen more than I did. He may have been looking around and seeing things that were not clean." As Connley understood it, Hilton was the problem. If the "air of the room [was] very unpleasant," as Hilton had complained, then it was because the women were crowded into a small space and forbidden access to sinks and mirrors with which they might have kept their faces and hair neat and because Hilton "looked for" reasons to deride the women under his command.[57]

This was not the only occasion in which civilians stepped forward as self-appointed guardians of women war workers.[58] In the aftermath of the Allegheny explosion, the newspapers repeatedly described the "appalling sight" of the burning bodies of the blast's female victims. "In some places [bodies] lay in heaps," read one story, "and burnt as rapidly as pine wood, until the flames were extinguished by the firemen. In other places nothing could be seen but the whitened and consuming bones, the intensity of the heat having consumed every particle of flesh. The steel bands remaining from the hoop skirts of the unfortunate girls, marked the place where many of them had perished."[59] As civilians rushed to the scene, they were pushed back by officers in Symington's command, including among them Lieutenant John Edie, a young officer who prevented family members from entering the grounds to identify their daughters' remains. In the process, Edie was involved in a verbal disagreement with the father of two girls employed at the arsenal, and the outraged father complained to the civilian commission investigating the blast. The commission voted unanimously to order Edie to "remove his presence from the midst of the community" on account of his having "made use of outrageous language concerning the female portion of the sufferers." There, in proximity to burning heaps of "delicate feminine beauty," Edie used "vile language" in reference to women employed at the arsenal; the *Gazette* joined "gentlemen" in town who called for Edie to leave town within six hours or suffer "a coat of tar and feathers, and a ride on the rail."[60] In the wake of this tragic disaster, there was a lot of blame to go around—for Symington for failing to adequately supervise the men he employed, for the civilians and army men who oversaw the women's work, and for townspeople for embracing the army's experimental policy of hiring women as cartridge formers. But in the first few days of the blast, the people of Pittsburgh focused their anger on one young man who had used inappropriate language when referring to the dead bodies of munitions workers. Even as the outcome of the investigation was still pending, the "gentlemen" of Pittsburgh were prepared to punish one young military officer for his savage disregard for women's delicacy.

Like Gooch's obsession with Hilton, civilian promises to protect the victims of the Allegheny explosion attempted to salvage antebellum relations of gender and class. As the theater of war expanded, it drew working-class women, men, and children more completely into the industrial economy and away from the benign influence of the middle class. Middle-class men who threatened vigilante justice against arsenal officers laid claim to the same aggressive masculinity as soldiers who described in detail what they would do to women's bodies and those would-be soldiers who showed munitions workers pictures of men with long penises and of women and men having sex.[61] Posed as virile protectors of women's bodies against the modern war machine, they closed the distance between themselves and those whose claims to masculinity rested on their active military duty. For the families of the Allegheny victims, genteel protection was small comfort; in the Watertown case, women had neither asked for this protection nor did they accept it.

Although Hilton's directive identified the source of the threat to masculine notions of war in the body of the munitions worker, the introduction of modern war-making technology increasingly rendered irrelevant the deeds of the individual soldier and upset antebellum notions of masculine war making. The introduction of new and more sophisticated guns and cannons that could be aimed and fired with deadly accuracy meant that death came anonymously to soldiers on the battlefield, where many were buried in large ditches where, as we shall see in Chapter 6, the anonymity they experienced in life was repeated in their death. Soldiers went to war, nonetheless, expecting to be heroes. With masculinity tied powerfully to active military service, men engaged in the production of war materiel recreated battlefield risk taking and brinkmanship, putting their own bodies on the line.[62]

Remarks about women's smells and stains can be read as fear of women's sexuality and men's close association with it. Women's sexuality—like the minié balls and rifle shot they assembled—was dangerous; it complicated easy identification between war making and masculinity. Dirtying women's bodies—either by exposing women to pornographic images or by imagining them as (willing or unwilling) objects of men's sexual desires—removed them from the protected status of mothers, sisters, and sweethearts and explained their exceptional position in the manufacture of war. The army's experiment with women war workers undermined nationalist claims of masculine protection when women's bodies became indistinguishable from men's—they were covered in dirt, they sweated, they got riddled with shot. When the explosion scattered women's bodies in the streets of Pittsburgh, the home front looked like a battlefield—a place where Hilton and regular army men had an advantage and where civilian authorities were distinctly outmanned.

Arsenal grounds remained a masculine testing ground for young men who resented the introduction of women into their midst. Through routine and institutionalized harassment of women war workers, male arsenal employees defended the space of the wartime arsenal as male. Though administrators were careful to employ and segregate women in certain jobs and enclosed spaces within the arsenal walls, men saw women as transgressors. They were, quite literally, bodies out of place. For men, arsenal appointments cemented local political ties, rewarded party fidelity, and reaffirmed masculinity in much the same way as military service. Women working alongside men confused these identifications. The wartime arsenal became a sort of no-man's-land between home and war, men and women. Women had not simply entered the arsenal space, remaining safely behind the walls of the cylinder room and the protection of men. They had moved purposefully throughout the space of the arsenal, finding allies and detractors among the men—and in Congress—and making themselves essential parts of the domestic war machine. Perhaps individually they, too, had participated in the sexual play described at the hearing, enjoying the attention of men and actively flirting with men with whom they worked in close proximity. Rejecting the protection of politicians and the harassment of military men, however, munitions workers sought collectively to make changes to the institutional culture by pushing issues of safety, linking reckless behavior with a needless waste of national resources, and condemning military men who failed to recognize their value as patriotic workers.

War Work as Women's Work: Survivors and Memories

Despite the political savvy of Abby Eldridge and the Watertown operatives, the charges they filed against Colonel Rodman and Major Hilton did not result in disciplinary action. Indeed, military success on the battlefield in the winter of 1864–65 validated the U.S. Army's willingness to expand the theater of war into the northern home front and reject the conciliatory policy toward southern civilians embraced early on in the Civil War. Carrying out raids designed to wreak havoc on the southern economy and terrorize southern civilians, U.S. Army Generals Grant and Sherman waged a different kind of war, one that pierced the "fragile barriers separating soldiers from civilians."[63] With this new approach yielding positive results, a complaint lodged by female arsenal operatives against military risk taking had little hope of getting a fair hearing. Indeed, the Committee on the Conduct of the War was waging a losing battle against army leadership whose manly spirit of experimentation had rescued the morale of a war-weary northern public.

The horror with which the northern public had responded to the specter of female casualties dulled as the war dragged into its fourth year; embracing hard war was preferable, perhaps, to facing defeat. Indeed, when a fire broke out at the Washington, D.C., Arsenal on June 17, 1864, the papers called it a "a most melancholy catastrophe," but the city moved swiftly to a matter-of-fact assessment of the causes of the fire and laid the victims to rest. The coroner arrived at the arsenal immediately and began to question witnesses even as bodies were still being pulled out of the rubble. Casualty numbers varied from seventeen dead to twenty-two.[64] The intensity of the blaze left little with which to make identifications; witnesses described a landscape of smoking hoopskirts where women had been.[65]

On the following day, the coroner found Colonel Thomas Brown, the arsenal's pyrotechnist, guilty of "gross negligence" for having left fire-

Monument to arsenal victims, Congressional Cemetery, Washington, D.C. This monument was erected in 1865 to commemorate twenty young women and girls who died at a fire in the Washington Arsenal on July 17, 1864. (Photo by author.)

works in the sun, just outside the cartridge room.[66] On June 19, two days after the fire, capital residents turned out en masse for the funeral, despite oppressive heat, crowding onto the streets and congregating at the Congressional Cemetery for the ceremony. President Lincoln and Secretary of War Stanton accompanied the processional. So quickly had the entire tragedy unfolded that surviving family members were still in shock at the loss of their sisters and daughters, resulting in some embar-

— Bodies out of Place —

rassing scenes as family members pressed through the crowds and tried to seize the coffins of their loved ones.[67] Distraught family members were kept in check by the capital's police force and by soldiers encamped in the city. By 1864, arsenal accidents involving girls and young women were perhaps no longer unusual, but families continued to experience these losses as tragic and unanticipated.

Like the Allegheny explosion two years earlier, the fire at the Washington Arsenal coincided with significant news from the battlefield, linking the fate of those involved in domestic war manufacturing with that of the men at the front and attesting to the blurred line separating home front from battlefield. News of Grant's capture of Petersburg made the front page of Washington papers on the day of the fire, followed by editorials predicting that Richmond would soon fall to Union forces. Southern papers carried positive predictions of their own, as Confederate forces kept Sherman out of Atlanta and residents of the besieged city remained resolved.[68] When a Georgia paper copied the news of women and young girls running from exploding shells in Washington, southern readers might have likened the women's fate to that of Atlanta's civilians, who were dodging shells lobbed on the city by Sherman's troops.[69] To be sure, Washington was not a city under siege and arsenal grounds were not battlefields, but the view from the ground must have made war seem rather close to home—where women and men, boys and girls, lived and worked.

Women working at U.S. arsenals saw their fates as intertwined not only with those of the men on the battlefield but also with those of other women and men engaged in similar work. Copied news stories of similar disasters reminded women of the dangers of the work and helped maintain their resolve.[70] Women who worked in soldier relief in the North also saw their work as intrinsically linked to developments on the battlefield—in particular women who collected supplies for the United States Colored Troops and who cared for the men when they became ill or injured. African American women faced considerable obstacles to this work, such as Jim Crow segregation policies that denied them access to public space, in particular streetcars. Like arsenal workers, African American women who boarded streetcars during the war found themselves in a hostile space. But here, too, they were not alone. We turn to their stories now.

FOUR

RIGHT TO RIDE

Women's Streetcar Battles and the Theaters of War

On the evening of April 17, 1863, Charlotte Brown entered a streetcar one block from her home on Filbert Street in San Francisco and took a seat inside with the other passengers, fully aware of car company policies prohibiting African Americans from riding in the cars. A few blocks into her trip, the conductor made his way through the car collecting tickets and stopped when he reached for Brown's. The conductor, Thomas Dennison of the Omnibus Railroad Company, refused to accept Charlotte Brown's ticket and asked her to leave the car. Brown insisted that she had "a right to ride" and that she had no intention of leaving the car before her destination. Dennison allowed her to stay, and the car resumed its route.[1]

Several blocks later, after a white woman passenger complained, the conductor resolved to remove Charlotte Brown from the streetcar. Brown once again refused to budge. This time, Dennison took hold of Brown and escorted the young woman out — either "with great force and violence," according to Brown's testimony, or by "gently touching [Brown's] shoulder," according to Dennison, who was later charged with assault and battery.[2] For his part, Judge Samuel Cowles believed Charlotte Brown's version of the encounter, and the jury in the city's police court found the defendant guilty. In a similar case that followed close on its heels, Judge Cowles angrily dismissed a streetcar company's claim that it had acted on behalf of its white passengers, in particular women, who needed to be protected from "objectionable" riders. Reflecting his thinking on both eviction cases, Cowles instructed the jury to disregard the company's claim unless its regulations against "objectionable riders" applied equally to "copperheads and secessionists who are much more oppressive to the community."[3]

Though the decision in Charlotte Brown's case sent a message to San Francisco's streetcar companies about the consequences of their continued exclusion of black passengers, Brown's stand against segregation did not end with the jury's guilty verdict. For the next two years, as the Civil

War raged on and emancipation became reality, her case was tied up in appeals as the Omnibus Railroad Company contested the verdict. Then on January 18, 1865, the 12th District Court upheld the lower court's decision and awarded Brown $500 in damages. Judge Orville Pratt referred to the practice of evicting black passengers as "a relic of barbarism."[4] Recognizing the decision as a dangerous precedent, the Omnibus Railroad Company was willing to continue to pursue its case rather than pay. But by then many similar suits were working their way through the city's courts, and news of the Brown decision appeared in black newspapers in other cities.[5] Seeing the writing on the wall, the company quietly agreed to pay Charlotte Brown. Even as the other cases remained undecided and evictions continued, San Francisco's black community dated the end of streetcar segregation from the day the white-owned Omnibus Railroad Company paid Charlotte Brown for the injury she suffered when forced to leave the car on account of her race.

Across the country, similar events were unfolding in a streetcar in Philadelphia. Early in April 1865—just a few months after the San Francisco court's decision in the Brown case—a "Mrs. Derry" boarded a Philadelphia streetcar, paid her fare, and took a seat among the other paying customers inside the car. Derry entered a car on the Lombard and South Street line around eleven o'clock on her way home from church where, as she testified later, a group of women "had been engaged in providing comforts for the wounded soldiers." After several stops, the conductor, a man named Lowry, asked her to get out of the car. Derry declined, pleading the lateness of the hour and the almost-empty car, and "asserted her right to remain." Lowry became increasingly agitated, called two men off the street to his aid, and "seized hold of [Derry], struck, kicked and finally ejected her from the car with great violence, tearing her clothes and inflicting some personal injuries." The conductor did not contest the facts of Derry's testimony; instead, he insisted that he was following company policy and that he "only used force when rendered necessary by her resistance." A police officer who had taken statements at the scene of the disturbance testified that Lowry had frankly admitted to having kicked "'the Nigger.'" Unconvinced by Lowry's defense of his actions, the court found in Derry's favor, instructing Lowry—or his employer—to pay Mrs. Derry $50 in damages for the injuries she incurred when she was wrongfully ejected from the train.[6] Mrs. Derry's case helped to build momentum for a movement in Philadelphia that eventually ended streetcar segregation there.

This chapter examines the confrontational politics deployed by women who identified segregated public space and freedom of movement as war issues. In neither San Francisco nor Philadelphia were the problems of segregation and harassment of black riders solved by litigation, but women's campaigns in both cities put segregationist proprietors on notice. The Philadelphia campaign ended with the passage of a law in March 1867 declaring streetcar segregation illegal in the state of Pennsylvania.[7] California's lawmakers moved rather more slowly, and segregation in public accommodations was not outlawed until 1893. Even so, as we shall see, the two campaigns hold important similarities—San Francisco and Philadelphia entered the war with dynamic black communities, and women took the lead in confronting white racism in both cases.

Although the acts described here seem individualized, evidence of similar confrontations and nearly simultaneous campaigns in a number of cities suggests a measure of cooperation or at least mutual support among women who had some experience of travel and who often knew and visited one another. Wartime benevolence work provided black women with spaces in which to share their humiliation at being denied access to the city, to experience a feeling of racial and gender solidarity over the issue, and opportunities to act on their convictions. In churches, soldiers' aid societies, black hospitals, and prestigious black schools, bonds of race and gender were reinforced by the retelling of stories. Experiences of racism and violence fortified bonds between women and strengthened their resolve. Black female spaces provided the context for collective activism—Patricia Hill Collins called these "safe spaces," where black women could indulge in self-definition, away from the racism and sexism of the larger culture.[8] Here, the contours of women's war experiences—not necessarily the desires of male leaders—shaped the form of their resistance. Choosing their bodies as sites of resistance, women defied a gendered and racialized urban geography and pushed freedom of movement onto the wartime agenda of state lawmakers. Women involved in streetcar battles embraced the politics of opposition, expanded the reach of emancipation, and helped to keep civil rights on the minds—if not the conscience—of the northern public.

Black women's street politics raised questions about what emancipation would look like on the northern home front. Charlotte Brown thought she had an answer when she defended her "right to ride," and by the time her case was decided, so too did Emma Jane Turner and Mammy Pleasant, fellow San Franciscans and women who traversed a similar wartime terrain. So did women in Philadelphia, New York, Cincinnati, St. Louis, and New Orleans, who—alone and together—staged similar protests.[9] As a result of these contests, racist streetcar company policies were reversed during the Civil War and afterward with a series of laws and precedent-setting court decisions that granted equal access to whites and blacks in many northern states. In his ruling in the Derry case, Judge Joseph Allison noted that the timing was key to women's success, for "the logic of events of the past four years has in many respects cleared our vision and corrected our judgement; and no proposition has been more clearly wrought out by them than that the men who have been deemed worthy to become the defenders of the country, to wear the uniforms of the soldier of the United States, should not be denied the rights common to humanity."[10] These were the same ideas that informed black men's eagerness to enlist—given the opportunity to prove themselves on the battlefield, African American soldiers expected to be repaid with emancipation and civil rights at home. To the judges who ruled in favor of black litigants, the path to legal equality was clear. But, as black soldiers discovered on the battlefield and women learned at home, the fight for civil rights was an uphill battle.

Choosing to confront the city's racism directly instead of under cover of male protection, women put their bodies in harm's way to carve out additional space for black communities. To emphasize the injustice of their treatment, black newspapers described the women as light skinned and "respectable," alluding to the elite class status of the victims of white conductors' brutality. Women counted on their status to fend off criticism from the black community and to win the sympathies of white judges, but they did not hide behind it. When women were publicly insulted and their bodies handled roughly by white men—as crowds of whites looked on—women threatened to derail the best-laid plans of male leaders. In Philadelphia male leaders worried that the attention could work against local civil rights campaigns based on lobbying and alliances with white business leaders, and in San Francisco, men also counseled patience. Women's actions charted a separate course.

Alone or with female companions, African American women traveled a hostile urban terrain, without male protection. As they moved to and from black churches and benevolence society meetings and delivered supplies to wounded and ill soldiers, women demanded freedom of movement and access to the city space as essential to that work and to black civil rights. With soldiers encamped outside of Philadelphia and an accelerated pace of wartime relief work in San Francisco, women reached outside of their neighborhoods, traveled with greater regularity, and moved with renewed purpose. In so doing, women engaged in an oppositional politics—infrapolitics—in which people who wield little power engage those who are powerful in everyday acts of resistance. What appear on the surface to be unrelated acts, James Scott argues, are often evidence of a collective basis of resistance.[11] Taking their battle for civil rights to the streets, Charlotte Brown, Mrs. Derry, and the others were not powerless, but their decision to draw attention to themselves, to use their bodies as tools of resistance, threatened to put them beyond the pale of respectability and block the one avenue of power they had—their connections to the black male elite. It was a chance they were willing to take.

The Streetcar as Theater

Streetcars served a wide variety of city residents, including those who could not afford private carriages or who traveled a greater distance than they could walk after a long day. Segregation rules varied from city to city, between competing companies, and on different lines. In New York and New Orleans, special cars were designated for African American riders.[12] In San Francisco and Philadelphia, streetcars were privately owned, and black riders were expected to stand on the platform next to the driver.[13] Conductors on Philadelphia and New York cars enforced segregation in the cars with sadistic pleasure, enlisting the help of white bystanders and police officers to forcibly remove black riders. In Cincinnati, where blacks were also denied service, a conductor dragged Sarah Fossett, a popular hairdresser and civil rights activist, for more than a block when she refused to get off the streetcar.[14] Seating was also the object of gendered and class-based tension among whites. Before women began their battle against segregation, Philadelphia newspapers covered a growing streetcar rivalry between working-class white men and middle-class white women in which editorialists chastised women shoppers for demanding seats from men returning from work.[15] In demanding a seat, a "lady" passenger enacted the privilege of her class among the largely working-class clientele—the point of her performance was not lost on men who tired of these interactions. This very public display of class and gender served as a reminder to all riders of the status of the seated woman.

As we have seen in previous chapters, the lines separating home front from battlefield became blurred as the Civil War required greater degrees

Streetcars as moving theaters. This 1890 picture of a Philadelphia streetcar illustrates the potential for streetcars to serve as "moving theaters." With all the passengers facing in the same direction, riders would be well aware of and easily drawn into confrontations between passengers or between a passenger and the conductor or driver. Women who confronted segregationist policies did so with an audience. (Reproduced by permission from Malcolm Kates, Allen Meyers, and Joel Spivak, *Philadelphia Trolleys* [Charleston, S.C.: Arcadia Publishing, 2003], 10.)

of war-related work on the home front and raised fears of the long-term consequences of these changes. "Wherever lines are precarious," anthropologist Mary Douglas observed, "we find pollution ideas come to their support. Physical crossing of the social barrier is treated as dangerous pollution."[16] Like white arsenal workers, black women were border crossers; their movements raised fears among northern whites at a time when borders seemed particularly vulnerable. Within the context of a war of emancipation, protecting the nominally white space of the streetcar was important to working-class women and men, on whose bodies hung the stain of work, who suffered daily reminders of their class, and who could simply not tolerate black women and men on the trains.

Segregated travel marked the status of those allowed in the cars to jostle for a seat and those who were forced to stand on the platform outside. In Philadelphia, where a nascent labor movement helped foster a sense of identity among white working-class women and men, conductors and their male friends were joined by white working-class women riding to and from work in maintaining racial segregation in the streetcars. In response to a January 1865 petition submitted by black activist William

Still to the chairman of the streetcar companies, the companies held a vote in their cars. After two days of "balloting," the companies could argue that segregation was consistent with the desires of their Philadelphia riders.[17] Among San Franciscans who rode the cars, the battle lines were a little less clear, with some accounts showing white men and women coming to the *aid* of black riders.[18] With a less well-defined white working-class identity, it was just as likely that San Francisco conductors like Thomas Dennison found themselves defending evictions of black riders like Charlotte Brown as it was that white passengers came to their aid in removing "offensive" parties.

Streetcars became the platforms on which women of color interpreted the meaning of emancipation on the northern home front. When women took on the streetcar issue, they moved into a liminal space between the social worlds of elite white women, the white working class, and the black elite. In the intimate space of the streetcar, black women encountered the city's heterogeneity on a stage on which those present were simultaneously audience members and performers. Robin Kelley refers to streetcars in the Jim Crow South as "moving theaters," pointing out that the space was also a site of military conflict—the other meaning of the word "theater"—when police officers and armed soldiers just home from the battlefield climbed aboard.[19] This was the space where Charlotte Brown took a stand—and where so many others followed.

Act 1: Charlotte Brown Stands Her Ground

When Charlotte Brown climbed onto the whites-only streetcar on April 17, 1863, the ink was barely dry on a California state law allowing blacks to testify in court proceedings involving whites. Before the testimony law, Brown would not have been able to testify against Omnibus. The law was in part the result of lobbying efforts of the small but well-organized black community in San Francisco. Though constituting only 2 percent of the city's population in 1860—or 1,176 people—members of San Francisco's black community were nonetheless well established, literate, and resolutely middle class. Well-traveled and cosmopolitan, many black San Franciscans had emigrated from the West Indies, where their light skin and expensive clothes bespoke their class status.[20] The city's conspicuous heterogeneity—Chinese, Indian, and Mexican residents usually lived in their own neighborhoods but in close proximity to black and white city residents—gave San Francisco's race and class relations a sense of indeterminacy. Black San Franciscans adopted Italian or Portuguese names and affected foreign accents and manners, easily passing as white in the city's diversity. Adopting an American Indian or Hawaiian identity offered African Americans greater freedom and opened up possibilities of social mobility.[21] The city's fluid class structure and new institutions encouraged blacks to have high expectations for equality, but California prohibited blacks from voting, serving on juries, and attending public schools.[22] When state legislators overturned a state law prohibiting African Americans from testifying in trials that included whites, then, black San Franciscans welcomed the news as the beginning of the end of racial discrimination in the state.

There was much to celebrate in the 1863 campaign to overturn California's discriminatory court testimony law, but the editors of the *Pacific Appeal* advised African American readers to be "patient and conciliating" and to avoid "all causes of passionate resentment" from whites. Above all, the editors cautioned against readers "resorting to the law," for not "every offence that may be committed against us is altogether in consequence of our color."[23] Black elites did not want to jeopardize their business connections with the white community with a rush to litigate; such a strategy could do more harm to the cause of civil rights than good.

As a member of an activist family, Charlotte Brown was aware of her new legal status. Charlotte's father, James, was active in California's black convention movement, which had led the testimony law campaign.[24] Two churches served as headquarters of local activism in San Francisco, the Bethel African Methodist Episcopal (AME) Grace Church and the AME Zion Church. The size and grandeur of these institutions reflected black aspirations. Black San Franciscans conspicuously occupied public spaces with a calendar of festivals and celebrations, including an annual celebration of West Indian and Haitian independence and, beginning in 1862, a Grand Jubilee celebrating American emancipation for which James Brown served as marshal.[25] Women's financial contributions and benevolence work helped sustain black institutions and formed a web of self-help that tied the elite to those with fewer resources at their disposal.[26] Women and men served in a variety of capacities on committees that organized events and came to know one another well. San Francisco's primary black newspapers—the *Elevator* and *Pacific Appeal*—helped to extend this familiarity and insured that their readers knew that they were part of a larger civil rights community.[27] Both San Francisco papers regularly reprinted articles from Philadelphia's *Christian Recorder*, and the *Christian Recorder* did the same. In 1862, for example, the *Pacific Appeal* covered William Still's campaign to convince Philadelphia's eight streetcar companies to end segregation by enlisting the support of elite white business leaders. Predicting Judge Pratt's choice of words in the Brown decision, the San Francisco editor referred to Philadelphia's streetcar segregation as "a relic of barbarism."[28]

Charlotte Brown likely knew others who had been ejected from the cars, for the paper published news of ejections prior to hers. On March 14, for example, the *Pacific Appeal* noted with indignation the ejection of "two of our most respectable females" though no white passengers had made complaint.[29] Though careful to protect the women's anonymity, the paper repeatedly referred to the women's manners and dress, insisting on their class status and respectability in the face of the "course threats of eject-ments." Traveling together the pair might have hoped to ride unmolested; when this failed, they shared their story with the paper, counting on the outrage it would elicit from other members of the black elite. Following the news of Brown's ejection, the *Pacific Appeal* printed the story of a criminal case initiated by a New Yorker named Elizabeth Jennings, a school teacher and the sister of a "Mrs. Samuel A. Smyih" of San Francisco. Jennings was dragged from a Brooklyn streetcar by a police officer when she and a female companion refused to leave the car on their way to church. As the case made its way to the New York Supreme Court, Elizabeth Jennings's father sought the support of the New York black community. Mrs. Smyih may have seen something of her sister in Charlotte Brown and hoped that her fellow San Franciscans would do the same.[30]

Brown traveled alone that night, but she wore a veil as protection. Like an assumed identity, a veil worn as a complement to refined dress helped to foster doubt about Brown's racial identity, effectively allowing her to pass, at least temporarily. It was a tactic that Charlotte had used before. Other ejection cases made references to female passengers wearing veils, suggesting that this was a strategy that Brown learned from someone else. Fugitive slave women used the veil effectively during escape. In an image from William Still's *Underground Railroad*, Charlotte Giles and Harriet Eglin, two escaping slaves on their way to Philadelphia, are examined by their master, who is pictured "peeping under their veils." Convinced that Giles and Eglin are in mourning, however, the man fails to recognize them and moves on.[31] With the veil drawn over her face, Brown entered the San Francisco streetcar undetected alongside other passengers and laid claim to a seat inside. Once in the car, Brown was in a good position to demand her "right to ride," for the conductor now faced a seated and ticketed passenger in a car in motion. He had to choose between playing along with her deception and confronting her.

In the indeterminate space of the streetcar, where "copperheads and secessionists" rubbed elbows with less unsavory city residents, there were risks to Thomas Dennison in choosing to confront a well-dressed woman traveling alone. In his defense, Dennison claimed to have been protecting white women from an objectionable passenger, and any white jury would read in the term "objectionable" the coded language of racism. With a veil covering the upper half of her body, Dennison had to move in close to Brown to examine her. And when she "wholly refused to go out," Dennison did something he likely would not have done had Brown been white—he put his hand on her shoulder.[32] Whether it was a "gentle touch" or forceful grab, Dennison's contact with Brown served as an unpleasant reminder to black San Franciscans of the denial of black women's bodily integrity. White men assumed the right to scrutinize passengers and to touch African American women, as in Brown's case, or to drag and beat them as the conductor did in removing Mrs. Derry.

But this contact could backfire if it startled or insulted white passengers, like the one pictured below just to the left of Giles and Eglin, who appears to have believed the female passengers were in mourning. As the streetcar battle heated up in Philadelphia, white passengers complained to the local papers about the mistreatment of female passengers. Conductors who used harsh language and physical violence to remove women made streetcar travel unpleasant for all passengers.[33]

The strategy of passing carried over into the courtroom, where neither Brown nor her attorney made reference to her race, leaving that to the defense. When Judge Pratt learned that Brown had been veiled that April night, he concluded that Brown's race could not have been obvious to Dennison before he moved in and asked her to disembark. As a consequence, Judge Pratt insisted that the defense prove that Brown was objectionable in "some other way," which the Omnibus lawyers failed to do. On January 18, 1865, the jury in Pratt's courtroom decided for Brown—awarding her not the $5,000 she had requested but $500 and $54 in court fees.[34] Within a year of appealing the case to the state supreme court, the Omnibus Company gave up and paid Brown.

The significance of the victory was not lost on the black community who hailed it as an end to segregation. Whites reacted, too. One local paper responded to the Brown decision with a cartoon and accompanying

"Charlotte and Harriet Escape in Deep Mourning." Charlotte Brown wore a veil when she rode the San Francisco streetcars. In her case against the Omnibus Railroad Company, Brown's veil complicated the defense's argument that it had denied her service as a routine policy of racial exclusion. Instead, Omnibus attorneys were instructed to prove that Brown was "objectionable" in some way other than race. In the above illustration from William Still's *Underground Railroad*, two fugitive slaves ride in a train car undetected. The accompanying text explains that their master—the man with the top hat—fails to recognize them even after he lifts their veils and asks their names. Still describes this as "an excellent strategy." ("Charlotte and Harriet Escape in Deep Mourning," Still, *Underground Railroad*, 215. Photo courtesy of the Historical Society of Pennsylvania.)

editorial entitled, "The Effect of Judge Pratt's Decision." The image portrays the inside of an Omnibus streetcar in the aftermath of the Brown decision. The accompanying text insists that Brown was in it for the money and implies that Pratt's interests were in Charlotte:

> Our artist this week gives us a glimpse of that "good time coming,"
> when all the narrow distinctions of caste and color shall be abol-
> ished, and when our colored brethren shall come into the full in-
> heritance of their rights,—shall sit in the cars and the dress circles
> of our theatres, with none to molest them or make them afraid. For
> the inauguration of this happy era, we are mainly indebted (under

Providence) to Judge Pratt. Poor Charlotte Brown, in spite of the efforts made by the *Gaz[ette]* to influence the jury, only got one tithe of what she demanded as a salve to her injured feelings. She said that her sensitive feelings were hurt to the amount of $5,000 by being led out of the car by a conductor and a jury only gave her $500. Try again, Charlotte, you may do better next time; and above all don't pay the editor of the *Gaz[ette]* to write editorials in your favor, it will only injure your case. You owe a lasting debt of gratitude to Judge Pratt for putting you in the way of making an honest penny. He is very partial to niggers, is the Judge, the darker the complexion the better it suits Pratt and the family. You are a real nigger, are you not, Charlotte? You did not use burnt cork for the purpose of gaining your point, did you? Having received $500 from the Omnibus Railroad Company, you will, of course, think it your duty to show your gratitude by patronizing them. Invest the money in car tickets, and you may possibly have the luck to be turned out again.[35]

In a few venomous words, the author(s) deftly illustrated the context in which women who chose to confront streetcar segregation operated. The text indicts Brown for being manipulative and incapable of earning "an honest penny," until she finds a willing white man to help in her scheme and to whom the young woman will owe "a lasting debt of gratitude." In a reference to Charlotte Brown's veil or her courtroom performance as a victim, the editorialist casts doubt on her racial identity when he asks, "You are a real nigger, aren't you?"[36]

The cartoon exploits contemporary pollution fears, emphasizing the danger to white women that would come with integrated cars. The image depicts two white women victimized by the intimate contact that now will be commonplace on the cars. Sandwiched between a leering black man on the left and a large attentive black woman on the right, the white women are separated by another black man who is oblivious to the role he is playing in the tragic comedy that unfolds around him. The sexual danger to white women of sharing space with black passengers is highlighted by the white woman on the left whose skirt is slightly elevated and who can only escape the advances of the black man to her right with great difficulty.

Of course, as Brown and others knew all too well, the greatest danger to integrating the cars was faced by African American riders who stepped into a space that was imperfectly marked as white and in which they could

"The Effect of Judge Pratt's Decision." In the cartoon and accompanying text, a San Francisco newspaper lampoons black reaction to the Brown decision, showing black passengers enjoying the "good time coming" on an integrated streetcar. ("The Effect of Judge Pratt's Decision," undated newspaper clipping, scrapbook #3, Wellington C. Burnett Papers, California Historical Society, San Francisco.)

expect to meet with violence. The cartoon attests to the potency of the space and the tendency to conflate racial conflict with sex. Finding no suitable way of portraying Charlotte Brown as threatening, the cartoonist depicted danger as a black man. Having gone to court to assert her right to ride and to secure her own personal safety, the paper implies, Brown effectively made the cars unsafe for white women. The implication is that white women should avoid the post-Brown cars, or at least not travel in them alone.

Though the *Pacific Appeal* did not respond to the invective leveled at Charlotte Brown, the white editorial and accompanying cartoon seemed to underscore the black paper's warning against litigants using the courts to combat racism. Nothing could be gained for black San Franciscans, one might have argued, from having white readers laugh at this joke. Stepping into the car and refusing to leave, Charlotte Brown had exposed herself to physical danger and public humiliation; taking her case to court, she had opened a door for white San Franciscans to see all African Americans as shylocks and bungling opportunists. But she had also *won*. And this message was not lost on those who read the papers, whether black or white.

Interlude: "Vindicating Manhood:" Men's Streetcar Campaigns in the City of Brotherly Love

Members of Philadelphia's large black community understood clearly the import of the Brown decision. The city's 22,000 black residents and the many institutions they supported made Philadelphia a destination for escaping slaves, placed the city at the heart of abolitionism and civil rights activism, and bolstered the City of Brotherly Love's reputation as the antebellum capital for free blacks. Elite black Philadelphians lived in the center of the city, near important urban institutions and adjacent to elite white neighborhoods.[37] Women and men, black and white were involved in abolitionism and the Underground Railroad through the Pennsylvania Antislavery Society and the Philadelphia Female Anti-Slavery Society, an interracial cooperation that brought together local luminaries such as the daughters of wealthy sailmaker and Revolutionary War veteran James Forten—Sarah, Harriet, and Margaretta; southern white ex-patriots, Sarah and Angelina Grimké; and white Quaker activist, Lucretia Mott.[38]

Despite the strength and influence of the black community and a history of abolitionism, white racism was as palpable in Philadelphia as in San Francisco—and perhaps more firmly entrenched. Strong business ties with the South and white fears of black migration kept white Philadelphians ambivalent about the war. It was only in the summer of 1863, when the Confederate army invaded Pennsylvania, that Philadelphians closed ranks in support of war against the South.[39] Still, strong differences of opinions about emancipation continued to divide city residents. Racist violence plagued the antebellum city, as it had in 1838 when angry whites burned

Pennsylvania Hall and the Friends Home for Colored Orphans after a meeting of the Philadelphia Female Anti-Slavery Society.[40] During the war, draft resistance in Pennsylvania was not uncommon, and criticisms of the Republican administration were often distinctly racist.[41]

A few days after the Brown decision, William Still—famous for his work in the Underground Railroad and president of the Social, Civil, and Statistical Association of Philadelphia, a broadly conceived civil rights organization—held a public meeting to discuss the streetcar problem in the city. At the meeting, black men—many of whom had been victimized by car company policies themselves—spoke of their "shame and sorrow that decent women of color have been forced to accept a standing position on the front platform of these cars, while visiting their relatives who have been wounded in the defence of the Country."[42] Since 1861, Still had led a petition campaign aimed at overturning Philadelphia's streetcar segregation by enlisting the support of white business leaders. But by 1865 little had changed for black passengers in the City of Brotherly Love, where Still's petition had convinced only one streetcar company to admit black riders, and then only on the platform.[43] Philadelphians watched as court cases in New York and San Francisco struck down Jim Crow streetcar policies, but Still remained convinced that litigation was ill-advised provocation. In 1861, a man named George Goines lost a criminal case against a conductor who ejected him, and the case reaffirmed the legality of maintaining segregated public spaces.[44] Still condemned Goines for bringing his case to court before other methods were exhausted and remained convinced that the best strategy was enlisting the support of white business leaders.[45]

William Still's plea for caution contrasted sharply with the news reaching Philadelphia from the West Coast and with the intentions of a younger generation of activists. Young black veterans returning home from the front had less patience with Still's approach than he believed was necessary to court the support of white Philadelphia. Among them was Octavius Catto, a young veteran who framed the problem of streetcar segregation as a civil rights issue. Through the Pennsylvania State Equal Rights League, Catto convinced Republican state lawmakers to draft a law outlawing segregation on streetcars and railroads. But in 1865 the law stalled before the legislature, a victim of the same resistance exhibited by California state lawmakers. In a rousing speech before a packed Union League of Philadelphia, Catto challenged his black and white audience to take up the issue as a matter of masculine self-defense. "Vindicate your manhood," Catto demanded, "and no longer suffer defenseless women and children to be assaulted or insulted with impunity by ruffianly conductors and drivers."[46] Catto's audience responded warmly to his youthful impatience and strongly gendered language, but, with public opinion unchanged and no law to protect black passengers, women and men who made decisions every day about riding the cars were largely left to defend themselves. After enjoying some initial success, the campaigns sponsored by William Still and Octavius Catto stalled, having attracted little attention beyond the black community.

Act 2: Philadelphia Women and the Streetcar Battle

Black women took seats in Philadelphia's streetcars in a steady stream early in the war. And when black soldiers began to return home, women continued to play an essential role in these moving theaters. The *Christian Recorder* reported the names of at least ten women who had been forcibly ejected from streetcars between 1862 and 1867 as they traveled to and from their work at relief societies or on their way to visit soldiers at city hospitals; among them were Mary Ann Miles, Anna Adams, Amelia Mills, Elizabeth E. Adger, Harriet Forten Purvis, Caroline LeCount, and a "Mrs. Palmer."[47] All of the women were active in a variety of benevolence organizations and were related to men prominent in black businesses, churches, and civil rights organizations.[48] But in almost all of the cases, women stood up to conductors alone and filed suit on their own behalves.[49] Perhaps some of it was simply a pragmatic assessment of benefits and costs—with crowded cars and schedules to keep, conductors could not possibly watch all passengers carefully. But their decisions to confront the issue also suggest the emergence of a collective consciousness among women who worked in wartime relief.

Women justified their demands for equal access to the cars as part of their work for the United States Colored Troops (USCT). Philadelphia raised fourteen regiments of USCT, and many of the men lay injured and wounded in hospitals and camps at a distance from black neighborhoods—such as Camp William Penn, which was located more than thirteen miles north of the city in Chelten Hills.[50] Before Philadelphia began raising regiments of black soldiers, a group of women formed the Ladies' Sanitary Association of St. Thomas' African Episcopal Church in anticipation of supplying soldiers and supporting their families; this organization was followed by a number of others promising to meet the needs of escaped slaves, wartime refugees, and black soldiers, including the Ladies' Union Association of Philadelphia, the Soldiers' Relief Association, the Colored Women's Sanitary Commission, and the Pennsylvania Freedmen's Relief Association, to name a few.[51] As they traversed the city with great regularity, women in these organizations emerged as leaders in women's streetcar battle.[52] In the absence of access to formal politics, black women helped to shape an oppositional politics through this work.

Brief snapshots of the work of a few of these women will give some sense of the intense personal and professional connections between the women and of their community visibility. Jane Johnson was president of the Soldiers' Relief Association, an organization that collected supplies for African American soldiers.[53] Amelia Mills served as president and Caroline (Carrie) R. LeCount served as corresponding secretary of the Ladies' Union Association (LUA) of Philadelphia, an organization that enjoyed considerable success raising money exclusively within the African American community and then using that money to tend to the needs of black soldiers.[54] At least three LUA women routinely ignored streetcar segregation orders —Mills, LeCount, and Anna Adams—and in their first annual report, the LUA identified restrictions on freedom of movement as the greatest obstacle to their continued success. "We hope that our friends will make some efforts to gain us admission to the city cars," the women closed the report, "as we find great difficulty in reaching the Hospitals."[55] Schools were particularly fertile ground for discussing the limitations of segregation, as teachers were involved in several confrontations. Carrie LeCount was the principal of Philadelphia's Ohio School, and Elizabeth Jennings, whose sister was active in San Francisco's black community, was a New York City teacher when she fought the streetcar company.[56] Charlotte Brown opened a school some time after she won her case against Omnibus.[57]

Women spent long hours together in the churches and elegant parlors of the black elite, but their work carried them into parts of the city where their fine clothes and cultivated manners did not protect them. It is not difficult to imagine women who spent so much time together exchanging advice on which car routes to take and which to avoid, the names and schedules of sympathetic conductors, and the best times during the day to enter a car and avoid coming into contact with rowdy white passengers likely to be policing the cars. Within these safe spaces and the cadence of these conversations, the form of women's resistance took shape. Having only indirect access to politicians and boardrooms, women's politics was expressed in these confrontations over public space. Together and alone elite black women dressed up and took back their bodies—for themselves and for their community—by refusing to move from their seats until they reached their destinations.

Women's streetcar battle began more inauspiciously in Philadelphia than it did in San Francisco, with women experiencing little success in criminal cases and receiving small compensatory awards in civil suits. But in Philadelphia—more than San Francisco—the evidence suggests that women who worked for black soldiers linked their work with the nation's and approached the question of whether or not to ride the cars in that context. In both cases, women reported using the cars to travel to and from church. These admissions served two purposes: first, they established women's class status and respectability and, second, they served as a way for women to establish a history of ridership and to suggest that the conductor's actions were unexpected. "I had purchased the ticket on the Sunday before that," Charlotte Brown testified, "while going to church, from one of the conductors of one of this company's cars."[58] And in Philadelphia, women offered this information as an additional way to claim their "right to ride," as the Mother Bethel AME Church and St. Thomas' African Episcopal Church provided essential supplies and medical care to the men of the USCT. Derry had just come from Mother Bethel Church, where, she explained, "she and others of her race were engaged in providing comforts for the wounded soldiers."[59] The judge in Derry's case found compelling the connection between women's demand for freedom of movement and the brave service of black soldiers.

Sometimes these connections were particularly obvious, as was the case in New York involving Ellen Anderson. Anderson's case suggests that, at times, streetcars did indeed reflect the physical violence of the theater of war. Going beyond a condemnation of company segregation policy, Anderson's case took aim instead at the city's willingness to use force against noncompliant passengers. After being evicted from a streetcar, Anderson, a Civil War widow, filed assault charges against a police officer who helped the conductor wrench her hands from the straps of the seat in front of her and drag her from the car. Veiled and dressed completely in mourning attire, Anderson appeared before the New York City Police Commissioners' Board to testify against the officer. Anderson's testimony must have made for good conversation among women at Philadelphia's Ladies' Union Association and other wartime organizations, for the papers printed it in full. "I am the widow of Sergeant Anderson, of Co. F, 26th Regiment, who died in discharge of his duty at Beaufort, S.C.," Anderson began. After she had boarded the streetcar, the conductor asked Anderson to get off and wait for the "colored car," but Anderson declined to move. What happened next shows how easily these confrontations escalated into violence:

> I told him I wished to ride in that; he started up and put his hands on me; I told him not to touch me; then he went out and brought in a policeman; this is the man here he came in and told me there would be another car along soon; I said I knew nothing about another car, and had a right to ride there as well as anywhere else; he said I could not ride, and must go out, and then he got hold of me and dragged me, and called to the conductor for assistance; the conductor came, and they got me off the seat; I got hold of the straps of the car, and then they both pulled me and dragged me so that I was very sore, and they tore my hand and at last succeeded in dragging me into the street; the conductor said he did not care for me or my husband; I had money with me to pay my fare; no one asked me for any money; I had a basket in my hand.[60]

Anderson was successful on both counts. The streetcar company reversed its segregation policy, and the police commissioner concluded that there was no "order requiring policemen to do the dirty work of these conductors." In fact, the commissioner explained, "it was [the officer's] duty to preserve the peace, and there was no breach of the peace until he broke it. It was rather his duty to have arrested the conductor than the woman."[61]

The striking image of a war widow forbidding a white man to touch her and then courageously facing her abusers in a public hearing attested to the power of women's politics and the body as a site of resistance. These messages were not lost on women in the midst of a heroic effort to supply hundreds of black soldiers camped in and around Philadelphia, women who fended off daily assaults on their own bodily integrity as they went about their work, baskets in hand, and who after having heard Anderson's story and Charlotte Brown's decided to take their assailants to court.

Act 3: The Theater of the Courtroom:
Carrie LeCount, Emma Jane Turner, and Mammy Pleasant

In the next year and a half—from 1865 to 1867—women in Philadelphia took their cases to the courts, ignoring William Still's warning that the battle would not be won if women sacrificed their respectability. Like Anderson, Derry made a striking presence in the courtroom, for the court reporter described her as "a very respectable woman, almost white." In his instructions to the jury on awarding damages, however, Judge Allison hinted that Derry did more than resolutely assert her right to remain. Alluding to injuries Mrs. Derry inflicted *on* Lowry, Allison recommended that if the jury found that the violence inflicted by the plaintiff upon the defendant "was used in defence of her person when assaulted by the defendant," then the jurors should not let that influence their willingness to award her damages. Perhaps in the struggle Mrs. Derry hit the conductor, or perhaps Lowry was defending himself when he claimed that Derry assaulted him.[62] It takes little to imagine William Still—perhaps even Mr. Derry—wincing at the accusation that a respectable woman such as Derry had raised her hand against a white man. But for women who fought daily to defend themselves against attacks like the one Derry suffered, it takes even less to imagine their urge to strike back.[63]

Courtrooms served as another form of theater, one where women performed for a judge, sometimes a jury, and often journalists and other curious onlookers.[64] Police courts tended to be rather informal, and lawyers were not always present. Facing a white judge, jury (if one was called), and defendant, a black woman appearing in this space was at a decided disadvantage. In San Francisco, at least, women were accompanied by lawyers at the appeals courts. Facing considerable odds, often alone, women armored themselves by taking care with their appearance and their comportment. Women sought to distinguish themselves from the defendants in these cases—streetcar conductors who played bit roles in the drama. The papers regularly carried sensational news of defendants at police court, but the novelty of these cases made it likely that reporters would scrutinize the plaintiffs. When Sarah Fossett, the Cincinnati hairdresser and civil rights activist, took her case to a court in that city, for instance, the white community took a keen interest.[65] Judging from her portrait, Fossett was likely an impressive presence in the courtroom. When Charlotte Brown entered a California courtroom she was not only contesting streetcar segregation, she was venturing into unchartered territory, testifying against a white man and seeking damages from a white-owned company. Like Mrs. Derry, women had to describe their injuries and answer questions posed by the judge, including inquiries that referred to the parts of their bodies where they had been touched or sustained injuries. These questions

Courtrooms as theater. Women took care to present themselves as respectable, even as they described rough handling by conductors and the injuries they sustained to their bodies. In this picture, Sarah Fossett of Cincinnati strikes a pose that belied the humiliating treatment she received when a conductor ejected her and then dragged her behind the car as she clung to the steps. (Dabney, *Cincinnati's Colored Citizens*, 350.)

might have rattled women's modesty, their self-confidence, but women's courtroom performances helped to foster a culture of opposition within the black community.

Black women's infrapolitics continued to take the demand for an end to Jim Crow to the courts and to the court of public opinion. In a September

1866 meeting of the Philadelphia Female Anti-Slavery Society, the women in attendance turned to the topic of the streetcar campaign and Catto's Republican Party lobbying. Harriet Forten Purvis concluded that the men's campaign had made "little, if any, apparent progress [toward] the abrogation of this form of injustice" and questioned the men's willingness to work with the Republican Party, whose "faithfulness in applying the principles of justice" remained unproven.[66] Having chosen the cars as the space in which to extend the national conversation about emancipation and civil rights, women had little faith in the boardroom or the statehouse to alter the balance of power in the streets.

Even after Pennsylvania lawmakers had passed the law prohibiting discrimination in the city's cars, the point had to be made again. On March 22, 1867, Pennsylvania governor John Geary signed a law outlawing segregation on streetcars and railroads. The law allowed judges to either fine or imprison (or both) conductors who denied service to black riders or those who employed subterfuge in order to avoid serving black riders on an equal basis with whites. Reflecting the humiliating experiences of black riders during the war, the law explicitly stated that *any* service given or withheld on account of race was prohibited, including compelling riders to sit in special seats or seating them apart from other riders.[67] Three days after the law was signed, a conductor on the Lombard Street line refused service to Carrie LeCount, taunting her by saying, "We don't allow niggers to ride." LeCount lodged a complaint with the nearest police officer, who knew nothing of the new law. LeCount must have anticipated this confrontation — or perhaps she intended to share the news with her students that day — for she carried a notice of the law with her and showed it to the officer. The police officer arrested the conductor and fined him $100.[68]

As after the 1865 decision in favor of Charlotte Brown, Philadelphia editors could barely contain themselves in the aftermath of LeCount's stand. The *National Antislavery Standard* concluded that "henceforward, the wearied school-teacher, returning from her arduous day's labor, shall not be condemned to walk to her distant home through cold and heat and storm; henceforward invalid women and aged men shall be permitted to avail themselves of a public conveyance, even though their complexion may not be white."[69] The passage of the state law confirmed Octavius Catto's logic; for, as he fought to get the law onto the Republican agenda, he had reasoned that as black men prepared to become voters, Pennsylvania Republicans would recognize that they could no longer afford to ignore their demands for civil rights protections.[70] A state law protecting streetcar and railroad travel would be an important tool in black men's arsenal of self-defense—so would the ballot. In gendered language that anticipated twentieth-century descriptions of Rosa Parks, black men stressed the need for political rights to protect women—"wearied" and "invalid"—from racism. Amelia Mills had appealed to this sentiment when, through the LUA, she had suggested that "friends" might want to see about getting women access to the cars. But she and others were also willing to put their bodies on the line to bring down the local Jim Crow administration. To the women who waged Philadelphia's streetcar battle, the LeCount decision proved what they had long ago figured out—that to claim their right to the streets, black Philadelphians had to ride in them. To do so required stamina and courage.

Women in San Francisco continued to make the point, too, that in the absence of a sea change in public opinion, black communities would continue to face restricted access to public spaces. Access to public space had to be continuously defended, not by law or legal precedent but by body politics. Unlike Philadelphia, San Francisco had no law outlawing streetcar segregation in 1867, and two cases initiated that year—Emma Jane Turner's and Mammy Pleasant's—indicate that the city's car companies remained recalcitrant. Both cases show an expanding African American demand for freedom of movement, beyond the black elite and those who were well-connected. Neither Turner nor Pleasant were members of elite families, nor were they educated teachers who might have seen the issue through the eyes of their young students. Indeed both Turner and Pleasant were domestics, and Turner was likely illiterate. Yet both women pursued their cases long after they might have hoped to gain financially from a settlement, suggesting that the suits were pursued as matters of principle.

On September 13, 1867, Emma Jane Turner, a widow, mother of three, and washerwoman, attempted to board a car at ten o'clock at night with her hands full of shirts to be laundered, when a conductor on the North Beach and Mission Railroad Company refused her entry.[71] When Turner refused to step down, "the conductor pushed [her] in the left breast with his right hand, violently," breaking her grip on the handle and causing her to rip her dress as she was forced off.[72] Though the conductor and the North Beach and Mission Railroad Company denied all the charges—particularly the accusation that Turner was denied service on account of her race—juries found in her favor twice, awarding her $750.[73] Two juries also ruled in favor of Mammy Pleasant, a maid who was awarded $500 in damages after she was denied service by a North Beach conductor.[74] Both cases were heard on appeal by the indefatigable Judge Orville Pratt, who saw in women's streetcar battle a connection to "the fierce strife through which the country has lately passed." Instructing his juries to use these cases to make a statement about the persistent denial of black equality, Pratt expected them to find in favor of "more enlightened and humane ideas."[75]

The California Supreme Court, on the other hand, was not convinced and reversed both the Turner and the Pleasant decisions in 1868, finding that there was no proof that the conductors or the company had intended to cause injury to either Emma Turner or Mammy Pleasant.[76] Two years after filing their original cases, Turner was widowed again with more children to support, and black churches appealed to the community on her behalf, recognizing in her case against North Beach an important service to the community. Mammy Pleasant was a successful businesswoman, recognized for her civil rights work. After 1867, black San Franciscans stopped reporting streetcar evictions and harassment.[77] Although the company was willing to engage in costly legal battles rather than pay individual litigants for their injuries, conductors seem to have made decisions that kept the peace.[78]

Conclusion: Charlotte Brown on the National Stage

Having made her stand against segregation in San Francisco, Charlotte Brown's successful stand against the Omnibus Railroad Company nonetheless resonated beyond the West Coast. Philadelphia's black community watched the case closely. Black communities on both coasts were connected, if not by marriage or birth then by ideals and aspirations. These ideals were reflected in Mammy Pleasant's claim, at the end of her life, to have been born in Philadelphia, though most who knew her believed she had been a slave.[79] Many women who fought the streetcar battles came from established and successful families, and they knew each other from abolitionism and their work on the underground railroad. Some adopted strategies of disguise and deception employed by slave women in resistance to slavery, such as wearing a veil or blending in with a crowd.[80] The work that women did to integrate the cars in their cities emerged from local abolitionism and civil rights work; with black enlistment and emancipation women came to see their local work reflected in the national

Mammy Pleasant. Mary Ellen Pleasant (pictured here in her eighties)—known as Mammy—took both the Omnibus Railroad Company and North Beach and Mission Railroad Company to court for denying her service. Pleasant dropped her case against the former after the company—the same one that had lost to Charlotte Brown in 1865—agreed to give up its policy of segregation. The North Beach case was ultimately lost in the California Supreme Court in 1868. (Arthur Irwin Street, *Pandex of the Press*, vol. 1 [San Francisco, 1902], Bancroft Library, University of California at Berkeley.)

agenda. It is not surprising that women engaged in such work would seek to carry the national conversation about emancipation into their communities and into the rhythms of their everyday lives. It is surprising, however, to see one such local effort—a campaign that emerged from infrapolitics, women's day-to-day defense of their dignity, their bodily integrity—receive a national hearing. Yet, that is what happened in the case of Charlotte Brown.

Just a little over a month after the January 1865 Brown decision had been rendered, Senator Charles Sumner of Massachusetts invoked it in Congress, noting that the case had established an important precedent in the battle for racial equality. Referring to a number of ejections in the capital involving black women and black soldiers, Sumner argued that Congress should revoke the charter of the Washington, D.C., streetcar company responsible for the incidents. Sumner quoted at length from Judge Orville Pratt's ruling, which Sumner believed exhibited a clear understanding of federal law as it applied to segregation. "I thank the State on the Pacific for teaching us here in Washington the law of the land," Sumner exclaimed. His fellow senators were not as moved as Sumner to see the Brown case as a call to action, and, as a result, his proposal made little headway.[81] But for a moment, Charlotte Brown's stand against segregation attracted an audience beyond her fellow passengers on the moving theater of San Francisco's streetcars and beyond those who came to police court to hear her file charges against the conductor who had "with great force and violence" removed her from the car. We can imagine the elation people feel when infrapolitics suddenly gets a public hearing, when, like Charlotte Brown, they suddenly find themselves involved in a "charismatic act," the term James Scott uses to describe these political breakthroughs.[82] The school teacher had been given the opportunity to "teach" federal lawmakers to see her rights the way she did—among them was "the right to ride" where she wanted, on an equal footing with whites.

For years after the Civil War, residents of northern and western cities struggled to make sense of a war that had been fought mostly in the South but also at home. African Americans found the road from emancipation to civil rights in California, Pennsylvania, and elsewhere long and the route indirect. As civil rights legislation and activism in both states attest, battles won by one generation had to be waged and won again in the next. By claiming the streets as their space, black women helped the Civil War generation enjoy freedom of movement and expanded black access to urban space. Focusing the big political questions at stake in the Civil War onto local conditions, women engaged in acts of resistance and encouraged others to follow suit. Together and alone they remapped the terrain of the antebellum city during the Civil War, expanding the space accessible to African Americans in the postwar era. Streetcar battles in San Francisco and Philadelphia demonstrated the potential of a civil rights strategy that was based broadly in the community and that relied on an established tradition of black self-definition. Some years later, Nannie Burroughs of the National Baptist Convention captured one of the lessons of women's streetcar war in reference to a similar battle when she said, "men and women are not made on trains and on streetcars."[83] Black women and men might still occasionally endure indignation on the city's cars, but in the safe spaces of their community they were reaffirmed by the memory of a war bravely fought and won—and then fought again.

As they crossed wartime cities in their war relief work, Charlotte Brown, Mrs. Derry, and other women collided with antebellum understandings of race, class, and gender. Their white neighbors found black women's movements to be disturbing because they reminded whites of what they had to lose with an extension of the space occupied by the free black community and the emergence of a new black assertiveness. How white working-class women and men responded to wartime threats to their communities, such as the reordering of urban space, is the subject of the next chapter.

FIVE

MARTHA GOES TO WASHINGTON
Women's Divided Loyalties

In 1864, as Charlotte Brown was battling San Francisco streetcar conductors, President Lincoln was fighting to secure his reelection. Having
faced down challenges from Peace Democrats and criticism from fellow
Republicans, Lincoln remained anxious about his prospects for a second
term in office.[1] As always, Lincoln was willing to try new approaches,
such as ensuring soldiers' votes were counted and granting government
workers a one-day furlough to vote.[2] Lincoln intervened on a number of
occasions to help local Republicans facing serious Democratic competition.

In the midst of negotiating these various concerns, Lincoln met with
a group of visitors who would never vote for him and who wielded little power to convince others to do so. Indeed, some of them had been
openly critical of the Lincoln administration. They were a delegation of
Philadelphia seamstresses employed at the Schuylkill Arsenal, women
whose U.S. Army sewing work was exemplary but whose loyalties had
sometimes been suspect. Armed with a petition signed by 800 women,
the seamstresses had come to Washington to ask the War Department to
raise their wages and to persuade Lincoln and Secretary of War Edwin
Stanton to stop government contracting.

Contracting was a logical response to wartime shortages of supplies
of all sorts, as it allowed the expansion of war production without the
added costs of hiring new government workers.[3] Contracting was also politically expedient; it allowed Republicans to shore up political support in
cities where war fatigue was endemic and Democrats had made considerable headway. But the inequalities of the system bothered critics who saw
contractors as opportunists who paid soldiers' wives starvation wages for
their sewing work while their husbands risked life and limb on the battlefield. Many in the North suspected that individual contractors stood to
profit handsomely off of war manufacturing.[4]

In between Republican politics and popular grumblings about contracting stood the working-class women who sewed the shirts, drawers, pants, and jackets issued to U.S. Army soldiers fighting in the war, women employed at or near U.S. Army arsenals in Philadelphia, Cincinnati, St. Louis, Detroit, and New York. Sewing work was a poorly paid and crowded field of labor; by one estimate, sewing women earned as little as $1.50 a week in 1863, wages that were inadequate to support families with small children, particularly when inflation and shortages are taken into account.[5] Seamstresses' demands for higher wages evidenced women's collective sense of the importance of the skilled labor they provided for the state, work they believed defined their loyalty. But these demands put sewing women at cross-purposes with free-labor nationalists who had no patience for organized labor. The Lincoln administration regularly regarded northern labor organizations in the same light as southern rebels in the occupied South; both had to be pacified. Sewing women who organized meetings and petitioned the War Department risked being perceived as disloyal, as bad as southern "she-devils" who disrespected U.S. Army men. Indeed, at least one Philadelphia seamstress who called on President Lincoln, Martha Yeager, lost her government job after criticizing the U.S. Army's use of contractors, even though she had a brother in the Union army.[6] Others had become suspect after denouncing emancipation or the draft or when someone discovered their husbands at home instead of at the front.

When the president and secretary of war met with this group of sewing women from Philadelphia there was more at stake than the few extra cents the women would earn for their sewing. The election-year meeting was part of an ongoing conflict over space and power in wartime northern communities, one that engaged white and black working-class women, men, and local authorities who vied with each other to lay claim to scarce wartime resources such as jobs, relief money, soldiers, and civilian morale. Draft rioting was one expression of this conflict over resources; labor petitions and unionization were others. Like the streetcar campaigns, the stage for this conflict was the streets of wartime northern communities, where local and federal officials came to blows with residents over contracting, the draft, and other policies, further eroding the boundary separating home front from battlefield. Along that disappearing line stood working-class white women who tried to make sense of the shifting ground on which they stood, women who were used to allocating resources within their own households and who found the war to be an unwelcome drain. Lincoln's decision to meet with women who were stirring up resistance in their communities speaks to administration concerns about combating northern war disaffection.

In previous chapters, we have seen how women moved into new spaces vacated by men and how they expanded to fill the void left in old ones. This chapter returns to the old spaces and examines a different kind of spatial adjustment underway during the Civil War—one that came as a result of federal and state authorities reaching into working-class, immigrant communities and commanding resources, mostly in the form of men to fight but also in women's implicit consent to a variety of home-front changes. As wartime northern governments moved into this space, they upset an existing balance of power between women and men, black and white. The previous chapter considered how black women invited this change—precipitated it, even—as an opportunity to correct an antebellum order of race and gender that left them marginalized twice over and geographically confined; in this chapter we encounter women who attempted to stop it. The white women described here, those who engaged in draft riots, labor protests, and other wartime resistance, wanted to protect old spaces *from* change. Ironically, these women came closest to realizing the image struck by the enlistment poem that began this volume, "We are Coming Father Abraham," of stalwart women standing stationary in their doorways, as wartime scenes moved rapidly past.

This chapter argues that women sought to protect workplaces and urban streets as racialized spaces that were threatened by emancipation and to disrupt traditional connections between enlistment, masculinity, and upward social mobility. It comes as little surprise that a government intent on realizing the modernizing potential of free-labor nationalism would have found working-class white women's conservative politics intolerable. Lincoln called northern war disaffection the "fire in the rear"; combating it was as important to the president as employing a successful military strategy. Based on the assumption that loyalty—like morality—originated in the household, women stood at the center of Union efforts to extinguish the "fire in the rear." Like the policy employed to subdue civilian resistance in the South, the campaign to enforce northern women's loyalty developed on an ad hoc basis, alternating between periods of escalation and retreat, benign offers of charity and the use of coercion or force. Of course, unruly and disloyal women never posed a threat to military or political hegemony in the North as they did in the South. But, like in the South, women's opposition created an environment in which resistance flourished and helped convince President Lincoln and others in his administration that, absent a victory at home, none would be possible at the front.

She-Devils and Copperheads:
Women's Loyalties and Middle-Class Attitudes

As the sewing women who went to Washington well knew, Stanton's charitable words were contradicted by various administration policies that divided women against each other—characterizing some women as loyal and deserving of government work or relief and others as not. Attaching loyalty tests to employment or relief was in part a practical reflection of real scarcity, but it also served to keep order at home by holding women with absentee husbands responsible for containing familial disruption brought on by enlistment and the draft. Immigrant wives of enlisted or drafted men who navigated a confusing labyrinth of wartime relief and local charity understood the spuriousness of such categories as loyal and disloyal, deserving and undeserving. In the struggle over resources, women clashed not only with officials but also with each other, often along lines of race and class but sometimes across those lines. Emancipation and black enlistment, for example, offered African American women and men opportunities to rethink the dynamics of power in northern communities and to reorder the access to space and power. With the wartime coming of age of emancipationist sentiment, African American women and men became the beneficiaries of the white middle class's sympathetic imagination, and, in that regard, black women were particularly useful in drawing up the balance sheet on northern loyalties, one in which Irish women and others often fell far short of expectations.

Concerned to avoid charges of disloyalty, the seamstresses were nonetheless opposed to the characterization of their work as charity for soldiers' wives. The petition addressed to Secretary of War Stanton before the August 1864 meeting was prepared on behalf of "Twenty thousand Working Women of Philadelphia, [women] who have given *their all* to their country; and who now come to that country, not as beggars, asking alms, but as American matrons and daughters, asking an equitable price for their labor."[7] Referring to themselves as "American matrons and daughters," sewing women did not come in search of alms but of fair recognition of their own war service. When they met with President Lincoln in 1864, Philadelphia's seamstresses had been waging their campaign against contracting for nearly three years. By then, they were unionizing, and they had been joined by sewing women in cities throughout the industrial North. Even so, for Lincoln, there would have been no political consequences had he declined to meet with women. Indeed, after having successfully linked labor activism with disloyalty, it is surprising that anyone in the administration would have agreed to the meeting, much less have been willing to make concessions. Yet Stanton ordered the expansion of government work and a salary hike for seamstresses employed in public arsenals. In a letter to the women published in the papers, the secretary of war assured sewing women of his good intentions and promised to keep working for their "desired object."[8]

Northern public opinion about female loyalty was shaped in reaction to southern women's resistance to U.S. Army occupation. Since the occupation of New Orleans, southern women's disloyalty and unwomanly conduct had become the northern public's obsession. For months, northern papers carried stories about the battle between the women of New Orleans and occupying Union troops under the leadership of General Benjamin Butler, and northern commentators often summed up southern women's verbal and physical assaults on U.S. soldiers by referring to them as "she-devils," women who were "far worse rebels than the men."[9] Recognizing the political significance in these everyday acts of resistance, the army responded—sometimes with federal approval and other times without, with various levels of force and with mixed success—to women's unruly and disruptive behavior.[10] Officially, U.S. Army commanders tried a variety of approaches to dealing with hostile women, including cajoling, threatening, imprisoning, and banishing women who refused to accept occupation; unofficially, individual soldiers used an even wider variety of approaches.[11] Though divided about the particulars, the northern public generally agreed that southern women's disloyalty should not go unpunished. As the war dragged on, the U.S. Army became convinced that to win, the Union had to break the will of the southern people; to do so required extending the northern public's tolerance for employing military violence against civilians, including women.[12]

Northern newspapers helped in that regard by printing stories ridiculing women's loyalty to the Confederacy and portraying southern gender relations as degenerate. In a May 1863 cartoon from *Frank Leslie's Illustrated*, the paper lampooned elite white southern women's self-image as demure and deferential when they are portrayed "hounding" their men to enlist and then suffering the consequences of war. Published soon after the April 1863 Richmond bread riot, the cartoon fed northern prejudices about southern women as "she-devils" who, at least in this case, got their just desserts. The bread riot story made the front page of both the *New York Times* and the *New York Tribune*, under headlines reading, "Three Thousand Hungry Women Raging in the Streets" and "Three Thousand Women in Revolt," respectively.[13] Both papers also carried news in the same issue of a large Democratic rally held in New York the previous day. Whether readers made the connection between dissent in the South and in the North, the simultaneous newspaper coverage of bread rioting and the "Copperhead Rally" implied as much.[14]

In contrast to southern women, who were portrayed (and mocked) by the northern press as fiercely partisan, northern women seemed to be indifferent. With these concerns in mind, a group of New Yorkers formed the National Women's Loyal League to rally and organize women's po-litical loyalties and enlist them in combating disaffection and copperhead sentiments in their communities.[15] At a May 1863 meeting of the National Women's Loyal League in New York, Elizabeth Cady Stanton sought to inspire her middle-class audience to action by comparing them to south-ern women. Stanton warned northern women that they too might one day have to support themselves, and then "the question would be, not woman's sphere, but woman's bread." Striking a note that was by now familiar, Stanton criticized southern women's loyalty to slavery and the Confederacy and asked, "what ought not the women of the North do to maintain the best Government on earth?"[16] Stanton called on loyal women in the North to actively and demonstratively support the administration. Middle-class women responded by forming Loyal Leagues committed to identifying and rooting out disloyal and disruptive elements in their own communities.[17] Although women in the leagues repeatedly denied the comparison, the leagues' campaign implied that to win the war, northern women needed to be more like southern women. For, as one critic of female indifference charged, had the women of the North — like their southern counterparts — encouraged "a loyal and devoted spirit among us, the cop-perhead conspiracy in behalf of the enemy would have been strangled at birth."[18]

The National Women's Loyal League's call to women's loyalty un-leashed a new round of anger against southern women as unwomanly. In a well-circulated Loyal League pamphlet entitled, "A Few Words in Behalf of the Loyal Women of the United States," Caroline Kirkland at-tacked southern women, blaming them for supporting slavery, mistreat-

"Sowing and Reaping." In this cartoon published in the aftermath of bread rioting in the South, southern women are portrayed "sowing" the seeds of rebellion and "reaping" its effects. In the frame on the left, women are "hounding their men on to Rebellion," and on the right, they are "feeling the effects of Rebellion and creating Bread Riots." ("Sowing and Reaping," *Frank Leslie's Illustrated Newspaper*, May 23, 1863, 141.)

ing Union prisoners of war, and celebrating the violence of war. Southern women, Kirkland insisted, were not heroines whom northern women should emulate but were worse than "those terrible Parisian fish-women," hateful *"poissardes,"* who rejoiced in the escalation of violence during the French Revolution. Reflecting her own middle-class consciousness and that of her intended audience, Kirkland imagined that guilt did not fall equally on *all* southern women, but that "in times of war and commotion, bad women, like bad men, find an opportunity of coming to the surface." Throughout the pamphlet, Kirkland repeatedly entreated her readers not to imitate southern women who followed their passions in support of their men, but in the end, that was what she recommended. Kirkland called on loyal northern women to engage war critics and to treat draft evaders with disdain. That some of her readers had already taken Kirkland's advice and adopted a more demonstrative loyalty was clear in the kind of behavior she advised against. "We need not make faces at [draft evaders], or send them presents of female or infants' gear," Kirkland concluded, "for that would be imitating southern women."[19] Although she does not offer specific advice, she did not think her middle-class readership was above a little modest gender baiting in the war against female apathy in the North. Northern commentators had many words to describe women loyal to the Confederacy—she-devils, copperheads, *poissardes*—but they also hoped that middle-class women in the North would learn something about loyalty from their example.

Across town at another meeting, Democrats made their own calls to loyalty in a packed hall at the Cooper Institute. At the "Rally of the Democracy," former New York Mayor Fernando Wood railed against emancipation and the draft and called on his audience to resist the Lincoln administration's "revolutionary" efforts to "destroy our Government." One of the resolutions offered at the meeting condemned the administration's liberal use of "the terms 'loyal' and 'disloyal'," as a "base invention" intended to squelch dissent.[20] Instead, Fernando Wood offered a stinging criticism of groups in the North who stood to profit from a perpetuation of the war. Railroad company magnates and the New England business elite figured prominently in Wood's attacks, but so too did the private contractors and government employees who made up the civilian war machine. Wood estimated there were "over twelve hundred thousand persons," more people than there were U.S. soldiers, whom he described as "the army of office holders and contractors [and] Government employees," intent on "a patriotic and vigorous prosecution of the war." With such a formidable army deployed in communities throughout the North, the goal of the Lincoln administration and its friends, Wood insisted, was not southern defeat but a perpetuation of war. Those who would resist the draft were not copperheads but patriots intent on saving the nation from war without end. Though Wood did not single out African Americans as another group that would profit personally from the nation's ruin, the connection was obvious to those who attended and read handbills parodying Loyal League efforts to encourage enlistment that read, "Fight for the Nigger."[21]

The crowd at the Cooper Institute responded warmly to Wood's rhetoric, interrupting him on a number of occasions to applaud and inject their own commentary on administration policies. The *Times* reporter scanned the New York crowd and reported with satisfaction that "[a]midst the vast concourse, one—and only one—of the gentler sex was observed." Reflecting middle-class ideas about women's moral superiority—and the *Times*' close relationship to the Lincoln administration—the comment implied that the absence of women confirmed the illegitimacy of the copperhead cause. The Democratic *Herald* also noted the shortage of women at the rally but pointedly remarked that "all of our recent political war meetings have been largely attended by the fair sex." In the contest for loyalties in a politically divided city, women's attendance was carefully counted.

Draft Riots and White Working-Class Women's Street Politics

Although contemporaries (and modern historians) would disagree over whether or not Mayor Wood and other local politicians were partly responsible for the violent draft riots that wracked the city in July 1863, his characterization of the war corresponded closely with that of the working-class and immigrant women and men who took to the streets and perpetrated horrific acts of violence, mostly against black New Yorkers. Draft rioters believed they were protecting their families and their communities from a government intent on their ruin. Wood's speech had reinforced the culture of opposition that thrived in northern communities and was sustained by women's street politics. Encoded in the script of the riots were hints of entangled assumptions about race, gender, and wartime loyalty peculiar to these politics.

For five days in July 1863, New York City was wracked with violence as rioters took to the streets, first protesting the draft and then lashing out angrily at members of the Lincoln administration, wealthy businessmen, and black New Yorkers. Venting economic and racial frustrations, Irish and German immigrant workers led the crowds who destroyed property and tortured and killed more than one hundred African Americans, setting off a massive black exodus out of the city. Peace was not restored to the city until troops were called in from Gettysburg to patrol the streets and round up rioters. As historian Iver Bernstein has shown, the riots allowed white workers to fend off both the draft and Republican rule of the city and to extend their political influence; for black New Yorkers, the riots were an unequivocal disaster.[22]

Women figured prominently in newspaper accounts of the draft riots in New York and other northern cities, as both perpetrators and victims. On the first day of the New York riot, the *Herald* reported that "quite a large number of females . . . armed principally with bricks and stones" were "prominent among those who made the first attack and who urged [on] their relatives and acquaintances."[23] White women likely also participated in the destruction of the Colored Orphan Asylum later that day, as the institution served as a symbol of middle-class poor relief dispensed, as Mary Ryan has pointed out, "magnanimously to those they deemed the 'worthy poor,' and rarely to Irish Catholics."[24] On the second day of rioting in New York, rioters attacked and killed Colonel Henry O'Brien of the Eleventh New York Volunteers after he had ordered troops to fire on a crowd, resulting in the death of a woman and her child. A man in the crowd clubbed the U.S. Army officer from behind, and then women beat O'Brien's face to a pulp, dragged him through the streets, and stripped and mutilated his body before leaving him to die in his own backyard.[25] The torture and murder of Colonel O'Brien was a rehearsal for the widespread racially and sexually charged attacks on black men and boys that followed in the days to come.

But white women were not the only ones who took to the streets in self-defense. On the fourth day of the riots, the *Herald* described "a white woman partially intoxicated, with disheveled hair, loose dress, and the swagger of one of the 'b'hoys'" confronting "a throng of colored women who had gathered opposite of their homes." Here, in a black neighborhood of the Fifth Ward, the white woman tried unsuccessfully to goad a group of African American women into a fight by cussing at them and calling herself a copperhead. "'I can fight too, by damned,'" the woman shouted, "who'll take me up?" It seems unlikely coincidental that a group of black women gathered across from their homes in the midst of the extraordinary racial violence that gripped the city; more likely, the women had come together to exchange information about friends and neighbors and to watch out for trouble. In any case, the women did not take the rioter's bait, and the latter was eventually led away by a white man, sparing the neighborhood a fight.[26] In the same ward, African American women with small children in tow could be seen making their way to police station houses or other safe places to ride out the storm.[27] With rioters perpetrating the worst violence against black men, families made difficult decisions about how best to defend themselves from assault, like splitting up and charging women with patrolling the streets.[28] In the midst of the riots, no black New Yorker would have wanted to risk being spotted alone on the street by a white mob, but perhaps some were emboldened to stand together.

Despite what newspaper accounts suggest, white women were never more than a minority of the participants in draft riots, but they were disproportionately important.[29] Their participation is consistent with the dynamic of antebellum street politics; in the street women watched over their families, policed their neighborhoods, and served as important

Women in the New York City draft riots. In this illustration, a woman figures prominently in the artist's rendition of the murder of Colonel Henry O'Brien on July 14, 1863. ("The Rioters Dragging Col. O'Brien's Body through the Street," from Headley, *Great Riots of New York*, after 198.)

sources of information and the first line of defense. As the war drew men out of these communities, women's work in home protection redoubled. During the riots, white women played key roles in identifying targets and instigating violence, and, of course, women's participation was symbolically important. It served to underscore the crowd's unanimity of purpose and the essential nature of the threat for which the rioters were seeking redress—that as the war drew away male wage earners, it drove working-class and immigrant women to destitution. Democratic demagogues played on fears of that threat in political speeches such as at the "Rally of the Democracy," at which they had anticipated female attendance.

As on streetcars, the riots enacted a kind of public theater in which working-class women and men, draft agents, policemen, and soldiers performed various roles; so too did onlookers and newspaper men. Wartime riots followed a script, the outlines of which had been set well before the New York City rally and the July 1863 draft. By then, some scenes were well rehearsed in communities far removed from the working-class neighborhoods of New York's Fifth Ward. Resistance to enlistment was not uncommon in industrial regions of Pennsylvania beginning in 1862 and in rural areas of New York, Connecticut, and Ohio, for example, and these earlier episodes suggest a certain pattern of resistance. Tension began to escalate at or near the scene of the enrollment or draft lottery, where women and men waited to receive the news. In Lancaster, Pennsylvania, for instance, more than one hundred women—the local paper called them "Amazons"—came to the courthouse where the draft was being administered. "Armed with knives, heavy spoons, and other kitchen implements," the women "rapped the boy who was turning the wheel over the head and knuckles."[30] In many cases, women began collecting information in advance of the official draft announcement. The Saturday before the New York riots, for example, city papers noted that groups of "workingmen's wives" had gathered nervously in the streets waiting for news about the conscription.[31] The list of draftees' names was then carried by formal and informal channels—newspapers and rumor—to the rest of the community, where people braced themselves for the worst. When draft marshals appeared in the streets of working-class communities, women were ready for a fight. Men were usually bystanders or witnesses up to this point, until rioters rounded up supporters from neighboring homes or workplaces or they responded to the sounds of the fight. Several hours underway, draft riots often became gender-integrated expressions of white working-class infrapolitics.

The timing was important in the riot in Boston that occurred on the second day of violence in New York. When draft marshals entered the heavily Irish North End community on Tuesday, July 14, men were away at work. The women who answered the knocks at their doors had just returned home from a large requiem mass held to mourn the losses in Boston's popular Irish regiments at Gettysburg. Two of the women attacked the agents, alerting men working nearby and setting off a day of violence that resulted in some fourteen deaths and considerable damage to the Cooper Street Armory.[32] Among those who attacked the armory, an observer described "one Amazonian woman" with extraordinary strength. "A dozen men were trying to get her away from the scene," one paper reported, "but she tore herself from their arms, and with hair streaming, arms swinging, and her face the picture of phrenzy, she rushed again and again to the assault."[33] Some news accounts may have exaggerated women's prominence in riots, reflecting nativist assumptions about degenerate immigrants, but the consistency with which women are described at the head of rioting crowds in Boston, in coal-mining towns in Pennsylvania, and in New York City prevents us from discounting this assessment outright.

Women instigated riots when they verbally and physically humiliated draft agents and egged on bystanders, and sometimes they continued to direct them even after men joined in. This pattern seems to have been the case in the coal-mining regions of Pennsylvania southwest of Scranton and in and around the city of Wilkes-Barre, where miners settled in tight-knit ethnic communities and Irish women patrolled the streets, carefully cultivating and enforcing a culture of resistance. In one town, rioting women forced residents out of their homes "to turn out and join them" or have their houses "pulled down."[34] Violence here was highly gendered, indicating that women sought not only to humiliate enrollment agents but also to chasten men who witnessed the violence—and who might have considered enlisting. An agent named Charles Rossler arrested a man in Archbald, Pennsylvania, who refused to give his name for a state enlistment. After the man enlisted and was released, however, his neighbors beat him.[35] Rossler had himself been a victim of the women of Archbald just a few weeks prior to this incident. Late in August 1862, when he first came to the town, the women attacked Rossler with stones, beat him in the head, and tried to remove his pants, offering their own interpretations of the connections between masculinity and military service. When miners tried to stop the women they too came under attack.[36] One wonders what—besides the military escort—compelled Rossler to return to the town for a second try. An agent named Otis was subjected to similar violence and gender-specific humiliation in Mauch Chunk, Pennsylvania, when twenty-five women stoned him with pieces of coal. One woman approached Otis, struck him in the mouth, and attempted to seize him by the hair. When his "'hair' all came off in a body," the woman retreated quickly, believing that in her rage, reported the local paper, she had scalped the now-wigless Otis.[37]

Such accounts served as excellent fodder for copperhead newspapermen, but the men who witnessed women's violence did not find the attacks amusing. Women who sought to punish or humiliate draft agents and recruiters performed a public critique of popular rhetoric crediting military service with turning boys into men—in the riot script, men who would leave their families to join the army, or convince others to, were not men but boys. Chasing men with knives and removing their pants, women directed this street theater, in which men were either villainous outsiders or women's hapless victims.

Women's street politics took place within the context of local political and racial tensions. In Pennsylvania's anthracite communities, Democratic loyalties ran as deep as did working-class white racism. Local papers helped to stir the pot of resistance by employing military terms to describe the rioters' actions: the women "advanced in columns" on the unsuspecting agent and "outflanked" him when he tried to escape. Referring to the women as "rebels" allowed the Democratic *Luzerne Union* to play on Republican rhetoric about loyalty; at the same time, papers compared "wild" Irish women to Indians, employing a racial trope to describe white women rioters who were wont to express their own racism.[38] Women were observed surrounding their victims, chanting "Indian-like yells," and, in the case of the Mauch Chunk agent, scalping him.[39] Men (and women) joined in; or sometimes, they interceded to protect the victims, as when the miners tried to stop the women of Archbald from pulling off Charles Rossler's pants. Emphasizing women's "savage" and unpredictable behavior allowed local Democrats to portray the coal fields as enemy territory where enrollment officers or other agents of the administration would be treated accordingly. But it also underscored the point that when it came to enlistment, working-class women and men might have differences of opinion.

White women were responsible for both witnessing and perpetrating sexual humiliation and violence against male victims. In New York, male rioters castrated or sexually mutilated black men in front of crowds of cheering onlookers.[40] Explicit attacks on black men's bodies were likely aimed at protecting a racial and sexual order that rioters believed was threatened by the improved status of black men postemancipation. With white women among the witnesses to these acts, white men enacted their fears of miscegenation and gender disorder and attempted to underscore women's sexual vulnerability. Similar concerns informed the gender and racial dynamic in Pennsylvania's coal fields. Miners in Mauch Chunk were incensed when four women were arrested and jailed after they attacked and "scalped" the state enrollment officer. The men—who had been unable to stop the women from attacking the agent—gathered outside the jail and demanded their wives' release. Why, they asked, were their wives in jail while a black man charged with knocking down a white girl had been set free? Here, predominantly Irish coalminers asserted their racial prerogatives and posed as white women's protectors, hoping that a judge would see things their way. He did. The women were released with the understanding that their husbands would prevent further disturbances.[41] "Woman without her man," the local paper declared, "is but a savage."[42]

Inasmuch as men attempted to superimpose an alternative narrative on wartime riots, one that focused on correcting a temporary gender and racial disorder, that narrative only partly covered over the economics of enlistment that formed the basis of women's riot script. According to the script, draft rioting was an expression of loyalty to family and to community. Individually, immigrant men might consider enlistment as a means of upward mobility or as an opportunity to disprove nativist assumptions about their manhood. But in communities such as Pennsylvania's coal fields and the Irish neighborhoods of Boston and New York, where the culture of resistance flourished, men who enlisted or were drafted had to face down considerable resistance both in and outside their homes. When Michael Kelly was recruiting in Connecticut and upstate New York, he found men willing to talk with him but women hostile. "One woman chased [me] with a large meat knife," Kelly recorded in his diary, and "another daubed in the face with cow manure" while Kelly "talked with her husband in [the] barn yard."[43] In the short term, enlistment meant more work and worry for wives and children. And as it drove families to the brink of destitution and into the hands of middle-class dispensers of charity, military service risked *confirming* nativist prejudices about degenerate immigrant domesticity.

The riots provided a number of opportunities for middle-class observers to link Irish women's disloyalty to an absence of appropriate feminine qualities—and, by extension, a lack of masculinity in the men. References to the women as inordinately strong "Amazons" and to faces full of "phrenzy" served to underscore the irrational and unruly nature of draft rioters—"bad women," as Caroline Kirkland, spokeswoman for loyal Yankee women, would have referred to them. Focusing on the presence of children in the crowds added to this characterization. The discriminating *Pittston Gazette* repeated a story told by a beleaguered marshal in that town who had faced down considerable resistance from women, including one—"a woman of that class"—who thrust "into his face a small child which had the small pox in the most loathsome form."[44] Some years later, Boston resident Emma Sellew Adams had forgotten many of the details about that city's wartime riots, but she recalled how several women had held "their babies in their arms . . . daring the soldiers to fire at them."[45] Stories like these helped convince middle-class observers of the necessity of resorting to force in putting down women's resistance, for once women in these crowds ceased to be women, they no longer deserved protection. The *Gazette* offered these "Amazons" a word of advice about how best to respond to the next marshal who they met: "Quiet submission then is the only course that will show you are worthy of the protection which this Government affords you."[46]

That children were often present at these street conflicts speaks to the particular context of working-class women's lives and the communities where they lived and worked. When a husband and father enlisted or was drafted, he left his wife in charge of providing for and protecting the children—from illness, injury, orphanhood. These were the same women who toted their children along to relief offices where middle-class agents judged their fitness—their "worthiness"—to receive aid. In painting a picture of draft rioters as "bad women," Adams and other observers forgot that children had suffered serious injuries as a result of soldiers firing into the crowds.

Voters did not forget. Responding, or failing to respond, to women's street politics could have political consequences for officials linked closely to the Lincoln administration. In July 1863, Mayor Frederic Lincoln and Governor John Andrew ordered out soldiers who fired on a Boston crowd composed mainly of women and children and garrisoned troops around the affected areas. The city's response to the riot became an issue in the fall 1863 reelection campaigns for both Massachusetts Republicans. Yet mayors, governors, and local law enforcement ignored the threat posed by women's disloyalty at their own peril. Officials took women's threats to public order seriously, despite disclaimers suggesting that they were ambivalent about enforcing female loyalty through the barrel of a gun. The governor of Pennsylvania called soldiers to the anthracite region in response to the string of attacks on draft agents in the fall of 1862.[47] In a letter to Edwin Stanton, Governor Andrew Curtin explained, "notwithstanding the usual exaggeration, I think the organization to resist the draft in Schuylkill, Lucerne, and Carbon counties is very formidable. I wish to crush the resistance so effectively that the like will not occur again."[48] Having been stung by their attempt to "crush" their own draft resistance, politicians in Boston considered a more conciliatory approach in the months after the one-day riot. The Common Council and the Board of Aldermen considered a bill authorizing the city to pay "the commutation fee of such of the citizens of this City liable to military duty and drafted into service of the United States, who have families dependent on them for support."[49] In New York, the draft was suspended, and eventually troops were called out to restore order. Tammany Hall Democrats stood alongside elite Republicans and condemned the draft riot, but they also passed a measure promising to pay the $300 exemption of New York conscripts.[50] Although neither measure went into effect, they suggest that city leaders considered meeting rioters halfway when they demanded an end to the draft.[51]

As an expression of infrapolitics, draft riots are best understood as a conflict over resources. Local officials were at odds with women whose conduct was disruptive and disrespectful and who drained urban resources earmarked for wartime urban protection from enemy invasion, for recruitment, and for other inevitable wartime expenses. The added costs of policing a city's female population took on political significance as women's actions redirected attention and sometimes manpower from the war front to the home front. Any explicit measures taken to police women's behavior or to respond to their critiques accepted that women's actions were politically significant. Hence the ambivalence in Governor Curtin's dismissal of reports of women's draft resistance as "exaggeration," followed by his promise to "crush" it. When he threatened to treat the women of occupied New Orleans like prostitutes, Benjamin Butler employed gendered language to refer to the problem of disloyalty, but he took seriously the need for the U.S. Army to enforce women's loyalty. Confederate officials struggled to balance the need to respond decisively to threats to public order and their desire not to make too much of women's politics. In Virginia, Governor John Lechter and President Jefferson Davis insisted that the Richmond bread rioters were outsiders and prostitutes, but when Lechter called out soldiers and threatened to fire on the crowd of women, his actions too spoke louder than words.[52] Local officials learned that enforcing women's loyalty, or at least their "quiet obedience," required using scarce resources—city and state funds, for example—but it also came with a potential cost to northern morale and at the expense of some political capital.

The negotiation that took place between working-class, largely immigrant communities and local officials during and after draft riots suggests that these engagements were also contests over space. Charged with the protection of their homes and families, women verbally confronted and then attacked the draft marshals who appeared at their doors or in their communities. Marshals, police officers, and even soldiers, at times, operated at a distinct disadvantage in streets patrolled by women and governed by different rules. In Pennsylvania, residents of working-class immigrant communities came out of their homes and into the streets on the day of the draft, making it difficult for marshals to confirm their identities and residences and add their names to the state enrollment lists.[53] Like the veils worn by black women riding wartime streetcars, white working-class rioters made use of the fluidity of wartime identity. Using the familiar spaces of their own communities, locals could evade officials or help others to do so. Rioters also contested the assignment of space and power outside their own neighborhoods when they selected targets such as the Cooper Street Armory in Boston, for instance, or New York's Colored Orphan Asylum. In the former case, the building was easily associated with the war—a visible, daily reminder of the unequal demands made on the working class to enlist or be drafted. In the latter, the asylum represented a kind of middle-class charity for which working-class Irish women were rarely deemed worthy. Working-class women and men attacked these structures in order to register their discontent with how the war had opened up new conduits to power for some and exaggerated the powerlessness of others.

The Sewing Women and the President

In the midst of the five-day New York City riot, a few elite members of the Republican Union League pushed President Lincoln to declare martial law and to appoint General Benjamin Butler military governor of New York.[54] The specter of a military occupation of New York spoke more to the extreme fantasies of a few embattled Knickerbockers than represented the wishes of a Republican majority, nonetheless, the seriousness with which the proposal was pursued indicates that some among the northern public saw no reason to treat treasonous New Yorkers any different from the Confederate loyalists Butler had suppressed in New Orleans. Less radical solutions to the street violence were pursued by Union League members and fellow elites who, in the days after the riot, generously reached out to the city's beleaguered African Americans with what historian Iver Bernstein has described as "an unprecedented liberality to the black poor." Seeking a way to model appropriate class relations for the Irish working class, elite Republicans lavished praise and charity on black New Yorkers as a reward for their "'pure' loyalty."[55] To working-class whites, there was nothing new about the divide-and-conquer approach that relied on drawing lines separating the loyal working class from the rest, a strategy that had often focused on managing women's behavior in particular. This latest outpouring of charity served as a reminder that working-class women and men were losing the battle to defend the white spaces of the streets but had not yet given up the war.

Union League activities in Philadelphia focused too on enforcing loyalty on the home front, from the inside out. One week after the riot in New York, the assistant quartermaster in charge of the Schuylkill Arsenal—the largest employer of women in Philadelphia—announced that the arsenal would no longer employ seamstresses who could not prove their loyalty to the Union. Within two days, Colonel George Crosman had discharged more than one hundred sewing women who could not provide written evidence of their relationship to U.S. Army soldiers or who "belong[ed] to families opposed to the war."[56] That the laid-off women did not hurl bricks at the Schuylkill Arsenal buildings or take to the streets to protest was Crosman's good fortune, and that of Philadelphia's large black population, whom the crowd also might have targeted. Local officials perhaps anticipated that the order would meet with little resistance in the aftermath of the Confederate invasion of south-central Pennsylvania earlier in the month, a time when many in the state still feared for their safety. The order was a novel attempt to ferret out any remnants of copperheadism in the city by reserving arsenal sewing jobs for loyal women and soldiers' wives and letting other sewing women fend for themselves among the many private contractors.

Once again, city officials and local military authorities were surprised by organized and articulate female resistance, for the U.S. Army's decision to lay off members of disloyal households backfired. Two days after the initial layoffs, 145 women signed a petition to Edwin Stanton demanding their jobs back and strongly refuted the army's spurious linking of the layoffs with a lack of patriotism. Next to their signatures, each woman described her circumstances and gave her address: Ann Nugent, "widow, two sons at the war"; Maria Hale, "three children, husband killed at war"; Margaret Jackson, "two children, son killed at war"; Mary M. Kelley, "lost husban and son at war."[57] The petition explained, in no uncertain terms, that women who had lost their jobs were experienced seamstresses who stood at the center of loyal households. At least two women—including Martha Yeager ("brother at war") and Anna Long ("Widow, 5 children") had criticized Crosman at a public meeting; surely they wondered if their assertiveness, rather than any evidence of disloyalty, had lost them their jobs. At an even larger meeting held a few days later, seamstresses drafted a series of resolutions addressed to Stanton demanding Crosman's removal and an immediate end to the new loyalty policy, which they described as "oppressive and prejudicial" because it did not apply equally to the men employed at the arsenal who had "neither friends nor relatives in the service."[58] If the army was worried about enforcing loyalty among its employees, then the women would offer their own suggestions.

Under Crosman's new loyalty mandate, women who had worked at the arsenal for years now had to apply along with others in a process that proved contentious and divided women against each other. Applicants were required to bring a letter of reference verifying their claims to the work and testifying to their loyalty. Women resisted the army's surveillance by forging documents and misleading referees.[59] Women who had lived and worked in the neighborhood for many years colluded to keep control over their share of the government work. Seamstresses who managed to retain their Schuylkill jobs shared the work, "handing off" some or all of their sewing to friends, sisters, or daughters who they believed needed the money more.[60] At the same time, within their communities women continued to police each other carefully, despite the new protocol placing the army in that position. Like the text of the draft riots, seamstresses' letters reveal little unanimity of opinion about the war in the working-class neighborhoods and homes of Philadelphia. Though her husband was a discharged soldier, Mary King was fired when an arsenal colleague overheard her "abusing the Government and every person around her" and exclaiming that she "'was sorry she ever came here to live under a nigger Government.'"[61] Schuylkill seamstress Sarah Cosgrove had to defend herself when a neighbor overheard her "dancing for joy" when she heard news of Lincoln's death.[62] A woman who signed with her initials and the words "a Soilders wife" relayed rumors about a woman who had no legitimate claims to the work. She "gets the work and has no children small she owns two houses and sets in market she gives it to her daughter in law and her husband is living and is a bricklayer and at home," the anonymous seamstress explained.[63] Even so, Crosman's divide-and-conquer strategy was only partly successful; while it clearly divided women against each other, women with questionable loyalties still worked at the arsenal more than a year after the directive. And sewing women continued to make use of every opportunity to police the community and control access to government sewing work.

African American women seized the moment opened up by the new loyalty directive to make their own demands for the work. Based on their connections to United States Colored Troops, a group of black women led by "Mrs. M. R. Smith" addressed themselves to Union League member George Boker, who wrote directly to Crosman on their behalf. In an ingenious plea to the league's ethnic and religious prejudices, the women asked whether it was Crosman's official policy to hire only Irish women to work at the arsenal. Also a Union League member, Crosman denied the charge and promised to give black women applicants equal consideration.[64] Although it is not clear whether they ever secured government appointments at the Schuylkill Arsenal, African American women recognized an opportunity in the Protestant Union League's growing scrutiny of white working-class—largely Irish Catholic—women's loyalties and moved to secure government jobs for themselves. Crosman's response was predictable, but it was nonetheless significant that with sewing women scrambling to keep their jobs, the colonel was willing to integrate the arsenal—or at least consider it. Like those Union Leaguers who reached out to New York's black community after the riots, if Boker and Crosman did indeed see to it that African American women were allowed into the white space of the arsenal, they further unsettled the white working-class community and reinforced the administration's effort to enforce loyalty on the home front, from the inside out.

In the struggle over wartime resources, white sewing women were not yet willing to relinquish control over their workplace to army bureaucrats; nor were they willing to admit defeat to the new business relationship forged between the army and private investors. They insisted that Crosman's loyalty directive was a pretext to drive more women out of public arsenals and into the hands of private employers, contractors who demanded the same work and paid half the wages. One local paper estimated, for example, that whereas the Schuylkill Arsenal paid twelve and a half cents for a haversack, contractors paid women only five cents. Even with costs, contractors profited handsomely.[65] To make matters worse, many contractors insisted that women sew uniforms on sewing machines, an innovation that women strongly resisted as machines produced inferior products. As long as contractors were profiting from government money, working women harder for less money, and producing "shoddy" products, who, sewing women asked, was monitoring *their* loyalties?

Having found no suitable solution, the petition campaign against contracting picked up momentum. Philadelphia seamstresses were joined by women in New York who were trying to hold on to government work.[66] The following spring, sewing women initiated an intense round of institution building, forming protective organizations and unions in New York, Philadelphia, and other northern cities with large public arsenals.[67] By the summer of 1864 Philadelphia's sewing women were in the middle of a growing movement applying pressure on local and federal officials on multiple fronts simultaneously, and from cities where Republicans could hardly stand to lose any further public support. So when Philadelphia's sewing women addressed a petition on behalf of "Twenty-Thousand Working Women" to Secretary of War Edwin Stanton, he responded with an invitation to the White House. Characterizing their grievances in terms of loyalty, the petitioners were "American matrons" who had "given *their all* to their country."[68] What they wanted was for the government to set a minimum wage for all seamstresses—those working in the private and public sectors—a move that would have given them job security and would have relaxed the fierce competition for the few jobs reserved for "loyal women." What they got was an audience with the president, a raise, and Stanton's promise to consider the matter.[69]

Stanton's assurances did nothing to disarm the situation or discourage the sewing women. Indeed, in September members of the Working Women's Union in New York held the first of a number of large and raucous meetings to draft a response to Stanton's offer. "We do not ask charity," the New York seamstresses explained to the Secretary of War, "we come to you as American women, many of whom have sacrificed the dearest treasures of their hearts on the altar of freedom."[70] Seamstresses in Philadelphia were also unsatisfied, and in January 1865 they appointed a new delegation to take their demands directly to the president.[71] Accordingly, on January 26, 1865, President Lincoln met for a second time with Philadelphia seamstresses, but the president offered the seamstresses the same solution as had Stanton—more government work and a raise in the per piece rate.[72] No sooner had Lincoln met with the women when seamstresses in Cincinnati sent a petition reiterating the demands of women in New York and Philadelphia, suggesting again that sewing women were aware of movements afoot in other cities.[73]

In the end, the seamstresses' campaign yielded mixed results. On the one hand, neither Stanton nor Lincoln was willing to slow the changes that were being made to the public clothing industry, namely the creation of a close alliance between the War Department and private manufacturers, for such an intervention would have been inconsistent with free-labor nationalism.[74] Local officials, too, continued to pursue policies that divided women against one another, keeping sewing women insecure about their wages and ambivalent about the war and the administration that pursued it. On the other hand, sewing women met with federal lawmakers twice, and at both meetings members of the Lincoln administration interceded on their behalf. Local authorities thought it important to publish Stanton's and Lincoln's assurances, suggesting that they too were convinced that the movement was bigger than a few disgruntled seamstresses who might disturb the good order of an otherwise loyal home front. On these occasions, sewing women successfully set aside the question of loyalty in order to draw attention to the effects of a reallocation of resources on the northern home front.

Conclusion

Calls to loyalty might propel middle-class women to a greater consciousness and perhaps more support for the war, but they could only partly disguise the real issues at stake for working-class women who saw much in the war to resent and little to support. As men went to war and workplaces were reordered to meet the expanded needs of a modern army, more of the responsibility for family survival was shifted on to working-class women with fewer resources. Local and state governments reached deep into these communities, reordering antebellum relations of race and gender and unsettling the ground on which working-class white women stood. Black and white women now squared off over access to work, space, and public sympathy; and working-class white women and men at times went to blows over enlistment and the draft. When authorities responded, they tried to balance the morale of the deployed troops with the need for domestic order and political conformity at home. Women's resistance reverberated outward from their households and through the civilian community, creating problems that local authorities could not afford to ignore.

White working-class women lost the defensive war they waged against the draft, emancipation, and privatization. Standing solidly in the doorway, as the war marched by, they had won some concessions—even compromises—but in the end they had been unable to protect the spaces of their communities from change. U.S. victory settled many of the questions that had been raised about how a wartime government manages women who stand in the way of its prosecuting a war. As the country moved from war to peace, southern white women who had stood in the way of the U.S. Army moved rather quickly from being hateful "she-devils" to being once again the worthy recipients of middle-class northern sympathy. This shift helped to disguise the real threat southern women had posed to occupying U.S. forces and the seriousness with which the army had responded to that threat. Working-class Irish women, however, were remembered for having had misplaced loyalties and exhibiting degenerate gender behavior long after the war—and long after middle-class whites had run out of interest in the black poor. This explanation allowed the administration to explain women's resistance as resulting from an absence of female restraint rather than from the limitations of a war strategy that had relied on their consent but had never secured it.

White working-class women had tried to protect their communities from the war, by attacking draft officials and reclaiming the streets as their own. But the war came home nonetheless; husbands and sons enlisted and others were drafted. And when men did not return, as we shall see in the next chapter, women went in search of them.

SIX

PLATFORMS OF GRIEF
Widows on the Battlefield

When Maurice O'Connell arrived at the home of Mrs. McCormack on Hanover Street in Boston's North End in May 1863, McCormack showed O'Connell the coffin containing the remains of her dead son, a soldier in the 9th Massachusetts Regiment. Having no means to bury him, McCormack had written to Governor John Andrew asking for money to give her son a proper burial. The governor sent O'Connell to investigate her claim. Sitting in her darkened home, next to the coffin of her dead son, McCormack waited for O'Connell to arrive. In her grief, McCormack tore up her son's discharge papers, leaving her with only a few letters from him during his tour of duty. Having managed to retrieve her lost child's body from the battlefield, Mrs. McCormack wanted to give her son a decent burial, one close to home, near family and friends, living and dead.[1]

Maurice O'Connell might have been personally acquainted with the family, as his office was located near Mrs. McCormack's home. If he knew either Mrs. McCormack or her dead son, he did not admit as much. Nor was he particularly moved by the scene of a grieving mother tending to her dead son's uniformed body. Indeed, in his letter to Governor Andrew, O'Connell stressed that the state ought to protect itself from pressing demands such as Mrs. McCormack's, for he did not believe that burying dead soldiers was the responsibility of the state. "I would not that my pen should trace a word that could in the remotest degree lessen the humane desire of your Excellency to alleviate, by all means, the sufferings of the worthy poor," O'Connell began his letter to Governor Andrew. But he ended it with a recommendation that the governor resist his "humane desire" to help Mrs. McCormack bury her son.[2] The very circumstances of her grief—the darkened home, the dead body, the torn-up documents—convinced O'Connell that McCormack was unworthy of the state's largesse. Concerned about setting a precedent for others who might seek the state's help in burying dead soldiers, O'Connell advised the governor to extend relief only to those who kept their grief private; women who, O'Connell believed, "would no more think of seeking aid from the State House, than from Louis Napoleon." In effect, the government agent believed the state owed women like Mrs. McCormack nothing. Even so, O'Connell advised Andrew to pay for half the costs of burying the dead boy. Unable to shake the scene entirely from his memory, O'Connell begrudged Mrs. McCormack that much.

In making public her grief over the loss of her soldier son, Mrs. Mc-Cormack stepped outside the bounds of respectability, casting doubt on her request for aid and even on her motherhood. Employing the middle-class language of antebellum poor relief, O'Connell easily dismissed Mc-Cormack as unworthy, for the "worthy and respectable poor will perish, from want, rather than seek relief." But inasmuch as he wanted to overlook this mother and her grief, O'Connell could not. In requesting the state to bury her son, Mrs. McCormack insisted that his death and her loss be recognized. And in this she was not alone.

The death of a husband or son marked the end of his enlistment, but it marked only the beginning of the work of mourning. For surviving family members, the anguish of the distant death of a soldier relation was compounded by the absence of a body to bury and a grave to tend.[3] Throughout the Civil War and afterward, civilians retrieved bodies of dead husbands, sons, and brothers and brought them home for burial. In so doing, they worked against wartime rhetoric emphasizing the anonymity of soldier sacrifice and discomfited state officials who preferred private expressions of grief. Like the opening poem applauding men as they prepared to die—"to lay us down for freedom's sake, our brothers' bones beside"—northern women were encouraged to accept soldier death quietly. According to Caroline Kirkland, author of a popular 1863 pamphlet, northern women's "settled aversion to show in matters of the heart" distinguished them from their southern counterparts. Whereas southern women were guilty of an unfeminine tendency to express their loyalties and their grief in public, Kirkland applauded northern women who showed restraint, women "who have given their dearest blood to the war, received them back maimed, broken or coffined, yet never, even in their anguish, cried—'Submit to wrong, for why should we die!'"[4] Mrs. McCormack's decision to ask for recognition of her son's death worked against Kirkland's characterization of northern women's invisibility. Her grief was visible and uncomfortable; her claims on the state irrepressible.

This chapter follows women like Mrs. McCormack as they retraced the steps of husbands and sons who died far from home. To make these trips, widows commanded state and federal resources and took their grief into public spaces, where their appearance on battlefields, railroad cars, and statehouses stood as a sharp critique of the ways the war had objectified men's bodies, relying on the public's consent to the largely anonymous deaths of common soldiers. As a testament to the ways in which the war redrew the boundaries between public and private life, Mrs. McCormack's home became a site of contention, where a war that relied on anonymity was confronted with the individual circumstances of a soldier's life. Wherever women went with bodies of husbands and sons they created sites of everyday politics, places where their desire to retain some part of the good death confronted the state's need for military efficiency and nationalist sacrifice.

Women bringing bodies home—or laying them at the doorsteps of public officials—remapped the gendered terrain that divided home front from battlefield, North from South, safe from unsafe. Because women's respectability relied on the space they occupied, those, like Mrs. McCormack, who grieved in public fit awkwardly into the public space of wartime. In sacrificing their husbands and sons to the cause, they deserved the nation's gratitude and respect—perhaps even the state's efforts on their behalf. But in announcing their grief, they became disreputable, unfeminine at times. Like the women on streetcars in Philadelphia and San Francisco, widows and mothers moved about the landscape of wartime cities, train stations, and recently quieted battlefields. Historian Drew Faust has described "a uniformed sorority of grief" through which southern women visibly and publicly shared their anguish.[5] Absent the experience of collective mourning, grieving widows and mothers in the North were at times perceived as bodies out of place, not unlike women working in wartime arsenals, whose appearance in male spaces threatened their respectability, their femininity. Undaunted, widows claimed the right to move about and became part of a wartime conversation about the responsibility of the state to care for the soldier dead and their families.

Here, their movements intersected at odd angles with those of other women who were headed in the same direction but whose respectability was less likely to be questioned. Wartime nurses, or "angels of the battlefield," were applauded for their ability to see all wounded and ill soldiers as the same—young, helpless lads in need of a woman's soothing words and healing hands. The impersonal nature of their work shielded nurses from attacks on their respectability, and it reinforced the anonymity of soldier sacrifice. When an old woman tried to thank her for writing a letter on behalf of her dying son, Mary Livermore, of the United States Sanitary Commission, received the woman's crushing gratitude by insisting that she had tended so many soldier deaths that "it was hardly possible for me to recall any individual case."[6] Like so many other nurse veterans, Livermore maintained that the anonymous care given by middle-class nurses was a hallmark of the successful northern war machine. In their memoirs, nurses recalled how they stroked men's foreheads and tended to their final comforts, acting as surrogates for the wives and mothers who would have tended their deaths at home.[7] They defended a work ethic that valued efficiency over personalism. Even so, Livermore noted sadly how the condolence letter she could not remember writing had been read and reread by the wife and mother of the forgotten soldier and then circulated "to other women similarly bereaved" until the paper was "worn in pieces."[8] Widows' trips to the battlefield contradicted the notion that any woman would do—in seeking to give husbands and sons the good death, women insisted that surrogacy was inadequate recognition of a man's service to the state and of his family's loss, and worn-out letters from strangers hardly served to fill the void left by a body to bury.

ALTHOUGH we do not know how Mrs. McCormack retrieved her dead son, it is likely that she or one of her son's comrades dug up the body from its battlefield grave, bought a coffin, and accompanied it home. Soon after the fighting was over, soldiers formed burial squads and buried their dead comrades near where they had fallen, often with little other than a blanket wrapped around their bodies. Secretary of War Simon Cameron instructed quartermasters to place headboards at each soldier's grave and to keep careful record of the identity and location of all graves; commanding officers were responsible for informing the family of the soldier's death.[9] In practice, however, most soldiers were buried with no ceremony or markings on their graves; many were never buried at all; and thousands who were buried remained unidentified.[10] Common soldiers who knew the dead man or his relatives personally often notified the family before the official letter of condolence from a soldier's commanding officer was written.[11]

The U.S. Army's practice of battlefield burials profoundly disrupted the antebellum culture of death that centered on the home.[12] To experience a good death, a person died in the company of loved ones, remaining conscious and resolute until the end.[13] When the dying person faced death willingly, friends and family could be reassured of his salvation. As the final performance of life, death was an important family event in which survivors lent the dying man strength and said good-bye. After death, women washed and dressed the body for burial; indeed, Mrs. McCormack might have already prepared her son's body when Maurice O'Connell arrived to assess the circumstances of his death.[14] The family then accompanied the body as it was carried out of the front door of the family home to the burial plot or as it wound its way around the community to the cemetery. A soldier who died far from home, unattended, was denied the possibility of a good death; so, too, was his family deprived of the opportunity to share in his final moments and thereby ascertain the condition of his soul. As a consolation, family members wanted to give soldiers decent burials. Survivors sought to bring the remains of sons, husbands, and brothers home, where their bodies could be cared for by mothers and widows, and families separated in life could be reunited in death.

Government support for the shipment of soldiers' remains varied. Officers were more likely to be shipped home, offering their families one last opportunity to salvage some remnant of the good death. Until the creation of the national cemetery system, however, the War Department did not arrange for large-scale transportation of bodies from southern battlefields and camp hospitals; embalming was irregular, so families were anxious about finding the remains before identification became impossible.[15] States provided funding for families on an ad hoc basis. (In Massachusetts, Mrs. McCormack applied to the governor's office. Perhaps she had heard rumors that money was available for transportation and burial.) Where support was available, women were common petitioners, pushing commanding officers for details about the circumstances of a loved one's death and the location of the grave and requesting help from the state. Men, too, pushed for this information, but, despite antebellum proscriptions about women's travel and common perceptions about wartime space, women often assumed primary responsibility for finding and retrieving the bodies, even traveling to battlefields to do so. The work was too important to delegate. It was a lesson that Mary Raivley of Philadelphia learned the hard way. Raivley hired an undertaker to recover the remains of her son, but the man returned without a body. This did not shake Raivley's confidence that she would find his body, as she knew "for certin that he is buried wheir I said for I was sent word when he was killed that he was buried their by a dozen of his comrades."[16] Better to go herself than to entrust another, Raivley decided.

By the time Mary Raivley contemplated a trip to the South, women's travel was nothing new, but middle-class women were repeatedly cautioned against traveling alone and were socialized to feel helpless when they did.[17] White middle-class women were supposed to feel vulnerable when they traveled alone. The physical constraints of feminine dress—tight clothing and hoop skirts—increased the likelihood that women would seek help from strangers when boarding or alighting trains, coaches, and cars and helped to reinforce socialized notions of incompetence and dependence. Historian Patricia Cline Cohen has said of women's travel that "part of the price of respectability was a denial of female competence in negotiating public space."[18] Raivley and others who went in search of soldiers' bodies undertook trips they were warned against, weighing their own (in)competence against their desire to bury the dead. When they did, they tested cultural assumptions about respectability and the gendered geography of war.

To find the bodies, women like Mrs. McCormack and Mary Raivley relied on condolence letters from soldiers describing the terrain marked by rocks, trees, and fences and estimating the distance to the nearest town. This information had a powerful effect on women, as it reassured them that a husband or son had not died alone and unnoticed and allowed them to imagine that they, too, had attended the death. When Mary Hall wrote an official requesting transportation to retrieve the body of her husband, Emory Hall, she was sure that she "cold got to the verry spot where he lyes." Mary described his death and burial in great detail. "He is buried 10 miles from Lynchburgh on the tye river on the south side of bluridg," she explained. "His boddy lyes under an apple tree on bluridge." Mary expressed her desire to be with Emory, to witness his death, as confidence in her own ability to find him. Hall reassured state officials, "if I will go fore him they all say here that thire will not bee enney difficulty in findeng his grave."[19] Letters such as Hall's offer evidence of a change in women who would have had very little previous contact with state officials and no firsthand knowledge of the geography of war. As the war came home to them, women demanded the ability to move about within it, to navigate the terrain of the battlefield and the army camp to bring their own experience of war to an end. They knew they would find their husbands' bodies and bring them home.

Whereas soldiers had firsthand knowledge of how and when death occurred on the battlefield, civilians on the home front experienced wartime death through newspapers and photographs.[20] Wartime newspapers printed the names of the dead, and family members scanned the columns carefully. Newspapers' steady reporting of battlefield casualties kept women and men on the home front in a constant state of anxiety. Dead soldiers figured prominently in the battlefield photography of Alexander Gardner and Mathew Brady. Gardner's photographs of the dead at Antietam allowed people at home to stand among the dead.[21] At an exhibit of Gardner's Antietam photos at Mathew Brady's New York studio, a reporter commented on the realism of the images, suggesting that Brady had "brought bodies and laid them in our door-yards and along the streets."[22] Whereas reading the casualty lists in the morning paper was comparable to "a funeral next door," viewing the photographs was like having "the corpse carried out over your own threshold." Although the soldiers in Gardner's photographs were not identified, the clarity of the images allowed onlookers to lean in and study their features.[23] The *Times* reporter warned viewers that they "would scarce choose to be in the gallery, when one of the women bending over them should recognise a husband, son, or brother in the still, lifeless lines of the bodies, that lie ready for the gaping trenches."[24] Soldiers expressed fears of dying alone in their letters home; photographs of the dead brought that fear to life.

The anonymity of the deaths portrayed and the remoteness of any semblance of the good death, the reporter believed, was particularly shocking for women who saw the photos. Imagining the response of a woman who recognized her dead son in a photo, he wondered, "How can this mother bear to know that in a shallow trench, hastily dug, rude hands have thrown him. She would have handled the poor corpse so tenderly, have prized the boon of caring for it so dearly." To save him from the terrible anonymity of the soldier's death, surely this mother would give her life "but for the privilege of touching that corpse, of kissing once more the lips though white and cold, of smoothing back the hair from the brow and cleansing it of blood stains."[25] The deaths portrayed in Gardner's photos shattered any hopes that dying on the battlefield might retain some of the intimacy of death at home.

Women at home pleaded with husbands and sons to write often, for a sudden absence of letters raised their worst fears. Rumors that circulated in wartime communities could allay or aggravate these fears. Mary Walters heard from neighbors that her son had been engaged at the Battle of Wilderness in Virginia. When his letters stopped arriving, she assumed the worst. Having exhausted home-front channels of information, Walters wrote to the governor of Pennsylvania. "What has become of him," she asked, and answered herself, "no one knows (dead of course)."[26]

Along with reporters and photographers, women and other civilians appeared on battlefields soon after the fighting—and sometimes during—not only to nurse the wounded but to retrieve the dead. Seeking to confirm rumors or to deny their fears, women went in search of men who had fallen. "He was my right arm, [but] I must help myself," Barbara Burger of Harrisville, Pennsylvania, said of her decision to go to Virginia to retrieve the body of her son. Having received confirmation of his death, Burger got as far as Harrisburg, Pennsylvania, in March 1865 when "an order was issued for no civilian to go further then Washington City."[27] With fighting still occurring in and around the city of Petersburg, Burger was turned back. Civilians who tried to retrieve bodies at Fredericksburg in May 1864 were ordered off the battlefield because "there are not many burial places of the fallen that can safely be visited, except with a considerable force."[28] Women and men who arrived soon after battles had to navigate potentially hostile terrain. For her own safety, Margaret Bissell, a southern woman who traveled to Gettysburg to bury her husband, was advised against showing her grief or walking behind her husband's body as it made its way through town.[29] So soon after a battle, civilian desires to identify and bury the dead ran counter to military necessity and battlefield reality. Even when there was no immediate danger, women who planned these trips were warned against it. Mary Young was planning to go to Andersonville in November 1865 when she inquired whether "persons [will] be protected by a military guard while disentering the remains of their friends."[30] Young was likely responding to home-front information about the dangers of traveling south unprotected when she planned her trip to Andersonville.

In response to mounting public pressure to bring dead soldiers home for burial, Pennsylvania governor Andrew Curtin offered to reimburse family members for the costs of retrieving soldiers from battlefields and burying them at home.[31] Curtin announced the program in fall 1865, but women and men began writing to him to ask for travel money months earlier. Five days after the war ended, Eliza Williams wrote to ask for help retrieving the body of her husband, who had died two weeks earlier in Virginia. Having heard "something about state authorities bringing home the remains of Pennsylvania soldiers," Williams wrote to Curtin to find out the details.[32] Taking such a program for granted, Mrs. S. J. Kline wrote that it was "now drawing near the time for the removal of our brave dead from the battle field."[33] What had been a rumor became official in the fall when Governor Curtin offered to pay for one family member to travel beyond Washington to find and retrieve the body of a Pennsylvania soldier. The program recognized the strong civilian urge to provide sons, husbands, and brothers with some of the intimacies of the good death. Leaving the men buried where they fell was too much for Carrie Chamberlain, who wrote of her dead husband's body, "I cannot bear the thought that my best earthly friend's grave is in such a place and will soon be tilled by the hand of strangers."[34]

Soliciting state support for retrieving dead bodies was complicated and bureaucratic. Family members wrote in advance of their trips to the South, requesting railroad vouchers and passes. Upon return, the traveler filled out a form itemizing the expenses incurred and swore an affidavit to its authenticity. But sometimes women who had waited months to retrieve the bodies of loved ones could not wait any longer for transportation vouchers to arrive. Other times, women had to write more than once to get desperately needed reimbursements.[35] After Jane Deans traveled from Philadelphia to City Point, Virginia (ten miles from Petersburg), she hoped the state would reimburse her quickly, for she had not received her husband's back pay or pension. Having not yet paid the undertaker for burying her husband, she hoped reimbursement would arrive before she had to bury her sick child.[36] Women tried to expand the reach of the program that was limited to soldiers who had filled Pennsylvania state quotas and who died out of state. When Hiram Hull died in a hospital in West Philadelphia after his left leg was amputated, his wife Laura was at his bedside, but she did not have the means to bring his body along when she returned home. Hull then wrote to ask for a pass to travel within the state to bring her husband home to be buried in New Richmond, Pennsylvania, a town some 360 miles west of Philadelphia.[37] Mary Irwin wanted to get the body of her only son, David, who enlisted in Pennsylvania but died while serving in a Maryland regiment.[38] Although a resident of Pennsylvania, Mary Dresser's husband enlisted in a New Jersey regiment; the governor's office denied Dresser's request for travel vouchers to bring his body home.[39] If Mary Dresser was successful in bringing her husband home for burial, she paid for the trip herself.

After having been assured of the state's generosity, women and men bringing home the body of a loved one must have found the process of itemizing the costs — not to mention having a stranger testify to their legitimacy — alienating. Without railroad passes, family members had to pay for their own roundtrip tickets and a one-way ticket for the body; they also incurred fees for digging up the body and purchasing a coffin.

Women who were unable to travel hired others to go in their place. Often, they convinced an undertaker to extend them credit until reimbursement arrived. Involving a number of people outside of the immediate family in the burial ritual further complicated survivors' attempts to care for the dead. Because soldiers enlisted within their own communities, their families often knew one another. When regiments suffered heavy casualties grief was multiplied as neighbors mourned together. Funerals served as opportunities to share bits of news that women could use to press their claims. This was the case when Mrs. M. Kean applied for a reimbursement for the various fees associated with obtaining her son's remains from Virginia, which she did "without mutch trouble." When Kean learned that a neighbor received more money, however, she believed she deserved an explanation. "I had to buy a coffin he was buried in a blanket it cost 7.50 for transportation," explained Kean. "If there is eny mistake please to let me know."[40] The deaths of husbands and sons required women to navigate battlefields as well as bureaucracy, but they did not necessarily do so alone.

Armed with verbal maps and the confidence that they could find the "verry spot" where loved ones lay, women and men overcame considerable obstacles on these journeys. They also received help from a number of people along the way.[41] Some women going to retrieve their husbands' bodies traveled alone or with young children. Jane Deans's experience retrieving the remains of her husband, Mark, serves as an example. Early in October, after hearing about the governor's offer, Deans left Philadelphia for the hospital at City Point to retrieve "the corpse of my husband." Having five children at home, Deans brought the youngest with her and left the older children in charge of their siblings. Because she was traveling with an infant, Deans purchased a room on the steamer she took to City Point. Once she arrived, Deans sought the help of a doctor and an undertaker to have her husband's body disinterred and prepared for the trip. On the way back, Deans—now traveling with an infant, her dead husband, and the headboard that she found on his Virginia grave—left behind the travel pass; she realized her mistake just as the boat was pulling away from shore. We might have forgiven Deans this oversight, under the circumstances, but the boat captain did not. Fortunately, soldiers—perhaps some of her husband's former comrades—and a doctor on board helped pay her way. Back in Philadelphia, Deans gave her husband a funeral and buried him near his home. Understanding the considerable risks involved in making a trip like this, Jane undertook it anyway, for giving Mark Deans a good death had as much to do with fulfilling the desires of the dead as the wishes of the living. "Now I am content," Jane explained, "for his 5 littel orphans can go with me to see where thier Fathers bones do ly." Having her husband's remains close to home brought Jane Deans's Civil War to an end. Now Jane sought the money that would allow her to care for the children in Mark's absence.[42]

Women's trips could be complicated by obstructionist railroad officials or other unforeseen difficulties. Unembalmed bodies were not allowed on government transports, and railroad officials were often reluctant to transport them. Nancy Cotton took her son Alex with her to retrieve the body of her son James from Washington, D.C. Nancy paid for her own trip and used the pass for Alex. Their trip was uneventful, until they—Nancy, Alex, and James's body—reached Harrisburg, Pennsylvania, where a ticket agent confiscated Alex's ticket "because it did not read 'with body.'"[43] Like Maurice O'Connell, the ticket agent was not moved by Nancy Cotton's appearance at the station platform with her two sons—one standing beside her and one in a coffin—and no soldiers came to her assistance. Cotton had to buy three tickets to board the train, and James's cost more.

On battlefields and at camp hospitals, women confronted the anonymity of soldier death when they could not find bodies or identify them once they did. Whereas Jane Deans found her husband buried with a headstone, the graves at Andersonville and elsewhere were numbered—a system that led to some confusion. Graves were difficult to find, and some had been dug up. Newspapers carried stories of civilians looking for bodies in Gettysburg. A month after the battle, the *Gettysburg Compiler* took note of a woman digging up graves looking for her husband's body, until "her heart almost failed." Then, in the twenty-first grave, she found him.[44] Papers carried advertisements from family members, like Mrs. J. S. Whitcomb of Chicago who solicited help from "any person at Gettysburg, who can give information of the exact burial place of Liet. Hemphreyvlle, of the 24th Michigan Inf."[45] Sometimes family members looking for bodies had to make more than one trip to bring home the remains of a soldier. Mary McKenna arrived at her husband's grave at City Point only to find no body in it, so she returned with the soldier who had buried him.[46] Depending on the conditions, women would have found bodies difficult to identify. When Mary Williams prepared to retrieve her son's body, it had lain in a shallow grave near Spotsylvania Courthouse for more than three years.[47] We cannot know if Williams found her son, but if she did, there would have been little to distinguish him from his comrades buried nearby.

Women made these extraordinary trips at a time when social convention dictated that middle-class women should not travel alone without male companionship. Urban sociability, on the other hand, relied on working-class and poor women's mobility, as wives and mothers sustained connections between households, traveling alone for short distances by foot or by streetcar. Elite women too flouted convention as they boarded public conveyances with more regularity during the war to tend to the wounded at hospitals nearby or far from home.[48] Mary Ryan has argued that the coding of public spaces as dangerous was a reaction to women's antebellum visibility and mobility; the creation of safe places such as parks and ladies' cars on railroads was an attempt to impose order by segregating space.[49] Mary Douglas suggests that these attempts at segregation have "as their main function to impose system on an inherently untidy experience."[50] Wartime travel was an "untidy experience." As trains lurched forward or stopped abruptly, passengers and possessions shifted and collided. In crowded stationhouses, women and men, soldiers and civilians brushed past each other as they rushed to board and to disembark. These chance encounters between strangers signaled a shift in the marking of space and an unsettling of antebellum relations of gender and class. As Douglas has argued, attempts at segregation cannot merely be understood as a response to sexual danger but as "symbols of the relation between parts of society, as mirroring designs of hierarchy or symmetry which apply in the larger social system."[51] Segregated space and restrictions on elite women's mobility reflected antebellum attempts to shore up hierarchies of class and race that were threatened by immigration, working-class politics, and the specter of emancipation.

The novelty of women's appearances—with the coffined remains of soldiers—at railroad stations and on trains may explain the attention they received from newspapers, returning soldiers, and ticket agents. Novelist Rebecca Harding Davis, in her postwar memoirs, recalled a trip to Philadelphia when the train came to a stop at a rural station and "a poor, thin country girl" with a child stood waiting: "When we stopped the men took out from the freight car a rough unplaned pine box and laid it down, baring their heads for a minute. Then the train steamed away. She sat down on the ground and put her arms around the box and leaned her head on it. The child went on playing."[52] Davis's contemporaries surely had similar memories. As women—many, no doubt, veiled and dressed in black—crossed the country to bring home remains, they were notable additions to the postwar landscape. The exigencies of war disrupted traditional rituals of death that rendered grieving as a home-centered and deeply personal private act, but war would not deprive widows of the bodies over which they could grieve.

Women and men who traveled into the South to retrieve the bodies of loved ones endured lengthy trips and overcame considerable hardships along the way. Whereas travel in the North improved rapidly and noticeably during the war, the Confederacy could not keep up with the demands of repairing destroyed tracks and replacing cars. One historian of Civil War railroads described southern railroads at the end of the war as "a pitiable mass of wreckage."[53] Even when tracks were intact and cars ran, trips were split up into multiple legs, and train travel was combined with boat and carriage rides—even travel on foot. Stillman Wightman left New York City for Fort Fisher, North Carolina, the day he read in the paper about his son Edward's death. In a trip that took him three weeks and that by his estimate covered some 1,600 miles, Wightman traveled by rail, wagon, steamer, boat, horse, and foot. Along the way, he often had to wait for days for a train or boat to arrive, sleeping uncomfortably at saloons and other places while he waited. Ten days after starting out, Wightman arrived at Fort Fisher, walking the last three miles in a blinding rainstorm across a marsh to find his son. But his work had just begun.[54]

For the next six days, Wightman negotiated with U.S. Army generals and surgeons for permission and help disinterring Edward's body and preparing it for the trip home. Wightman used the professional connections he had made as a lawyer in New York and Connecticut to grease wheels and solicit favors, an advantage that would have been difficult for a female traveler. Once he had U.S. Army approval and all of the supplies he needed (including tent material treated with pitch to make the coffin airtight and a pine box to place the coffin in and to fill with salt), Wightman managed to dig up his son's body and deposit it safely in a coffin, with the help of some twenty soldiers. On the way back to New York, as on the original trip, Wightman booked passage and quarters on military vessels, and rode and took meals with U.S. Army officers, soldiers, and doctors. On a ship sailing from Fort Fisher to Fort Monroe, Wightman described his cabin as "a nasty, filthy place unfit for a human being to sleep in."[55] As difficult—indeed, epic—as was Stillman's journey, had Edward Wightman's mother gone in search of his body alone, she likely would have found it inappropriate to dine intimately in train cars and ship's cabins where she could hope to solicit favors from military men and business associates. Gendered restrictions on travel did not stop widows and mothers from making epic journeys of their own, but they added additional burdens.

Mrs. A. M. Hesser traveled from Philadelphia to Robertson's Tavern in four legs—Philadelphia to Baltimore, Baltimore to Washington, Washington to Fredericksburg, and Fredericksburg to Robertson's Tavern—to carry home the body of her husband, Lieutenant Colonel Theodore Hesser, logging 221 miles by her estimate.[56] Of course, we can only assume that she also made the trip in the reverse, although she did not include a return trip on her itemized reimbursement request, and, unlike Stillman Wightman, Mrs. Hesser did not write a memoir of her trip. Railroad travel would have carried Hesser as far as Fredericksburg, then Hesser would have arranged for a carriage or hearse to take her the twenty miles west to Robertson's Tavern.[57] Two years earlier, Theodore made the same trip, on the same roads, before he was killed in action when his regiment came under fire. At that time, in November 1863, Pennsylvania regiments moving toward Robertson's Tavern repeatedly delayed their advance because the rain had washed out the roads.[58] Now, his wife rode the same road in search of his body.

We can only imagine what went through Hesser's mind as she made her solitary journey, looking out over marshes and forests as she rode. She may have experienced some of the same difficulties in traveling as Theodore and his regiment two years earlier. Maybe the roads were muddy, making the trip more treacherous, and perhaps Hesser had to haggle with carriage drivers who were reluctant to drive her under those conditions. In Fredericksburg, she would have arranged for a coffin and found an undertaker—perhaps a willing embalmer. Because Theodore was an officer, his widow might have had an easier time finding his grave than did widows of common soldiers who, like her, went in search of the bodies of other men who died in the three-day battle. Like Stillman Wightman, who found a plank marked with his son's name, Theodore Hesser's widow likely would have relied on a headboard or some other marking to find him, for after her husband had been buried for two years in swampy terrain, it would have been difficult to identify him otherwise. After his son was dug up, Wightman lingered for a while at the open grave, looking into his son's partly decomposed face in disbelief, then broke down and cried as Edward's "whole life rushed upon my memory"; Mrs. Hesser

— *Platforms of Grief* —

likely felt similar emotions as her husband's grave was opened and she faced the reality of life without him.[59] With the added weight of the coffin, the return trip might have been more difficult for the driver, not to mention Mrs. Hesser. Perhaps, like Jane Deans, she would feel content to have Theodore home in Philadelphia, but in the meantime, the trip must have felt long and lonely. At least Deans's mind was in part occupied by the pressing demands of caring for her infant; Hesser likely had little to keep her thoughts off her husband's death, other than the war-scarred terrain she saw out of her window.

Rebecca Loomis traveled by train and steamer to retrieve the body of her husband, Captain J. B. Loomis, from Harrisburg, Pennsylvania, to Reams Station, Virginia, in at least six legs: Harrisburg to Philadelphia, Philadelphia to Baltimore, Baltimore to Washington, Washington to Acquia Creek, Acquia Creek to Petersburg, Petersburg to Reams Station, located ten miles south of Petersburg, Virginia.[60] Like Hesser, Loomis made the trip in late November or early December 1865, but Loomis covered more than 800 miles before she was done. From Washington, Rebecca Loomis took a steamer to the federal transport wharf at Acquia Creek, from which point she made the rest of her trip by rail and hired carriage. Like Wightman, Loomis may have waited for the steamer in Washington before continuing on to Virginia. She may have wished for more privacy aboard the boat, like Jane Deans who traveled with her infant. Rebecca Loomis shared the small space allowed her on the steamer with military supplies and personnel. Here she likely deployed strategies to maintain her respectability, staying to herself and "draw[ing] her cloak in close."[61] She might have worn a veil. Perhaps she was advised against taking her husband's body by steamer—or perhaps it was impossible to do so—for Loomis did not take river transportation on her return trip.[62]

Despite the difficulty and expense of these trips, women were likely heartened when word reached them of their neighbors' bringing home husbands and sons. News of the program in Pennsylvania spread by word of mouth, encouraging some who would not have attempted the trip otherwise. Hearing that neighbors' husbands and sons were returned home to be buried was too much for women who had experienced no such "contentment." "If he was laid in a Cemetary like those that fell at Gettysburg I could be content," Mary Raivley explained of her desire to retrieve her son's body herself, adding, "I know he died a honorable Death."[63] A burial at home was an appropriate way to repay the individual soldier for his sacrifice, and it recognized the strong connections between the living and

Wartime and postwar travel arrangements. This image of the Federal Wharf at Acquia Creek Landing, Virginia, captures one leg of the 800-mile trip Rebecca Loomis took from Harrisburg, Pennsylvania, to Reams Station, Virginia, to retrieve the body of her late husband, Captain J. B. Loomis, in fall 1865. ("Acquia Creek Landing, VA, 1860–1865," from Hirst D. Milhollen and Donald H. Mugridge, eds., *Civil War Photographs, 1861–1865*, No. 0168, Washington, D.C., 1977, American Memory Digital Library, Library of Congress, LC-B817-7643.)

the dead, connections that centered in the home. Bringing the body home allowed surviving family members the chance to begin to heal and to begin the process of reconstructing family and community connections around the loss. When her son Simon died at City Point Hospital, Barbara Burger was at his bedside, but she was unable to bring him home with her. Leaving him in Virginia, Burger experienced a loss that was at once emotional and corporeal. "He was my right arm," Burger explained as she prepared to go find his body.[64] Though the City Point graves were marked only by numbers, Barbara Burger knew she would find her son because he was part of her. As long as he remained in a grave marked only by a number, alone among strangers, Simon Burger's death remained anonymous and his mother's loss continued to be unreconciled. If going for him meant that Barbara Burger would make public her grief and endure public scrutiny, then so be it. "I must get his remains in some way," Mary Raivley insisted, "if I hav to beg my way to the battle field."[65]

As pitiful as was the image invoked by Raivley's threat to "beg my way to the battle field," it was not pity that widows sought but justice. They insisted that they had a right to tend the bodies of their dead husbands and sons and to see that they were buried decently—and that the state should respect that right. When Amanda Potter learned that her husband was among the dead at Andersonville, she pointedly described his death as "murder." Learning from federal officials that he was buried in grave number 12,479 did little to reconcile Amanda to the loss, so she wrote to the governor's office to get his body back. "His name is Benjamin Franklin Potter," Amanda Potter explained, and she expected to have his body sent home.[66] Benjamin Potter's death was personal, so should be his burial. "You promised to get my son George Hannaker," Mary Myers wrote to "Curnil Curtin," "please rite and let me know what you will doe."[67] Like Mrs. McCormack, Mary Myers had no documentation to prove her son's enlistment, but she did not equivocate. Returning her son was, Mary Myers believed, part of the original enlistment agreement; Mary Raivley, Amanda Potter, and Mrs. McCormack would agree. Whereas U.S. Army policy held that a man's enlistment ended with his death, women insisted that it continued until his body was returned to his family. Jane Deans retrieved her husband's body herself. "With pleasure I now site down to let you know that I arrived home safe with the corpse of my husband," she wrote the governor. Now, Deans explained, the state ought to pay her expenses and see to it that she received his back pay and pension. "I know that you will do me Justice in sending it to me," Deans explained.[68]

Like Deans, Mary Booth found the U.S. Army's battlefield burial arrangements inadequate and its treatment of widows unjust. Several officers were on hand to help Mary locate and retrieve the body of her husband, Major Lionel Booth, a white officer who died while in command of U.S. Colored Troops (USCT) at Fort Pillow, Tennessee, on April 12, 1864. But when the grave was opened, the party was unable to make a positive identification because of the advanced state of decomposition. One officer on hand concluded that the grave held the body of a black man, one of the many USCT men massacred by Confederate general Nathan Bedford Forrest after they had surrendered.[69] After some debate about the racial identity of the corpse, the consensus among those present, including Mary Booth, was that they had indeed found Lionel Booth buried in the grave.

While she scoured the Fort Pillow battlefield, Mary Booth likely interacted with other widows who had come to claim the bodies of husbands and sons, many of them in the USCT. After she buried Lionel, Mary Booth visited Lincoln to request that the army relax the requirement that widows provide proof of legal marriage before they could qualify for a pension because Booth believed that the requirement unjustly disqualified women who had married in slavery. Lincoln sent a message endorsing Booth's suggestion to Charles Sumner, who attached it to a U.S. Army appropriations bill in the Senate several days later.[70] Although the measure did not make it out of the House intact, this recommendation seems to have been the one foray that Mary Booth made into politics, suggesting that the experience of retrieving her young husband's remains from the battlefield provided her with a temporary platform with which to seek to influence army policy. And, whereas the army's initial assumption that Lionel Booth was a black man reflects a particularly noxious form of northern racism that associated African Americans with death and decay, the experience of identifying his body among so many convinced Mary Booth that widows had more in common than the state was willing to acknowledge, and that they all deserved "justice."[71]

Conclusion

It is not difficult to imagine overwhelmed state officials and commanding officers on the receiving end of a crush of letters and inquiries from women demanding the return of bodies — men who became inured to the details of husbands and sons who had served bravely and left hungry children to feed.[72] Men like Maurice O'Connell who preferred to extend the state's pity to women who did not embarrass themselves by requesting the state's help. Women's letters proved difficult to ignore; they were, as the *Times* reporter had said of the photographs of the dead at Antietam, "the corpse carried out over your own threshold." Letters like Amanda Potter's, which carefully juxtaposed her husband's POW number — 12,479 — with his name — Benjamin Franklin Potter — eliminated the possibility of treating soldiers' deaths as anonymous.

And when women like Mrs. McCormack brought home bodies, despite protestations and dire warnings, they invited a wider audience to consider the limitations of the wartime state — chiefly, the failure to provide expectant families with a body over which to grieve and survivors with the resources necessary to rebuild. Women who came out to retrieve bodies performed a kind of improvisational public theater in which they

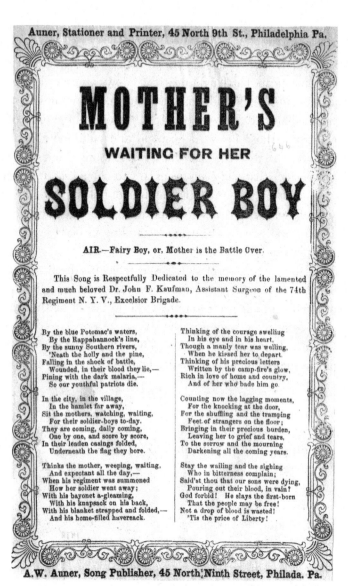

"Mother's Waiting for Her Soldier Boy." A popular song portrays mothers waiting quietly at home for the coffins to arrive — the remains of their sons, delivered to their homes by strangers. (Courtesy of the Library Company of Philadelphia.)

enacted the rituals associated with death at home in public spaces, creating conversations about where the line separating battlefield from home now stood. As long as nurses adhered to a careful anonymity in recognizing the death of soldiers, the rituals they performed in hospital and camp were consistent with the wartime state's demands for efficiency and nationalist self-sacrifice. And these rituals—stroking foreheads and writing letters—did not portend a rupture of the lines so much as an attempt, in part, to domesticate battlefield death. Widows and mothers boarding trains and scouring battlefields, on the other hand, reminded witnesses that the war had altered the relationships that formed the basis of northern self-identity—those between husband and wife, mother and child. These encounters became the basis for conversations about the extent of home-front sacrifice that had been necessary to uphold the wartime state. Fighting an industrialized war took the lives of thousands of anonymous soldiers and left some observers attempting to trace the outlines of postwar society in the silhouettes of women standing vigilant over coffins on train station platforms.

According to wartime protocol, respectable northern women gave "their dearest blood to the war" and "received them back maimed, broken or coffined" without protestation.[73] The figure of mothers awaiting the dead bodies of their sons was the subject of popular songs, such as "Mother's Waiting for her Soldier Boy." The lyrics portray a woman waiting motionless in her home, as if she need only wait to have her son's body returned to her:

> Counting now the lagging moments,
> For the knocking at the door,
> For the shuffling and the tramping
> Feet of strangers on the floor;
> Bringing in their precious burden,
> Leaving her to grief and tears,
> To the sorrow and the mourning
> Darkening all the coming years.[74]

Missing from the song "Mother's Waiting" were the women who did not wait, who could not. Women who did not wait invited public scrutiny. The brief celebrity of Lydia Bixby, the widowed mother of five soldiers, marked her forever as disreputable, and it did not remove her marginality. Surely, failure was a possibility that Mrs. McCormack considered in May 1863, as she put a clean shirt on her son's dead body and tried to reassemble the pieces of his discharge papers lying scattered on the floor. Not trying would have been worse.

CONCLUSION

Women were, as W. H. Hardy described them during the Civil War, the "army at home." In the South, women's willingness to sacrifice, to go without, was essential to sending more men to the battlefield and keeping them there despite considerable hardship—and, near the end—despite declining prospects for military victory. When growing numbers of southern women withdrew their support for the war, victory became illusory and the collapse of the southern home front, certain. In the North, the survival of the "army at home" was also tied to military success—when women made accommodations for enlistment, but also when they worked on farms, in arsenals, and in factories sewing uniforms. Middle-class women, too, extended themselves during the war, engaging in voluntary works on behalf of soldiers and civil rights political activism on behalf of freedmen. Like the subjects of this book, middle-class women who served as nurses, worked as government employees, and volunteered to teach the freedmen accommodated themselves to altered domestic circumstances, serving as part of the North's "army at home." The willingness of women of all classes to work in the breach in new ways and in different settings, in the domestic war machine and elsewhere, helped to determine the success of the Republican experiment in free-labor nationalism, a belief in the redemptive possibilities of male economic independence.

As the Civil War became part of life on the home front, it became clear that women did not experience the war with unanimity of purpose. Not all women welcomed the war or the changes it wrought in their lives and communities. Some believed the war had not changed enough and sought to make change more extensive and permanent. Others protested the war's disruptions, the way it redistributed space and power in their communities. Women encouraged desertion and created safe spaces for deserters—remaking the North into "deserter-country," as one historian has put it.[1] Whether they tried to stop change or to extend it—or simply to negotiate their own terms—women's actions disturbed home-front cohesion, distracted the war's civilian administrators, and sent reverberations of dissent onto the battlefield.

Understanding how women negotiated the war in their everyday lives complicates our understanding of who won and who lost the Civil War. Elizabeth Cady Stanton was sure that, in the long run, women had won —but she did not take into consideration working-class women's extra work and worry, their displacement and loss. Nor did she recognize the battles for freedom of movement that African American women had already waged and won before war's end. Women on the northern home front both won and lost with Union victory. Absent the experience of defeat, perhaps we cannot know how northern women's dissent affected the war's outcome, but we should not overlook how unruly women fed war disaffection that was serious, although not fatal. Knowing that battles for integrated street travel had to be waged again by another war generation of African American women and men should not prevent us from detecting the roots of that later struggle in the Civil War. The Civil War changed the way people on the home front saw space and moved through it. And, having shattered antebellum experiences of space, the Civil War remained an important historical reference point for twentieth-century wars that would prove similarly disorienting and would produce new moments to reconsider how gender was marked in time and space.

Remembering and Forgetting the Army at Home

When 132 women died in an explosion at the Eddystone Ammunition Plant in Chester, Pennsylvania, (near Philadelphia) on April 10, 1917, the scene was eerily reminiscent of Civil War Pittsburgh. Fearing that they were under attack, civilians rushed into the streets to identify the source of the explosion. There they discovered the gruesome truth. "What shocked one most," a reporter from the *Chester Times* wrote from a makeshift morgue near the blast, "was the knowledge that most of the bodies were those of young women. A rubber shod foot here and there protruded. It was a small foot, perhaps, indicating that the victim was a female. There were dozens of such feet in evidence."[2] As they had in Pittsburgh fifty years earlier, townspeople once again scrambled to place blame. Rumors circulated about German, Austrian, and Russian spies infiltrating the factory, and some blamed the explosion on Mexicans working at the plant.[3] Chester residents struggled to explain the gruesome evidence of violated gender norms by reinforcing lines of class, ethnicity, and race; seeking to blame immigrants for the blast shielded the businessmen who employed the women in unsafe conditions and the town leaders who had approved their employment. When the plant reopened a few days after the blast, papers announced that "Nine Hundred Girls" were ready to work and that many others had applied for work; but this time, German girls were turned away.[4] In 1862, city leaders had entreated Pittsburgh residents to accept the gross amalgamation of male and female, human remains and the materiel of war at the gravesite of the victims of the Allegheny Arsenal blast, where a stone tablet marked the spot where "female beauty and manhood's vigor commingle." In 1917, as in 1862, seeing women and girls as war's victims was a powerful reminder of how war threatened hierarchies of all sorts.[5] As civilians averted their gaze from scenes of the war come home, they focused their attention on borders that could still be protected.

Yet even as commentators recalled the 1862 Allegheny Arsenal explosion and the resulting panic, the more sanguine tone of the 1917 newspaper coverage evidenced a new sensibility about the overlapping experiences of soldiers and civilians, women and men in wartime. During the U.S. Civil War, boundaries of gender—policed by local authorities and celebrated in popular culture—failed to contain the war experiences of northern working-class, African American, and marginal rural women who repeatedly crossed over the boundary into the theaters of war. The same would be true of women in World War I. Remarking on the crowd of local residents who rushed to the offices of the *Chester Times* for news about their daughters, a reporter explained, "it was their first taste of what war means, for this is war. It is just as much war as is a battle on the British front in France."[6] Just four days into America's entry into World War I, the battle lines were drawn. To win, the reporter implied, Americans would have to accept that modern war did not respect separations between battlefield and home front. Women and men would be drafted to the effort, and their blood would "commingle." Next to news stories of the plant's reopening even as the investigation into the blast continued, Chester residents read excerpts from President Woodrow Wilson's April 16 speech to the nation about winning the war. "The industrial forces of the country, men and women alike," Wilson explained, "will be a great national, a great international, Service Army—a notable and honored host engaged in the service of the nation and the world, the efficient friends and saviors of free men everywhere."[7] Wilson's description of the "service army" whose members were enlisted to the national effort to protect democracy abroad must have been particularly poignant for some local families who had lost loved ones in the blast. Women and girls from Chester and surrounding communities had enlisted in this service army, and on April 10, 132 of them had become the war's first American military fatalities.

As Americans tallied their first casualties of the Great War, Mrs. Mary McGraw of Pittsburgh remembered how she had enlisted to serve her nation—it was part of the story that she and other women had told often. McGraw was sixty-eight when the *Pittsburgh Gazette Times* interviewed her in 1917 about the Civil War explosion that had taken the lives of so many of her friends, but she remembered that day clearly. "My sister and I walked to work from our home . . . that morning as usual," McGraw recalled. She remembered that "there was a great hurry for ammunition on account of the battle of Antietam, then being fought, and orders from Washington were to rush ammunition with all possible speed to the front."[8] Indeed, in the rush to complete their work, McGraw—who was thirteen at the time—and her colleagues worked through lunch, leaving their posts briefly at two o'clock to collect their pay right before the explosion ripped through the room where they had been working. Mary McGraw and her sister escaped the burning building alive, but many of their friends did not. Hearing of the accident in Chester, McGraw hoped her experiences would help prepare young women and men for the work and the hazards that lay ahead of them as they, too, enlisted in the war effort.

Spectacular economic growth in cities such as Pittsburgh testified to the spirit of modernism that swept through the urban North in the last decades of the nineteenth century and reconfigured the streets and neighborhoods in which women and men had experienced the Civil War on the home front. By 1913, electric streetcars moved workers to and from work, steel manufacturing had brought extraordinary wealth and grinding poverty to the city, and immigration had dramatically reshaped the experience of life and labor. Wage labor had long ago become a permanent condition for a majority of Americans, burying expectations of upward mobility for all but the most naïve. Industrial workplaces remained sex-segregated, but women continued to work in all sorts of occupations that middle-class Victorians had once thought inappropriate or dangerous. By the turn of the century, though, the Pittsburgh arsenal was a relic, and only local nostalgia kept the building largely intact until the city began destroying it in 1926.[9]

— *Conclusion* —

The powder magazine at the former site of the Allegheny Arsenal. The building stands next to Arsenal Middle School and across from the park pictured below. (Photo by author.)

The scene of the 1862 Allegheny Arsenal explosion is now a playground and baseball field. It is a bucolic scene, with nothing to remind the girls and boys who play there of its past. (Photo by author.)

Local historical society members tried to save parts of the old structure—a tablet from the entrance, part of the gate, the gatehouse—but with little success. The Allegheny Arsenal was destroyed, in some cases dismantled stone by stone. By the 1920s, an elementary and junior high school stood in its place. Today the neighborhood that was German and Irish is predominantly African American; Asian, Latino, and white families also send their children to Arsenal Middle School.[10] The powder magazine still remains on the arsenal grounds, though the building now houses playground and baseball equipment. As the space of the former arsenal was carved up and sold at auction, survivors of the 1862 blast—like Mary McGraw—witnessed the final act in a long process of forgetting.

By the time the school was opened, on the spot where so many girls and women had lost their lives, townspeople had settled on a story about the Allegheny accident that fit the triumphant spirit of modernism of the postwar industrial city. Pittsburgh residents, who in 1862 had paused briefly to consider the consequences of waging a modern war in which battlefield and home front became one, effectively left these uncomfortable questions behind them.[11] With the voices of survivors silenced, contemporaries and later generations remembered parts of the story. Alexander McBride, former superintendent of the Allegheny Arsenal, remembered thinking as he heard the sounds of the women fleeing the collapsing building "that some of the women or girls were skylarking."[12] "The great explosion of 1862 blew the roof from this building," an account concluded in the 1930s, "and though there was no immediate danger from fire many women and girls lost their lives or were crippled by leaping through the windows."[13] In both of these scenarios, the story downplayed the dangerous conditions under which women worked and the extent to which the army's success in the field relied on women working in munitions.[14] It is almost incidental that women were casualties in this "great explosion," and had they had stronger nerves, perhaps they would not have perished. Like shrapnel-riddled remains carried off by "curiosity hunters," bits and pieces of the story of women's war work were scattered throughout the town, leaving townspeople to supply their own meanings. In the years following World War I, reporters tried to interest readers in this forgotten piece of local Civil War history.

But McGraw and other survivors sought more than the town's episodic interest in them. For several years, women worked to shape the memory of women's contributions to victory in the Civil War. In 1913, fifty years after the original disaster, McGraw and a group of survivors raised money for a plaque that was placed at Arsenal Park, as the site was known to young residents unfamiliar with the role the town played in the Civil War. School children sang, bands played, and some 2,000 residents looked on as McGraw's granddaughter unveiled the plaque paid for by the survivors. The new plaque included the names of all seventy-eight victims of the blast—unlike the one erected in 1863 that only commemorated the forty-five women whose remains were never identified.[15] This was an ambitious effort by eighteen elderly women to pass along their war stories to a new generation. The plaque expressed aging survivors' wishes to be remembered even as the arsenal building was being dismantled, the city of Pittsburgh having decided against preserving the site of the loss of young women's lives.

McGraw and other survivors' efforts to mark the site where "American women"—their sisters, mothers, and friends—lost their lives worked against these strong currents of dismemberment and disorientation.[16] The plaque imagined and paid for by the survivors reclaims war work as women's work and tells a story that is both powerful and dangerous. Erected at the scene of the explosion—instead of at the cemetery on the outskirts of town—the plaque reestablished women's central position in Pittsburgh's proud history of domestic war manufacturing. Gathering the names of all of the blast's victims worked against previous tendencies to memorialize them in various spaces—some in a mass grave at the Allegheny cemetery, others in a Catholic cemetery nearby, and still others in individual graves. The blast had scattered women's bodies; the survivors sought to gather their memories in one spot. An enormous winged angel with the words "In Memory Of" emblazoned across her chest is the central focal point of the plaque; extending her protective wings above the names of the victims, the angel embodies survivors' promises to remember their sisters' patriotic sacrifice. The angel's size and steady gaze defy stories of women fleeing needlessly or skirting their duties—she stands steadily at her post, both in the past and at present. Her powerful body both remembers and re-members women—such as Abby Eldridge and Mary McGraw—who were capable of simultaneously serving their nation and caring for their families and who, in the aftermath of the U.S. Civil War, sought to give the war meaning. Placed in the public space of a bustling modern city, the plaque took its place alongside other Civil War monuments that told the stories of local war heroes. Moved to a new

Plaque to the Allegheny victims. This plaque, featuring a large winged angel as its focal point, was placed at the site of the Allegheny Arsenal in 1913 to commemorate the seventy-eight explosion victims, mostly women, who died there in 1862. Since the 1930s, it has hung in the entranceway of Arsenal Middle School. (Photo by Lynn Parrucci.)

spot just inside the front door of Arsenal Junior High School after World War I, the plaque held the potential to help a new generation of young people make sense of their war. City leaders hoped that adolescents who came through those doors would "learn the arts of peace that will lead them to be useful, valuable citizens of our great nation."[17] No doubt city leaders who were at pains to cover over the site's history of war making had their own understandings of what it meant to educate girls and boys for "useful citizenship." The plaque assures that the memory of women war workers would continue to enter conversations about gender, citizenship, and national identity.

Because the war described in this book was fought in the spaces of everyday life, there are few monuments to it, no maps marked with blue and gray arrows tracing the movement of northern women as they fought. But here they are, in rural courthouses, on urban streets, in wartime arsenals and street cars, and on train platforms, moving in lines that at times paralleled those of marching troops but often traced different paths. Women fought every step of the way—to keep their homes or to return home, to support their families and work with dignity, to move about freely, and to bring home their dead. Along the way, they left little evidence of their work and wrote no memoirs, leaving would-be memorializers little to work with. Memories were just about the only thing left behind to guide the survivors of the Allegheny blast in commemorating lost sisters and friends.

Southern women, by contrast, have been well memorialized and remembered for the multiple ways they fought the war in their everyday lives. The ordinary and unexceptional mothers who gave their sons to the Confederate army attracted the attention of veterans groups and purveyors of popular culture early on and continued to do so long after the war. Indeed, in 1912, at the same time as the Allegheny survivors were collecting money and commissioning a monument to be dedicated to their fallen comrades, a committee of Confederate army veterans dedicated the Mississippi Monument to Confederate Women in Jackson. The monument was intended to be the first of a series of statues that were to be placed on the grounds of every state capitol in the South.[18] Though the woman depicted in the monument is young, discussion surrounding it focused on southern women as mothers who bravely sent their sons into battle. Some saw the pose as too passive and called for a depiction that captured how "our mothers met the call of the hour courageously." Others were reminded of how Confederate mothers sent forth sons who stuck out the war, though "far outnumbered, poorly equipped, almost starved, and often barefooted, [and] thrilled the world with their deeds of courage and daring."[19]

Lydia Bixby, whom we met at the beginning of this book, lost two or perhaps three sons in the war and took care of her younger children and

Monument to Confederate women, Jackson, Mississippi. Dedicated in 1912, this statue depicts a southern white woman laying a palm leaf at the feet of a fallen soldier, unaware that she is simultaneously being crowned with a wreath by Fame. The Confederate veterans who erected the statue in Jackson, Mississippi, intended to place one at every state capitol in the South. In the end, only two were erected—one in Mississippi and one in Tennessee. (Courtesy of the Mississippi Department of Archives and History, Jackson.)

grandchildren with little or no support from all five of her soldier sons for the duration of the war. To do so, she moved often, though never very far. Bixby left her neighborhood to look for work and to apply to state officials for relief. She faced hunger and homelessness, inflation and wartime shortages. Yet her five sons enlisted and reenlisted, and some were promoted to officers, a testament to their worthiness and hers. Lydia Bixby never recovered from the poverty she experienced during war, and when she died, her contemporaries did not mark her grave—nor has anyone done so since. We know her because President Lincoln thought her life worthy of the nation's attention, as a mother of exceptional patriotism whom he believed served as an example of extraordinary feminine self-sacrifice. In death, she did not fare as well, as indicated by the three numbers—423—that mark her otherwise anonymous grave.

What accounts for the postwar South's willingness to commemorate the anonymous women who helped fortify the Confederate armies with their sons (and husbands) and their stalwart patriotism? Why were there no parallel efforts afoot in Boston or Harrisburg or Albany?[20] Why, on the eve of World War I, were the Allegheny veterans alone in championing women's war work during the U.S. Civil War? And why are there no monuments to Union women?

The turn-of-the-century monument gap is perhaps indicative of the uncertainties that lay beneath the celebratory spirit of modernism that would be reflected in the sanguine reporting of the first female military fatalities in World War I and the matter-of-fact reception of Wilson's call to women to join the service army. Because southern white women were popularly understood as standing somewhere between, as historian Thomas Brown has described it, "tradition and the forces of change," they became canvasses on which to project a national memory of the Civil War as having been shaped largely by tradition.[21] This memory resonated with many Americans still trying to make sense of the last war and the industrial society it had helped to usher in. Northern women, on the other hand, were likely to be remembered by turn-of-the-century feminists who embraced nurses, teachers, and spies for their devil-may-care flaunting of middle-class convention and their thoroughly modern sensibilities. Accordingly, they lobbied for monuments to Clara Barton and Mother Bickerdyke, for example. Of course, this memory was no more representative of the experiences of the vast majority of northern women than the one of southern white women who never regretted sending sons to their death nor gave up faith in southern victory. Indeed, northern women were pulled by similar forces of change and tradition, seeking at times to hurry change on the home front and other times to stop it. Still, remembering northern women in all their complexities posed significant challenges for Americans who saw them as harbingers—or at least the grateful beneficiaries—of changes that many still found unsettling. For the three years that the United States stubbornly stayed out of the war in Europe, Americans did not prepare themselves for the prospect of battle-field fatalities—female or male. Instead, they attended the dedications of monuments that portrayed an image of war that no longer existed, one that was strange perhaps even to the southern white women remembered in it.

Women's conspicuous absence from Civil War monuments in the North served the desires of veterans groups and city leaders who insisted that lines separated battlefield from home front, that battles waged at home were unrelated and insignificant to the war's outcome, and that south-ern women's wartime experiences—their support in the face of consid-erable deprivation, their willingness to wage partisan war against the enemy at their doorsteps, and their extraordinary endurance—were unique and not comparable to women in the North. It did not prepare Americans for the wars of the new century that would once again violate those boundaries. The winged angel dedicated to Pittsburgh's cartridge formers confounded that insistence; instead it recognized that northern women faced down similar enemies at their doorsteps in a war that also had been waged on the northern home front. It did not portray women as tradition-bound—like monuments to Confederate women—nor was it dedicated to the individual achievement that spoke to the generation of New Women. Instead the memorial celebrated women's collective hero-ism and patriotic work. Throughout World War I, the winged angel hung outdoors, where city residents passed her on their way to and from work at one of Pittsburgh's many war-related industries. We cannot know if Mary McGraw's heroic angel spoke to a new generation of war workers as they rushed past it early in the morning, between factory shifts, or at night, on foot or in electric cars. Or maybe they moved past the plaque too quickly to take note of its message of women as saviors of the nation.

In a move that paralleled the post–Great War rejection of modernism abroad, Pittsburgh city leaders moved the plaque—not entirely indoors but nearly so—to the foyer of the middle school, where it still hangs. In this liminal space, one not entirely private, nor public, city leaders hoped it would instruct young people in the arts of peace. Here, once again, city leaders attempted to shape the story told by veterans of the Civil War on the northern home front, turning the angel of war into an angel of peace—a more appropriate message for women to bring to children, per-haps, than one that celebrated war making. But Mary McGraw's angel is about war. It is about how women and men—or in McGraw's day, girls and boys—worked in factories making war, how they returned home to families and communities changed by that war, and how they no longer recognized the world in which they grew up.

Free Labor and Women's Civil War

For Mary McGraw's generation, the Civil War remained a defining moment in the way women (and men) understood space and moved about within it, a moment of time in which relations of power and gender had been reevaluated. Disfranchised and subordinate, nineteenth-century women were self-schooled in alternative approaches to politics, using letters, petitions, and protest as tactics, and personal relations, community networks, and sociability as their conduits to power. James Scott's term "infrapolitics" is useful in this regard as it challenges historians to recognize the politics in everyday acts of resistance, among women, people of color, or the working class.[22] Women's class status determined their approach to political work and shaped its impact, but not always in predictable ways. The war opened up spaces for women to use their class status—or to transcend it. Caroline LeCount, to whom we were introduced in Chapter 4, counted on both white racism and the outrage of men of her class when she boarded a segregated Philadelphia streetcar. LeCount and other elite African American women did not imagine that their politics would translate across class lines, yet it did, as women of modest means such as Emma Jane Turner and Mammy Pleasant took to the streets to demand the same freedom of movement as Caroline LeCount. Mary Booth's privileged class position eased the burden of retrieving her husband's body and allowed Booth to negotiate a meeting with President Lincoln to discuss the plight of African American widows, as we saw in Chapter 6. Lydia Bixby also garnered political attention, stepping briefly out of networks of working-class sociability and informal politics into the halls of power before she slipped backward into anonymity.

Ties to racial and ethnic communities shaped women's experience of war as much as did their gender identity. Immigrant identity shaped patterns of enlistment in the rural North, as men enlisted within communities and counted on extended family and the larger ethnic community to support their wives and children in their absence. Those same ties had catastrophic effects for women when regiments suffered high casualty rates and ethnic communities were hit with multiple, simultaneous demands on their benevolence.[23] Ethnicity and race shaped the experiences of working-class immigrant women in the urban North in ways that were sharply different from their rural counterparts. As part of "the army at home," women moved into new industrial spaces from domestic labor, textile work, or other traditionally female occupations.[24] Surnames suggest that Watertown's cartridge formers were a mixture of Irish and working-class Yankee women; Washington's cartridge chokers were mostly Irish; and at Allegheny they might also have been German and perhaps African American.[25] Cartridge forming was not defined as white women's work, but with popular fears about race mixing tied closely to antebellum attempts to provide separate spaces for women and men, white and black, in northern schools, churches, parks, railroad cars, and other public places, wartime arsenals were likely spaces where working-class women carefully guarded their own claims to whiteness by keeping out women of color. Emancipation aggravated these fears, and women spearheaded efforts to protect the racialized spaces the war had violated. Race shaped the way women saw space and moved about within it, and racial conflicts over space were often riddled with gender consciousness.

Working-class and poor women—many of them new immigrants—were likely to feel the impact of a withdrawal of male wages immediately and to recover slowly. The war did not draw these women out into public; they were veterans of living along the borders of public and private life, having never had the resources to live solely in the latter nor access to power in the former. That working-class and poor women are overrepresented in the records of relief agencies and public institutions that served the war's displaced peoples is perhaps not surprising in and of itself, except that it suggests that the image of a northern home front, constant and stable, was a useful wartime fiction. If the northern home front did not sustain the nationalist self-image of free-labor male independence and dependent female domesticity, then perhaps the wartime North looked more like the South than the North. The dramatic cases of women working and supporting families—or failing to—exposed deep flaws in the free-labor ideology and threatened to disrupt the foundation on which the North's wartime consensus was built.

Women's wartime paths overlapped in ways that suggest that regional differences did not matter as much as those defined by race and class. Working-class and poor northern women lost their homes and were displaced; in the South, white (and sometimes black) women fled advancing troops, and those without friends or family to turn to became refugees.[26] Black women who escaped slavery brought little with them, arriving

— Conclusion —

at Union camps or Northern cities with little to begin their new lives. Freedwomen were strangers in wartime cities and as vulnerable as Irish immigrant women who spent the antebellum years raising children and living on the margins of respectability only to lose it all when their husbands enlisted. Urban institutions such as almshouses, shelters, and relief offices served purposes similar to freedmen's camps—they provided emergency food and shelter to displaced women and children and often expected labor in return. Resources to support marginal women were scarce, so it is not surprising that the dispensation of relief or sympathy created conflicts between northern women as severe as those that surfaced between southern women. The destruction of homes and fields in the South turned refugees into permanent émigrés and complicated the process of postwar family reconstruction; the bounty gamble and the lottery of soldier relief left northern families facing similar postwar conditions.

Years ago, historians stopped taking southern women's loyalties for granted and recognized how the disintegration of the southern home front led to considerable female disillusionment, male desertion, and, eventually, to defeat. Of course, not all southern women gave up the cause, as historian Gary Gallagher has noted, but neither did all northern women support it.[27] At the same time, the North's military victory was made possible by the willingness of army commanders to wage hard war, of businessmen to reach deeper into the working class, and of the public to tolerate the evidence of a profound disruption to domestic relations. Northern victory, it could be argued, came at the *expense* of free labor, for it signaled the triumph of modernity—evidenced by the impermanence and fluidity of northern home-front relations described here. Immigrant, working-class, and African American women made use of rumor and infrapolitics to express their opinions in antebellum cities, and in the undetermined political climate of the war, their actions took on added significance. If the North fought, in part, to prevent change, then women's work and the increased visibility of everyday politics contributed to defeat in this theater. Working in new industrial occupations, negotiating the increased fluidity of modern life, and expanding the parameters of their enfranchisement, women's Civil War is not simply a story of unrewarded loyalty or unassigned blame. It is, rather, the stories of the adjustments, large and small, women made to a war they had not been asked to fight but joined nonetheless.

NOTES

Abbreviations

BCA	Boston City Archives, Hyde Park, Mass.
CHS	California Historical Society, San Francisco
CSA	California State Archives, Sacramento
HSP	Historical Society of Pennsylvania, Philadelphia
HSWP	Historical Society of Western Pennsylvania, Pittsburgh
JSH	Johannes Schwalm Historical Association. *Johannes Schwalm, the Hessian.* Lyndhurst, Ohio: Johannes Schwalm Historical Association, 1976.
LibCo	Library Company of Philadelphia
MHS	Massachusetts Historical Society, Boston
MSA	Massachusetts State Archives, Dorchester
NARA	National Archives and Records Administration, Washington, D.C.
NARA-MA	National Archives and Records Administration, Mid-Atlantic, Philadelphia, Pa.
NARA-NE	National Archives and Records Administration, New England, Waltham, Mass.
OR	U.S. War Department. *The War of the Rebellion: A Compilation of the Official Records of the Union and Confederate Armies.* 128 vols. Washington: Government Printing Office, 1880–1901.
PCA	Philadelphia County Archives, Philadelphia, Pa.
PHMC	Pennsylvania Historical and Museum Commission, Harrisburg

Prologue

1 Barton, *Beautiful Blunder*, 67.

2 Emerson, "America's Most Famous Letter."

3 Bullard, *Abraham Lincoln*, dedication.

4 Ibid., 44–45.

5 Schouler, *History of Massachusetts*, 577–78.

6 Bullard, *Abraham Lincoln*, 20.

7 Mrs. Andrew C. Wheelwright (formerly Miss Sarah Cabot) quoted in ibid., 43–44. Bullard estimated that Wheelwright wrote her memoirs between 1878 and 1917.

Wheelwright likely came in contact with Bixby through the Ladies Industrial Aid Association begun by Anna Cabot Lowell. Miller, "For His Wife," 96.

8 Bullard found that only two of Bixby's five soldier sons died while in U.S. Army service—one was honorably discharged, one deserted, and another may also have deserted. Bullard, *Abraham Lincoln*, 33–34. He also found that Bixby had one son who was too young to enlist and two daughters. Ibid., 33–34 & 46.

9 Barton, *Beautiful Blunder*, 129.

10 Bullard, *Abraham Lincoln*, 34.

11 Holzer, "Bad as She Could Be."

12 Miller, "For His Wife," 80.

Introduction

1 Boritt, *Gettysburg Gospel*, 86.

2 J. Cullen Bryant (lyrics) and D. A. Warden (music), "We Are Coming Father Abra'm, 600,000 More!" LibCo, Song Sheet Collection, 1862.

3 Stanton quoted in Stanton, Anthony, and Gage, *A History of Woman Suffrage*, 23.

4 A representative sample of work considering northern women follows, in chronological order: Gallman, *Mastering Wartime*; Vinovskis, "Have Social Historians Lost the Civil War?"; Venet, *Neither Ballots nor Bullets*; Clinton and Silber, *Divided Houses*; Oates, *A Woman of Valor*; Leonard, *All the Daring of the Soldier*; Schultz, *Women at the Front*; Creighton, *The Colors of Courage*; Venet, *A Strong-Minded Woman*; Whites, *Gender Matters*; Silber, *Daughters of the Union*; and Gallman, *America's Joan of Arc*.

5 Ginzberg, *Work of Benevolence*; Leonard, *Yankee Women*; and Giesberg, *Civil War Sisterhood*.

6 Silber concludes that "the war did not emancipate women so much as teach them about their second-class status." This study focuses on the experiences of middle-class white women who worked as nurses and government employees and African American women who taught in freedmen's schools. Silber, *Daughters of the Union*, 284. See also Attie, *Patriotic Toil*.

7 Faust, *Mothers of Invention*.

8 Bynum, *Unruly Women*.

9 Clinton, *Tara Revisited*; Schwalm, *A Hard Fight for We*; and Edwards, *Scarlett Doesn't Live Here Anymore*.

10 Amy Stanley explores, among other things, how southern black women explicitly rejected the notion that the marriage contract would necessarily mean "freedom" for black women. Stanley, *From Bondage to Contract*.

11 Glymph, "The Civil War Era," 171.

12 W. H. Hardy quoted in Ramsdell, *Behind the Lines*, 30.

13 James McPherson concluded that northern victory was possible because "the

Union developed superior managerial talent to mobilize and organize the North's greater resources for victory in the modern industrialized conflict that the Civil War became." McPherson, *Battle Cry of Freedom*, 857.

Many scholars have taken issue with McPherson's characterization of the war as modern or "total." Mark Neely insists that "no Northerner at any time in the nineteenth century embraced as his own the cold-blooded ideas now associated with total war." Neely, "Civil War a Total War?" 49. In the same volume, Stanley Engerman and J. Matthew Gallman examine the northern economy and argue that the South made more definitive moves toward modern or total war than did the North. Engerman and Gallman, "The Civil War Economy," 217–48.

For very good reasons, historians do not generally refer to the Civil War as a total war because the intentions of civilian leaders on both sides were rather limited, in particular Lincoln's. Additionally, scholars have been careful to point out that military men agreed to and generally adhered to rules of war that exempted civilians from violence. Finally, the continued reliance on private enterprise and volunteer efforts, at least in the North, suggests that the Civil War did not result in the birth of a modern state, as had been argued previously, and hence does not really qualify as a total war.

14 Neely, "Civil War a Total War?" 36.

15 Lefebvre, *Production of Space*, 25. Significantly, Lefebvre insists that in addition to class revolution, "it is also necessary to produce a space within which a revolution in everyday life can be carried out."

16 Douglas, *Purity and Danger*, 36.

17 Scott, *Arts of Resistance*, 183.

18 State governors' papers are one of the best sources for understanding how women experienced the war in their everyday lives, for women (and men) addressed their questions and concerns about enlisted men, relief, taxes, shortages, and all manner of military policy to state governors—and often received responses. City archives in Boston, Watertown, Philadelphia, and Pittsburgh contained the records of relief agencies, almshouses, and temporary shelters, as did the state archives in Dorchester, Massachusetts, and Harrisburg, Pennsylvania. The records of women employed in government munitions work and textile manufacturing are in the National Archives in Washington and in Philadelphia and Watertown. Local newspapers carried news of this work, in particular when something went wrong, like it did in Pittsburgh, Watertown, and Philadelphia. Newspapers also covered news of draft riots and labor protests.

Chapter 1

1 Northern farmers experienced unprecedented prosperity during the war, in part due to what one historian has characterized as the Union army's "voracious ap-

petite for food and animal feed." Women and other family members continued to produce the food crops they had produced before the war, only now these staples commanded higher prices. Ransom, *Conflict and Compromise*, 261–62.

2 Newton, *Report of the Commissioner*, 3.

3 Ibid., 4.

4 Ibid., 546.

5 Livermore, "Western Scenes." This story is reprinted in Livermore's *My Story of the War*, 145–49. Page numbers here refer to 1889 version.

6 Livermore, *My Story*, 148–49.

7 Elizabeth Schwalm to Samuel Schwalm, April 24, 1864, *JSH*, 272.

8 Esther Jane Campman to Governor Curtin, April 28, 1865, Records of the Adjutant General, PHMC, RG 19.29, Box 25.

9 Data collected by Bell Wiley found that 47.8 percent were farmers, whereas the USSC's data concluded that the number was slightly lower at 47.5 percent. Wiley data quoted in McPherson, *Battle Cry of Freedom*, 387. For marriage estimates, see Holmes, "Widows and the Civil War," 174.

10 Livermore, *My Story*, 149.

11 Faust, *Mothers of Invention*, 247.

12 Bercaw, *Gendered Freedoms*, 115.

13 Ibid., 112.

14 Giesberg, *Civil War Sisterhood*, 164–68. Venet, *A Strong-Minded Woman*, 127.

15 Hoogenboom and Klein, *History of Pennsylvania*, 193.

16 In her study of dairying along the Northern Tier (Chester and Delaware Counties), Joan Jensen found that women played a significant role in commercial butter production in the antebellum period, and Sally Ann McCurry showed that male-run factory dairying did not begin to replace home-based manufacturing until 1860. Jensen, *Loosening the Bonds*; Sally Ann McCurry, *Transforming Rural Life*.

17 Weiner, "Rural Women," 153–54.

18 Osterud, *Bonds of Community*; Jensen, *Loosening the Bonds*. Julie Roy Jeffrey and Glenda Riley, on the other hand, differ from Jensen and Osterud about how well rural women escaped the gendered limitations of domesticity. Jeffrey, *Frontier Women*; Riley, *Women and Indians*.

19 Samuel Schwalm to "My dear wife and children and brothers and sisters and Israel Klinger and Mariah Klinger and all my friends," Beaufort, South Carolina, January 30, 1862, *JSH*, 262.

20 Ibid.

21 Samuel Schwalm to Elizabeth Schwalm, June 13, 1863, ibid., 269.

22 Samuel Schwalm to Elizabeth Schwalm, n.d., Kentucky, ibid., 272.

23 Elizabeth Schwalm to Samuel Schwalm, August 7, 1864, ibid., 274.

24 Samuel Schwalm to Elizabeth Schwalm, June 13, 1863, ibid., 270.

25 Samuel Schwalm to Elizabeth Schwalm, June 5, 1862, ibid., 266.

26 Elizabeth Schwalm to Samuel Schwalm, April 24, 1864, ibid., 272.

27 Livermore, "Western Scenes."

28 Samuel Schwalm to Elizabeth Schwalm, June 13, 1863, and December 25, 1863, *JSH*, 269, 271.

29 Elizabeth Schwalm to Samuel Schwalm, August 7, 1864, ibid., 275.

30 Samuel Schwalm to Elizabeth Schwalm, June 20, 1864, ibid., 275.

31 This issue seems to have plagued many farm families. Levi Perry, a soldier serving in a Maine regiment, for instance, wrote home to his mother when he found out that his brother had enlisted. "I think [Chandler] has done wrong for he promised me when I left home that he would stay and take care of things at home." Perry worried that "now there is no one to look to things but you." Levi Perry to "Mother," July 26, 1862, in Silber and Sievens, *Yankee Correspondence*, 138

32 Damage Claim Applications, 1868–1872, PHMC, RG 2.69. Osterud, *Bonds of Community*, 11–12.

33 Surnames recorded in the 1860 census for Adams and surrounding counties suggest that, when the war came, many families had multiple generations living in the region.

34 Woodworth, *Beneath a Northern Sky*, 21–34.

35 The diaries of middle-class Gettysburg women indicate that many men fled town with livestock and other valuables in advance of the invading troops, leaving women with the responsibility of defending their homes and men open to charges of cowardice in the aftermath of the battle. Ericson, "'The World Will Little Note,'" 82–101; Creighton, *Colors of Courage*, 76–78.

36 Musser, Musselman, Hill, Deardorff, and Bowling Affidavits, Damage Claim Applications, PHMC, RG 2.69.

37 Bucks County Board of County Commissioners, Minutes of the Board of Relief, PHMC, MG 4.

38 Mifflin County Relief to Families of Civil War Soldiers, PHMC, MG 4.

39 Minutes for December 1863 and June 1864, Bucks County Board of County Commissioners, PHMC, MG 4.

40 Maria Thomas to Governor Curtin, April 29, 1865, PHMC, RG 19.29, Box 25.

41 Rebecca Snook, Application for Relief, January 3, 1865, Mifflin County Relief to Families of Civil War Soldiers, PHMC, MG 4.

42 Lavina Rheam, Application for Relief, Mifflin County Relief to Families of Civil War Soldiers, PHMC, MG 4.

43 Sarah Kile and Martha Ann Beacer, Application for Relief, Mifflin County Relief to Families of Civil War Soldiers, PHMC, MG 4.

44 Minutes for July 1864, Bucks County Board of County Commissioners, PHMC, MG 4.

45 Minutes for February 1865, Bucks County Board of County Commissioners, PHMC, MG 4.

46 Sarah "Hufner" to Governor Curtin, April 11, 1865, PHMC, RG 19.29, Box 25. In the 1860 and 1870 census, the last name appears as Heffner. Sarah is listed as twenty-six years old in 1860, and Daniel is thirty-three. The couple had three children, Mary (nine years old), Daniel (6 years), and Christiana (3 years). Sarah's sixty-year-old mother-in-law was also living with the couple in 1860.

47 Ibid.

48 Mrs. M. H. Roberts to Governor Curtin, January 10, 1865, PHMC, RG 19.29, Box 24.

49 Here I am borrowing from Linda Kerber's analysis of how women's obligations have been discounted on a number of occasions, allowing the state consistently to deny women's rights. Kerber, *No Constitutional Right.*

50 Anne Sloan to Governor Curtin, March 9, 1865, PHMC, RG 19.29, Box 24.

51 H. B. Whiteman to Governor Curtin, January 30, 1865, PHMC, RG 19.29, Box 24.

52 Stephanie McCurry, "Citizens, Soldiers' Wives," 112.

53 The 1870 census is ambiguous. Frederick Campman appears in the census living in a tavern keeper's house, but not with Esther Jane Campman.

54 Mrs. Sedesa Cochran to Governor Curtin, January 7, 1865, PHMC, RG 19.29, Box 24.

55 Claims applications were checked against the 1860 and 1870 census. Thirty percent of female petitioners owned property before the war, and another 30 percent became property owners after the war. Fourteen out of a total of 48 female claimants were listed as property owners in the 1860 (and 1870) census. Thirteen out of the total of 48 were listed as new property owners in the 1870 census. Damage Claim Applications, PHMC, RG 2.69.

56 *Laws of Pennsylvania of the Session of 1848*, No. 372, Section 6, 536–37. *Laws of Pennsylvania of the Session of 1851*, No. 331, Section 5, 613.

57 *Laws of Pennsylvania of the Session of 1865*, No. 1118, Section 1, 1227.

58 Wistler and McElroy Affidavits, Damage Claim Applications, PHMC, RG 2.69.

59 Suzanne Lebsock showed that married women's property acts developed in the postwar South emerged not out of concern for women's rights but out of men's attempts to protect their property from debt. Lebsock, "Radical Reconstruction," 195–216.

60 Osterud, *Bonds of Community*, 134–35.

61 Lebsock, *Free Women of Petersburg*, 15–53.

62 Braukman and Ross, "Married Women's Property."

63 Brands, *Masters of Enterprises*, 35.

64 Stanley Engerman challenged the conclusion that the Civil War accelerated mechanization. In farming, Engerman found that sales of McCormick reapers were flat during the war and only picked up afterwards. Engerman, "Economic Impact," 186.

65 Samuel Schwalm to Elizabeth Schwalm, January 30, 1862, *JSH*, 263.

66 Sarah Heffner to Governor Curtin, April 11, 1865, PHMC, RG 19.29, Box 25.

67 Mrs. Hannah C. Main, Grahamton, Clearfield County, PA to Governor Curtin, May 23, 1865, PHMC, RG 19.29, Box 25.

68 Campman to Curtin, April 28, 1865, PHMC, RG 19.29, Box 25.

Chapter 2

1 Susan Hinckley to John Andrew, March 15, 1862, 9th Regiment Records, MSA, vol. 25, no. 30.

2 Sarah Heffner to Governor Curtin, April 11, 1865, PHMC, RG 19.29, Box 25. Norristown is in York County, Pennsylvania. Information about ages of children is from 1870 census.

3 Ibid.

4 Ibid. Sarah Heffner's youngest child, Abraham, was nine years old in 1870, placing his birth date in 1861. It is possible that Sarah was pregnant when Daniel Heffner enlisted.

5 Governor Andrew approved Chapter 222, entitled "An Act in Aid of the Families of Volunteers, and for Other Purposes," on May 23, 1861, earmarking state funds to pay up to $12 a month to the families of state soldiers. Families were allowed $1 per dependent. Miller, "For His Wife."

6 Allport and Postman, *Psychology of Rumor*, vii–viii; Scott, *Arts of Resistance*, 140–52; Hahn, *A Nation Under Our Feet*, 57–61.

7 Scott, *Arts of Resistance*, 144.

8 Rachel Culbert to Andrew Curtin, April 14, 1863, PHMC, RG 19.29, Box 18.

9 Women continue to be the majority of the world's refugees. Domosh and Seager, *Putting Women in Place*, 134–36

10 "The Call for Troops—Obstacles to Volunteering," *New York Times*, July 2, 1862, 2.

11 For widows, there was the federal pension system. A number of historians have traced the expansion of the pension system during—and in particular, after—the war. Congress drew up a new pension law in July 1862, extending pensions to mothers and sisters of soldiers and doubling pension rates for privates from $4 to $8 a month. McClintock, "Civil War Pensions," 463.

In order to qualify for pensions, dependents had to maneuver a confusing bureaucracy and keep track of changing laws of eligibility. Whereas the 1862 pension law assumed that wives were dependent on their husbands, for example, widows had to produce proof of their marriage, and their pensions were not adjusted for family size. Mothers, sisters, and children of dead or injured soldiers were eligible for pensions after 1862, but they had to prove they were dependents. Dependent fathers and brothers became eligible in 1866. Ibid., 463–72.

And, until 1873, only one dependent was eligible at a time. After 1873, widows received extra money for each dependent child. Skocpol, *Protecting Soldiers and Mothers*, 107

Applicants for federal soldiers' pensions were hindered by limited language skills or their inability to produce proof of marriage, citizenship, or residency. In 1864, an amendment was added to the 1862 pension legislation extending pension benefits to widowed former slaves—and their children—who were unable to provide proof of marriage. Basler, "And for His Widow."

This change did not apply, however, to women who were slaves at the time of their marriage, immigrant women, or others for whom providing proof of legal marriage was either impossible or difficult. Widows and other dependents of dead or disabled soldiers who managed to meet the various requirements became eligible for $8 per month from the federal government, but if they remarried or their dependency status changed, they were in danger of losing this benefit. The pension rate varied based on the rank of the soldier, with privates receiving $8 and lieutenant colonels receiving $30 a month.

Indeed, the low "take-up rate" for pensions must in part be a result of confusion about eligibility, for Theda Skocpol has estimated that only about 25 percent of the eligible dependents of dead soldiers were receiving pensions in 1875. Skocpol, *Protecting Soldiers and Mothers*, 106–8; Basler, "And for His Widow."

Megan McClintock's work on pension applications, however, suggests that trading in the scrutiny of local relief agents for the surveillance of the Bureau of Pensions was a right many widows were willing to forego. McClintock explains how the Bureau of Pensions intruded on the lives of widows by policing marriage practices and acting as moral guardians. McClintock, "Civil War Pensions," 471–79.

12 McPherson, *Battle Cry of Freedom*, 491–92.

13 For New York, see "The New Call for Troops," *New York Times*, July 3, 1862, 5. For Philadelphia, see Gallman, *Mastering Wartime*, 17–18.

14 Miller, "For His Wife."

15 "Meetings to Aid Enlistments" (in re, Massachusetts) and "A Call to Connecticut," *New York Times*, July 13, 1862, 8.

16 James Scott cautions against our seeing the "hidden transcripts" of infrapolitics as merely a "prologue" for the moment of political breakthrough, when the politics of marginalized groups suddenly are given a public hearing. Scott, *Arts of Resistance*, 202–3.

17 Bremner, *Public Good*, 76.

18 Sarah Heffner to Governor Curtin, April 11, 1865, PHMC, RG 19.29, Box 25. In 1866 concerns about the irregularity of marriage practices led Congress to suspend widow benefits for women whose living arrangements did not meet Bureau standards of morality. McClintock, "Civil War Pensions," 476.

19 Sanborn, *Special Report on Prisons*.

20 Catherine Purelle to Governor Curtin, May 1, 1865, PHMC, RG 19.29, Box 24.

21 Charles Sanders estimates that 194,743 Union and 214,865 Confederate soldiers were taken as prisoners of war. If 30 percent of these soldiers were married, as historians have estimated for the war at large (see Chapter 1, n. 9), then perhaps as many as 58,000 women shared an experience similar to Purelle's and Heffner's. Sanders, *Hands of the Enemy*, 1.

22 Scott discerns between rumor and gossip, the latter usually spread among equals and intended to enforce certain kinds of conduct. Scott, *Arts of Resistance*, 143.

23 Joseph A. (illegible) to "Dear Father," April 23, 1865, Schuylkill Arsenal Letters, NARA-MA, Box 6.

24 Bucks County Board of County Commissioners, Minutes of the Board of Relief, PHMC, MG 4.

25 George Cadwalader Papers, Military Papers: Civil War, Civilian Letters Folder, July 1861, HSP.

26 Mrs. Mary A. Sanno to "Honrable Govener Certen," April 9, 1865, PHMC, RG 19.29, Box 25, 15.

27 "Suffie Ruckool" (corrected by Curtin's office to Sophia Rucstool) to "Sir," April 10, 1865, PHMC, RG 19.29, Box 25.

28 Ibid.

29 Schultz, *Women at the Front*, 56–59.

30 Constant Hanks to Mary Rose, September 26, 1862, quoted in Schultz, *Women at the Front*, 56.

31 Daily Admissions Records, City Temporary Home, July 12, 1862, MHS.

32 Giesberg, *Civil War Sisterhood*, chaps. 2 and 3.

33 Abbott, "Civil War and Crime Wave." An 1863 inspection of the prisons in Boston's Suffolk County, for example, revealed that women were the majority of inmates in the House of Corrections, Lunatic Hospital, House of Industry, and the House of Reformation. Women constituted 500 of the 997 inmates at these institutions. Women were concentrated in the House of Industry, where they represented 67 percent of the inmates; the Lunatic Hospital, where they represented 57 percent of the inmates; and in the House of Corrections, where they represented 51 percent of the inmates. There were 193 inmates in the city jail, but no information about the sex of the inmates was given. *Boston Daily Advertiser*, December 28, 1863, 2.

Matt Gallman found very modest increases in rates of female incarceration in Philadelphia. He found small increases in the numbers of white women arrested for crimes in wartime Philadelphia and more significant increases in the numbers of black women arrested. Gallman, *Mastering Wartime*, 201–3.

34 The Committee of Relief for Soldiers' Families Report, January 27, 1862, Records of the City of Boston, Mayor and Aldermen, Vol. 40, 1862, BCA.

35 Ibid.

36 Miller, "For His Wife," 80.

37 The Committee of Relief for Soldiers' Families explained the procedure in Boston as follows:

> Payments shall be made at Relief Office to those entitled to receive aid,
> as follows, viz:
> To those residing in Wards 1 and 4, on the first Monday of each Month.
> 2 and 5, Tuesday.
> 3 and 6, Wednesday
> 7 and 8, Thursday
> 9 and 10, Friday
> 11 and 12, Saturday.

Committee of Relief for Soldiers' Families Report, 1862, 10, BCA.

38 Aldermen called this "the evil of duplication." Ibid.

39 Records of the City of Boston, Mayor and Aldermen, December 21, 1863, Vol. 41, BCA.

40 Ibid., May 23, 1863, Vol. 41, BCA.

41 Stanley L. Engerman and J. Matthew Gallman found economic growth in the North rather flat. Engerman and Gallman,"The Civil War Economy," 217–47. See also, Gallman, *Mastering Wartime*, 251–53. On workers' social mobility, see Paludan, *A People's Contest*, 170–74.

42 Engerman noted, too, that the white birthrate decreased 10 percent from 1862 to 1866. He offered no comparable statistics for the nonwhite birth rate. Engerman, "Economic Impact," 194, n. 17.

43 Tewksbury is located twenty-four miles northwest of Boston.

44 Inmate Case Histories Microfilm, Massachusetts State Almshouse Records, Tewksbury State Hospital, MSA.

45 The median age for men was forty.

46 Inmate Case Histories, Massachusetts State Almshouse Records, Tewksbury State Hospital, MSA.

47 While taking interviews, almshouse employees often editorialized with comments such as "story doubtful," "been with other men," "strumpet," or other comments indicating their skepticism.

48 (History of) Mary Lee, 1864, Inmate Case Histories, Massachusetts State Almshouse Records, Tewksbury State Hospital, MSA.

49 The seduction claim was more common among native-born women than Irish-born women. The former were often ten years younger than the latter when they entered the trade. Carlisle, "Prostitutes and Their Reformers," 92–95.

50 "Prostitutes Register in the Female Register of the Almshouse," PCA.

51 Seidman, "Beyond Sacrifice," 124–25.

52 Sanger, *History of Prostitution.*

53 Jones, "A Tale of Two Cities," 257–69.

54 *Lowell Daily Courier*, February 13, 1864, 2.

55 Thomas Webster to Major Foster, March 22, 1864, quoted in Seidman, "Beyond Sacrifice," 47–48.

56 In addition to Douglas, the interviewer listened to twenty-year-old Amanda Lowry, who admitted to prostitution when she explained that she "was at the Battle of Gettysburg [and] got the Disease from the soldiers." Both Elizabeth Hall and Helen Clark, for example, got the disease from their soldier husbands. "Prostitutes Register in the Female Register of the Almshouse," PCA.

Rachel Seidman counted 37 of 164 respondents who claimed to have been infected by their soldier husbands. Seidman, "Beyond Sacrifice," 128.

57 *Manual for the Use of Overseers of the Poor in the City of Boston*, 152–58, BCA.

58 Women with children rarely found domestic positions that allowed them to take their children with them. This usually required that women bind/indenture their children out. Daily Admissions Records, City Temporary Home, MHS.

59 Placing displaced women as domestics did not guarantee them safe working conditions, adequate means of support, or protection from further exploitation. Case histories indicate that women came to the home seeking shelter from abusive employers. Bridget Doyle was admitted to the home on September 28, 1862, with two black eyes, an injury she incurred while serving a family in Roxbury. Nineteen-year-old Mary Swan, whose husband enlisted in a New York cavalry regiment, took a position with a family in Medfield but then sought help from the home when her employer stole her personal belongings. Daily Admissions Records, City Temporary Home, MHS.

60 Monday, September 14, 1863, Daily Admissions Records, City Temporary Home, 232, MHS.

61 Hinckley to Andrew, March 15, 1862, 9th Regiment Records, MSA.

Chapter 3

1 "Appalling Disaster!" *Pittsburgh Gazette*, September 18, 1862, 3.

2 "The Arsenal Catastrophe: Coroner's Investigation," *Pittsburgh Post*, September 20, 1862, 3.

3 "Appalling Disaster!" *Pittsburgh Gazette*, September 18, 1862, 3.

4 The coroner's investigation is reprinted in Carnprobst, "'Ye Know Not What Hour,'" 38.

5 Ibid., 40.

6 Although census research rarely yields definitive identifications of women, at least two of the victims of the 1862 blast were listed in the 1860 census as black females—Mary Bollman, who would have been fourteen years old when she died, and Sara Shepherd, who would have been seventeen.

7 The tablet was replaced in 1929 with one that included all seventy-eight names.

The one pictured here is the 1929 replacement. Wudarczyk, *Pittsburgh's Forgotten Allegheny Arsenal*, 77–78.

8 The fence that is visible just beyond the tablet marks the line separating Allegheny Rural Cemetery from the Catholic cemetery, where some of the victims were buried Still others were buried in individual graves.

9 Douglas, *Purity and Danger*, 115.

10 Ibid.

11 Lincoln quoted in Long, *Rehabilitating Bodies*, 20.

12 Eric Foner, *Free Soil*, ix–xxxix.

13 Angela Woollacott points out that working-class British women remarked that they had an easier time managing family budgets and spent more money on food and other necessities when their husbands were away during World War I then when the men were home spending money at pubs. Woollacott, *On Her Their Lives Depend*, 122–24.

14 On working-class respectability, see Rose, *Limited Livelihoods*; McClelland, "Time to Work"; and Ross, "'Not the Sort.'"

15 For the seventy-eight women finally identified as victims of the Allegheny explosion, few of their antebellum occupations could be gleaned from the census. I could identify six of the victims' occupations in 1860. These women worked as domestics, dressmakers, and washerwomen.

16 Of seventy-eight victims identified on commemorative plaques, sixty-six surnames are listed. Eleven local families may have lost more than one young person on September 17, 1862. Of course, the news stories reported that some family members who escaped were unable to save sisters or daughters. Estimates based on author's list of all victims identified in 1862, 1863, and 1913, when survivors commissioned a new plaque to be erected at the site of the explosion. After an explosion at the Eddystone factory in Chester, Pennsylvania, on March 22, 1917, the *Pittsburgh Gazette Times* reported on a ceremony held on the fifty-fifth anniversary of the explosion, in September 1913, that was attended by Allegheny survivors and included the erection of a plaque in Arsenal Park. "Arsenal Blowup Recalled By Big Blast," *Pittsburgh Gazette Times*, March 22, 1917, 1. Additional names of victims were added to this new plaque. And in 1927, the Arsenal Victims Memorial Committee, an affiliate of the Sons of Union Veterans of the Civil War and Auxiliaries of Committee raised money to erect a new plaque at the Allegheny Cemetery—the site of the original plaque erected in 1863—complete with the names of all those who lost their lives. A. G. Trimble, General Chairman of Arsenal Victims Memorial Committee to Omar Decker, (this letter seems to have been mailed out to potential contributors to the fund), undated (1927?), HSWP, MFF 309.

17 Carnprobst, "'Ye Know Not What Hour,'" 35–36.

18 The paper—or the plaque committee—might have gotten the spelling wrong,

for later she was listed as Eleanor Shepard. "Appalling Disaster!" *Pittsburgh Gazette*, September 18, 1862, 3.

19 The *Pittsburgh Gazette* reported Kate Dugan and her sister died, but neither plaque listed Mary's name. Perhaps this original report was inaccurate or later efforts to confirm Mary's death were inconclusive. The original newspaper story reported that Eliza and Mary Jane Lindsey (the spelling was corrected later) died in the explosion. In 1929, when the new plaque was posted at the site of explosion, survivors of the fire confirmed that the sisters' names were Elizabeth and Harriet. Some confusion continued to swirl around two Donahue sisters who were said to have died in the fire. Kate Donahue's death was confirmed, but her sister's remains a mystery. Ibid., 1. Carnprobst, "'Ye Know Not What Hour,'" 35–36.

20 "An Appalling Disaster!" *Pittsburgh Gazette*, September 18, 1862, 1. Gabby's death was never confirmed or her body was not identified, for her name was never added to the plaque.

21 Anonymous, "History of Allegheny Arsenal Explosion," n.d. (1905), HSWP, MFF 309.

22 Stansell, "Origins of the Sweatshop."

23 Workplace solidarity in part reflected the family connections between workers, as in antebellum textile mills. Dublin, *Women at Work*.

24 Estimates based on employment records for October 1861 to October 1864 at the Watertown Arsenal. T. J. Rodman, Return of Hired Men Employed at Watertown Arsenal, NARA-NE, RG 92. To compare these wages to women's work in the needle trades, see Paludan, *"A People's Contest,"* 182–83.

25 *Harper's Weekly*, quoted in *A History of Watertown Arsenal, 1816–1967*, Army Materials and Mechanics Research Center, 1977, 24, NARA-NE.

26 "The State Arsenal," *Indianapolis Daily Sentinel*, June 26, 1861.

27 Giesberg, *Civil War Sisterhood*, 41.

28 Schuylkill Arsenal Collection, NARA-MA, RG 92.

29 "Funeral for Victims of the Arsenal Explosion," *Baltimore Sun*, June 20, 1864, 4, America's Historical Newspapers (accessed 02/27/08).

30 T. J. Rodman, Commanding Officer, "Rules and Regulations for the Government of the Employees of the Magazines and Laboratories at Watertown Arsenal," Investigation into the Mismanagement of the Watertown Arsenal [Watertown Investigation], November 1864, 17–19, NARA, RG 92.

31 John Symington, Colonel of Ordnance, to General James W. Ripley, Washington, D.C., October 2, 1861, Symington Letterbook, Allegheny Arsenal Collection, NARA-MA, RG 92.

32 Rodman recorded the names of 158 women in his October 1861 pay book. The numbers of women on the payroll as cartridge formers varied throughout the war. Some months—October–December 1863, for example—no women were

employed in this capacity. Other months, the number of women employed as cartridge formers totaled nearly 250. Women were also employed stitching cartridge bags. The pay for this work was two cents per bag. Salaries recorded for this work at Watertown ranged from $2.50 to $23.50 per month. Stitching cartridge bags might have been done on an outwork basis, allowing women to stay home to tend to young children. No women sewing cartridge bags signed the 1864 petition complaining of work conditions. Rodman, Return of Hired Men, NARA-NE.

33 Here, too, women working in textile manufacturing throughout the New England area were an important precedent.

34 The much-maligned Frank Hilton, superintendent of the cylinder room, where most of the Watertown women worked, had two sisters and a sister-in-law employed at the arsenal. Testimony of Frank Hilton, Testimony Taken by the Committee on the Conduct of the War, Boston, MA, 1864, Watertown Investigation, NARA, 108.

At the Washington Arsenal, women who "choked" cartridges were often related to other arsenal employees, as well. These connections made it possible for family members to identify the charred remains of their relations in the hours after the July 17, 1864 explosion. "The Explosion Yesterday at the Arsenal Further Details and Particulars—The Coroner's Inquest," *Washington Star*, June 18, 1864, <http://www.congressionalcemetery.org/> (accessed 02/27/08).

35 Testimony of Violet Smith, Watertown Investigation, NARA, 69.

36 Various Testimonies, Watertown Investigation, NARA, 35, 56, 57, & 98.

37 At New England's textile mills, female operatives petitioned their employers in response to wage cuts in the 1830s, and women remained important in the early ten-hour movement, signing petitions alongside men demanding shorter work hours. Dublin, *Women at Work*, 122; Zaeske, *Signatures of Citizenship*, 21–28.

38 Susan Zaeske argues that women's antislavery petitioning "posed a serious threat to the political status of those who possessed the power to vote." Zaeske, *Signatures of Citizenship*, 28.

39 No cartridge formers appear in the employment records for September–November 1863. Rodman, Return of Hired Men, NARA-NE.

During the investigation, women testified that Hilton kept at least three female family members and several other of his "favorites" employed throughout the fall and winter of 1863. It was during this time, too, that Hilton allowed several arsenal employees to eat clam chowder on arsenal grounds. This event added insult to injury to out-of-work women. See for example Testimony of Leonard Gibson and of Jane E. Stanley, Watertown Investigation, NARA, 39–40 and 94–95.

40 Tap, *Over Lincoln's Shoulder*, 21–24.

41 In many parts of the country, Lincoln's support was lower in 1864 than it had

been in 1860, and other Republicans were in tight reelection races that fall. Donald, *Lincoln*, 543; Montgomery, *Beyond Equality*, 107.

42 Abby J. Eldridge et al. to Hon. D. W. Gooch, November 17, 1864, Watertown Investigation, NARA, 15–16.

43 Testimony of Abby Eldridge, Watertown Investigation, NARA, 58. Testimony of Margaret Connley, Watertown Investigation, NARA, 62.

44 For wage differential, see Rodman, Return of Hired Men, NARA-NE, 31. Carnprobst, "'Ye Know Not What Hour.'"

45 Hilton may have been biding his time at the arsenal until he could return to active duty. Watertown records indicate that in March 1863 and again in January 1864, Hilton requested to return to active duty from his Ordinance Department post at Watertown. Thomas R. Tannett, 14th Massachusetts, to Governor J. A. Andrew, March 7, 1863, and Waldo Merrian, Lt. Col 16th Massachusetts Volunteers, to Governor J. A. Andrew, January 2, 1864, Watertown Investigation, NARA, 20, 22.

46 See discussion of the Rodman gun, a new cannon that Rodman developed while working at Allegheny and Watertown. Wudarczyk, *Notes and Documents*, 24–25.

47 This spirit continues to inform the ways in which contemporary authors defend the service records of these men. Writing about the Allegheny explosion in a 1985 article in *Blue and Gray*, John Carnprobst defended two of the officers found responsible for negligence in the explosion—Lieutenants Jasper Myers and John Edie—as "two youngsters fresh from the Point, responsible for a largely civilian-staffed operation—women and young girls at that, who might serve as distractions for young officers—under extremely dangerous conditions." To this author, women were a distraction and proved disastrous for young men looking forward to distinguished careers in army ordnance. Carnprobst, "'Ye Know Not What Hour,'" 39.

At the Washington Arsenal, Colonel Thomas Brown was known for his superiority in pyrotechnics. Exploding fireworks flew into the cartridge room, setting off a rapidly moving fire from which the women workers had little hope of escaping. "Terrible Explosion at the Washington Arsenal," *Daily Columbus (Ga.) Enquirer*, July 7, 1864, 2, America's Historical Newspapers (accessed 02/27/08).

48 Officers condemned by a civilian jury in the Allegheny case were "quietly reassigned" to other posts, and at Watertown it is unlikely that any disciplinary action was taken in response to complaints filed by female operatives. Carnprobst, "'Ye Know Not What Hour,'" 39; *A History of Watertown Arsenal*, NARA-NE, 27–30.

49 Abby J. Eldridge et al. to Hon. D. W. Gooch, November 17, 1864, Watertown Investigation, NARA, 15–16.

50 Mitchell, *Vacant Chair*, 7.

51 Lyman quoted in Silber and Sievens, *Yankee Correspondence*, 123.

52 Henry Schelling to William F. Hertzog, November 21, 1863, William F. Hertzog Papers, Chicago Historical Society, 3.

53 Silber, *Daughters of the Union*, 118–19.

54 Testimony of Margaret Connley, Watertown Investigation, NARA, 62.

55 Testimony of "Miss Farnsworth," ibid., 79. Farnsworth was taken from Rodman, Return of Hired Men, NARA-NE.

56 Testimony of Mary E. Leonard, Watertown Investigation, NARA, 82.

57 Testimony of Margaret Connley, ibid., 62.

58 In the case of the Washington fire, an organization called the Knights of Pythias came forward to collect money for the victims.

59 "Appalling Disaster!" *Pittsburgh Gazette*, September 18, 1862, 3.

60 "The Allegheny Arsenal Disaster—Continuance of the Investigation," *Pittsburgh Gazette*, September 23, 1862, 5.

61 See the various descriptions of the pornography circulated at Watertown: Testimony of Leonard Gibson, 32–33; Testimony of Mrs. White, 54; Testimony of Mary Boyd, 71; Testimony of Frank Hilton, Watertown Investigation, NARA, 107. Gibson recalled seven or eight pictures, drawn by a Mr. Bowers employed at the arsenal, one "with a very long nose" with the words "to be continued" appended to it. White described a scene in which a little boy and girl had sex and "an old lady peeping in at the door."

62 Mitchell, *Vacant Chair*, 3–18.

63 Neely, "Civil War a Total War?" 36.

64 In "Funeral for Victims" published on June 19, 1864, the *Baltimore Sun* reported different casualty estimates in the same article, reporting seventeen deaths but estimating that the number would likely become twenty-two. Some of the injured escaped the building and were brought home, where they died of their injuries. In the July 17 article copied in the *Daily Columbus (Ga.) Enquirer*, the paper offered estimates of eighteen and fifteen to twenty before settling on twenty. Seventeen girls and three boys had not been accounted for. "Funeral of the Victims of the Arsenal Explosion," *Baltimore Sun*, June 20, 1864, 4; "Terrible Explosion at the Washington Arsenal," *Daily Columbus (Ga.) Enquirer*, July 7, 1864, 2, America's Historical Newspapers (accessed 02/27/08).

  The *Sun* listed the bodies that had been identified as of June 19 as those of Johanna Connor, Margaret Horace, Elizabeth Branegan, Julia McEwen, Bridget Dunn, Lizzie Brahler, and Eliza Lacy. The families of these girls had identified the bodies by "portions of dress still adhering to the remains, or shoes, or trinkets, not entirely destroyed." The bodies of Maggie Yonson, Ellen Roche, Melissa Adams, Mrs. Kate Bresnahan [*sic*], Mrs. Tippett, Susan Harris, Emma J. Baird, Emily Collins, Lizzie Lloyd, Mary Burroughs, Miss Murphy, and Willie Webster were not identified, though many bodies were so badly destroyed as to leave nothing with which to identify them. Finally, Sallie McElfresh, Annie Bates, and Rebecca Hull managed to escape the building but died later—McElfresh and Bates at the hospital and Hull at her home. All told, the paper printed twenty-two names of the dead and likely dead. The cemetery's brochure places the total number dead at twenty-one. For consistency, I have adhered to the *Sun*'s estimate of twenty.

65 The *Washington Star* warned arsenal workers against wearing these hoops, as they "caged" the bodies and allowed fire to enter the expanded dress, encouraging "the flames to fasten upon them with fatal effect." "The Explosion Yesterday at the Arsenal—Further Details and Particulars—The Coroner's Inquest," *Washington Star*, June 18, 1864, <http://www.congressionalcemetery .org/> (accessed 02/27/08).

66 "Further of the explosion—More of the Bodies Recognized—Preparations for Internment," *Washington Star*, June 18, 1864 (2nd edition, 4 o'clock), <http:// www.congressionalcemetery.org/> (accessed 02/27/08).

67 The sister of Melissa Adams, a young cartridge former who died in the fire, made her way through the funeral crowd, climbed up onto the platform in search of her sister's coffin, and then collapsed. "The Funeral of the Victims of the Arsenal Explosion," *Washington Star*, June 20, 1864, <http://www.congressional cemetery.org/> (accessed 02/27/08).

68 McPherson, *Battle Cry of Freedom*, 755.

69 "Terrible Explosion at the Washington Arsenal," *Daily Columbus (Ga.) Enquirer*, July 7, 1864, 2, America's Historical Newspapers (accessed 02/27/08).

70 After the Allegheny accident, workers at the Washington Arsenal took up a collection to help the survivors of the Pennsylvania blast. And on the day of the Washington Arsenal fire, news reached the city of a similar accident at the Watervliet Arsenal in New York. "Further of the explosion—More of the Bodies Recognized—Preparations for Internment," *Washington Star*, June 18, 1864 (2nd edition, 4 o'clock), <http://www.congressionalcemetery.org/> (accessed 02/27/08).

Women working in Confederate arsenals worked under similar circumstances. Explosions in Richmond, Virginia, and Jackson, Mississippi, suggest the dangers for women working in such facilities throughout the United States.

Chapter 4

1 Transcript, *Charlotte Brown v. Omnibus Railroad Company*, District Court of the 12th Judicial District, January 17, 1865, Charlotte L. Brown Papers, CHS, MS 278v, 1–2.

2 Complaint of Plaintiff, *Brown v. Omnibus*, Charlotte L. Brown Papers, CHS; Appeal of Defendant, *Brown v. Omnibus*, Charlotte L. Brown Papers, CHS.

In her original complaint, Brown emphasized the violent nature of her ejection; however, when she testified in the appeals court, Brown claimed that Dennison "did not hurt me at all." Brown was sixteen years old at the time of her ejection. Transcript, *Brown v. Omnibus*, Charlotte L. Brown Papers, CHS, 2.

3 "The Rights of Colored Men to Ride in the Cars," undated newspaper clipping, Wellington C. Burnett Papers, CHS, MS352½.

4 "The Rights of Colored People in California," *Liberator*, January 18, 1865, 187.

5 See, for instance, *Emma J. Turner v. North Beach and Mission Railroad Company*, January 23, 1867, District Court of the 12th Judicial District, January 17, 1865, Wellington C. Burnett Papers, CHS, discussed below.

6 The first names of the litigants in this case are not included in the court record. *Derry v. Lowry*, Court of Common Pleas, First Judicial District of Pennsylvania, 1865, in Wallace, *Philadelphia Reports*, 31.

7 (Pennsylvania) Act No. 21, *Making it an offence for railroad corporations, within this Commonwealth, to make any distinction with their passengers, on account of race or color, and punishing said corporations, and their agents and employees, for the commission of such offence*, March 22, 1867, in *Pennsylvania Laws*, 38–39; Speirs, *Street Railway System of Philadelphia*, 25–27; Philip Foner, "Battle to End Discrimination II," 368–72.

8 Collins, *Black Feminist Thought*, 95.

9 For New York, see below. For Cincinnati, see Dabney, *Cincinnati's Colored Citizens*, 145, 350–51.

Emily Elizabeth Parsons describes an agreement made with women in St. Louis, who were allowed on the streetcars on Sundays to visit their soldier husbands and sons. Emily Elizabeth Parsons to "Darling Mother," April 4, 1864, *Memoir of Emily Elizabeth Parsons*, 137–40. Also in St. Louis, a woman named Caroline Williams won her case against a streetcar company after she was shoved off a streetcar on which she was traveling—pregnant and with her other child in her arms. A jury awarded Williams a begrudging one cent, but the case set a precedent of which other companies took note. Greene, Kremer, and Holland, *Missouri's Black Heritage*, 93. For New Orleans, see "The Star Cars," *New Orleans Tribune*, May 4, 1867, 1; "The Public Schools," *New Orleans Tribune*, May 8, 1867, 1; and Ryan, *Women in Public*, 93.

10 *Derry v. Lowry*, in Wallace, *Philadelphia Reports*, 33.

11 Scott, *Arts of Resistance*, 183.

12 On New York, see "Justice Restored," *Christian Recorder*, July 9, 1864. On New Orleans, see "The Star Cars," *New Orleans Tribune*, May 4, 1867, 1.

13 Of the eighteen railway companies operating horse-drawn cars in Philadelphia in 1860, eleven excluded black passengers entirely, and eight allowed them to ride on the platform with the driver. Weigley, *Philadelphia*, 373–75.

14 This incident likely occurred in 1861 and created enough public outrage—particularly among the city's "wealthiest ladies" who counted on Fossett's beauty

expertise—that conductors began allowing African American women to ride. Dabney, *Cincinnati's Colored Citizens*, 145.

15 "Right vs. Politeness," *Philadelphia Sunday Dispatch*, August 27, 1865.

16 Douglas, *Purity and Danger*, 139.

17 Philip Foner, "Battle to End Discrimination II," 357. The referendum began on January 31, 1865, the day Congress adopted the Thirteenth Amendment. Weigley, *Philadelphia*, 415.

18 Douglas Henry Daniels argues that the black population of San Francisco began to decline in the postwar era as African Americans moved to Oakland in response to the growing labor movement. Daniels, *Pioneer Urbanites*, xiii.

19 Kelley, "'Not What We Seem,'" 75–112.

20 Daniels, *Pioneer Urbanites*, 17–19.

21 Ibid., 129.

22 For a discussion of California's short-lived romance with free labor ideals, see Gerald Stanley, "Civil War Politics in California," 115–28.

23 "Our Duty," *Pacific Appeal*, March 21, 1863, 2.

24 Mantilla, "'Hush, Hush, Miss Charlotte,'" 99, 113, 117–18.

25 San Franciscans celebrated West Indian emancipation on August 1 and emancipation in Washington, D.C., on July 18, 1862. The community held the first Grand Jubilee in celebration of the Emancipation Proclamation on January 14, 1863. "Celebration," *Pacific Appeal*, August 2, 1862, 2; "Celebration of the Emancipation by Colored Persons," *Pacific Appeal*, July 19, 1862, 2; "Emancipation," *Pacific Appeal*, August 9, 1862, 2; "Emancipation Celebration," *Pacific Appeal*, January 17, 1863, 2; Daniels, *Pioneer Urbanites*, 133; Hudson, *"Mammy Pleasant,"* 46–47.

26 Daniels, *Pioneer Urbanites*, 119.

27 The *Pacific Appeal* represented the interests of "Colored men" beyond "the Territories of the American government, but we include within the sphere of our duties the British possessions." "Our Object," *Pacific Appeal*, April 4, 1862, 2–3.

28 Hudson, *"Mammy Pleasant,"* 47.

29 "Prejudice," *Pacific Appeal*, March 14, 1863, 2.

30 "The Right of Colored Persons to Ride in the Railway Cars: Important Legal Decision of the Supreme Court of the State of New York," *Pacific Appeal*, May 16, 1863, 2.

31 Still, *Underground Railroad*, 214–15.

32 In her appeals court testimony, Brown claimed to have worn the veil up, not down, when she boarded the streetcar. Transcript, Brown Papers, CHS, 2.

33 In August 1865, a white man complained to the *Sunday Dispatch* about an incident that he endured riding on a streetcar when a conductor tried to remove two women on their way to visit their wounded soldier husbands. The man was personally insulted and made to feel unsafe when the driver drove recklessly, refused to let any passengers off, and used abusive language against the women.

Passengers joined in the insults, and the man was particularly offended by the foul language used by some female passengers, presumably white. Philip Foner, "Battle to End Discrimination I," 271–72.

34 Transcript, *Brown v. Omnibus*, Charlotte L. Brown Papers, CHS, 6.

35 "The Effect of Judge Pratt's Decision," undated newspaper clipping, Scrapbook #3, Burnett Papers, CHS.

Jeanette Mantilla suggests that the reference to the *Gaz* might be to the California *Police Gazette*, a newspaper published from to 1859 to 1865. Mantilla, "'Hush, Hush, Miss Charlotte,'" 28.

36 "The Effect," Scrapbook #3, Burnett Papers, CHS.

37 Weigley, *Philadelphia*, 368–90.

38 Yellin, *Abolitionist Sisterhood*, 116.

39 Weigley, *Philadelphia*, 402–11.

40 Dorsey, *Reforming Men and Women*, 153. See also Yellin, *Women and Sisters*, 48–49.

And, in 1853 deputies north of Philadelphia brutally attacked William Thomas, claiming that he was a fugitive slave. Bacon, *But One Race*, 122.

41 See, for example, "A Row in Mauch Chunk," September 10, 1862, *Luzerne Union*, 1, Luzerne County Historical Society, Wilkes-Barre, Pennsylvania.

42 Speirs, *Street Railway System of Philadelphia*, 24.

43 In June 1862, Still presented a petition signed by "hundreds of white citizens" to the company presidents asking the companies to grant equal access to the cars. By 1865, one company (the West Philadelphia and Darby Road line) had agreed to allow black passengers to ride on the platform, and two others began running separate "colored" cars periodically. Still, *Brief Narrative*, 5.

44 "The Rights of Colored People: Decision of the District Court against Colored People Riding in the City Railway Cars," *Christian Recorder*, January 26, 1861.

45 Ibid.

46 "Home Affairs: The Cars and Our People," *Christian Recorder*, June 30, 1866.

47 Additionally, conductors attempted to eject Harriet Tubman and Frances Ellen Watkins Harper from cars in Philadelphia. Tubman suffered injuries to her arm and shoulder when the conductor, with the help of friends, threw her out of the car, and Harper referred to her and Tubman's treatment aboard Philadelphia railroad cars in an 1866 speech to the Eleventh Women's Rights Convention. Humez, *Harriet Tubman*, 69–73. See also, Speech of Frances Ellen Watkins Harper, *Proceedings of the Eleventh Woman's Rights Convention*, New York, May 1866, in Sklar, *Women's Rights Emerges*, 196–98.

48 Harriet Forten Purvis, for example, was a founding member of the Philadelphia Female Anti-Slavery Society and the daughter and wife of prominent abolitionists, and she was married to Robert Purvis, a founding member of William Lloyd Garrison's American Anti-Slavery Society. Bacon, *But One Race*, 30–31, 40–42.

49 It is not my intention to shift credit away from male leaders. In the end, women's direct actions complimented men's approaches to lobbying for civil rights at home. Here, I want to suggest that women in streetcar battles helped foster what Stephanie Camp has described as a "culture of opposition." Camp, *Closer to Freedom*, 116.

The streetcar campaign waged by William Still (famous for his work on the Underground Railroad), Octavius Catto (Civil War veteran and voting rights martyr), and other male leaders has been described in Philip Foner, "Battle to End Discrimination against Negroes on Philadelphia Street Cars, I" and "Battle to End Discrimination against Negroes on Philadelphia Street Cars, II."

50 Weigley, *Philadelphia*, 415.

51 Forbes, *African-American Women*, 77–78.

52 In San Francisco, too, women already active in antebellum race work found a broader platform for their work when the war began. Here, women organized the Ladies Union Beneficial Society and the Daughters and Sons of Zion Benevolent Association, among others. Hudson, *"Mammy Pleasant,"* 45–46.

53 Forbes, *African-American Women*, 96, n. 110.

54 First Annual Report, Ladies' Union Association, 1864, HSP; "Sick and Wounded Soldiers," *Christian Recorder*, September 3, 1864; Forbes, *African-American Women*, 97.

55 Forbes, *African-American Women*, 97.

56 Carrie LeCount was also an ICY graduate, a well-known public speaker, and engaged to Octavius Catto. Ibid., 80. Biddle and Dubin, "Octavius v. Catto," 8–20. Controllers *Annual Report*, 120.

57 Mantilla, "'Hush, Hush, Miss Charlotte,'" 311.

58 Transcript, *Brown v. Omnibus*, Charlotte L. Brown Papers, CHS, 2.

59 *Derry v. Lowry*, in Wallace, *Philadelphia Reports*, 30.

60 "Justice Restored," *Christian Recorder*, July 9, 1864.

61 When William Still requested Philadelphia mayor Alexander Henry to forbid police officers from helping conductors eject black passengers, the mayor declined, explaining that he did not want "the ladies of his family to ride in the same car with colored people." Apparently, Henry had no qualms about the women in his family witnessing violence. Of course, they likely never rode the cars. Philip Foner, "Battle to End Discrimination II," 357.

62 Ibid., 32.

63 The awards in the Philadelphia settlements were small—Derry was awarded fifty dollars, and Anna Adams was awarded five, for example—in comparison to San Francisco's cases and hardly worth a streetcar company's appealing the decision. There was little financial incentive for women to file these suits in the Philadelphia streetcar battle. Even so, city railroad companies appealed a fine of five dollars awarded to Anna Adams of the LUA and Harriet Tubman eventually gave up her suit. *West Chester and Philadelphia Railroad Company v. Miles*, April 1,

1867, Supreme Court of Pennsylvania, CSA, 209–15; "Before the Supreme Court," *Christian Recorder*, November 16, 1867; Humez, *Harriet Tubman*, 73.

On Adams' affiliation with the LUA, see Forbes, *African-American Women*, 97. Adams was traveling with Mary Ann Miles to Oxford from Philadelphia. Ashmun Institute—later Lincoln University—was located in Oxford. Perhaps one of the two had business to attend to at this African American school.

64 For a discussion of gender as performance, see Butler, *Gender Trouble*, 24–25.

65 Dabney, *Cincinnati's Colored Citizens*, 145.

66 Minutes of Philadelphia Female Anti-Slavery Society, October 11, 1866, HSP.

Indeed, some time in January Purvis herself had been asked to leave a streetcar. "The Meanness of Complexion Prejudice," *National Antislavery Standard*, January 28, 1865, 2.

67 The law set a standard fine of $500 for companies who denied service to black riders, and it established a scale of $100 to $500 in fines and/or imprisonment "for a term not exceeding three months, nor less than thirty days" for "any agents, conductors, or employees" of companies who denied service. Among other things, the law warned against a conductor who might "throw any car, or cars, from the track, thereby preventing persons from riding." Act No. 21, March 22, 1867, in *Pennsylvania Laws*, 38–39.

68 Philip Foner, "Battle to End Discrimination II," 373.

69 *National Antislavery Standard*, March 30, 1867, 2.

70 Pennsylvania ratified the Fifteenth Amendment in 1869. African Americans began voting in 1870 in the state.

71 On Turner's background, see Mantilla, "'Hush, Hush, Miss Charlotte,'" 311–16.

72 Plaintiff's Deposition, *Emma Jane Turner v. North Beach and Mission Railroad Company*, January 23, 1867, Wellington C. Burnett Papers, CHS.

73 The attorney for the defense even asked Emma Jane Turner if she was wearing a veil, which, Turner explained, she never did. Mantilla, "'Hush, Hush, Miss Charlotte,'" 321.

74 Hudson, *"Mammy Pleasant,"* 51.

75 W. W. Crane, Jr., Attorney, *Emma Jane Turner vs. North Beach and Mission Railroad Company*, Appeal to Supreme Court of California (San Francisco: Alta California Printing House, 1867), 12–13, CSA.

76 *Pleasants [sic] v. North Beach and Mission Railroad*, Appeal, California Supreme Court, 1868, (WPA 16249), CSA; and *Turner v. North Beach and Mission Railroad*, Appeal, California Supreme Court, 1868, (WPA 15360), CSA. Hudson, *"Mammy Pleasant,"* 54.

77 Broussard, *Black San Francisco*, 19.

78 Cincinnati's conductors made similar adjustments in the wake of an incident involving Sarah Fossett, who was dragged from a streetcar as she clung to the steps after a conductor refused to allow her to board. In addition to being a popular hairdresser, Fossett and her husband, Reverend Peter Fossett, a former

slave, were active in the city's civil rights community. Elite whites in Cincinnati were outraged at Sarah Fossett's treatment, and, as a result, conductors eased segregation policies to maintain public peace. An undated newspaper clipping in the Wellington C. Burnett Papers refers to this case, indicating that it likely occurred in 1861. "The Rights of Colored Men to Ride in the Cars," undated newspaper clipping, Wellington C. Burnett Papers, CHS; Mantilla, "'Hush, Hush, Miss Charlotte,'" 102–5; Dabney, *Cincinnati's Colored Citizens*, 145.

Absent a court case or other legal precedent, the 1861 Fossett incident did not resolve the problem of segregation in Cincinnati. The *Cincinnati Daily Gazette* reported an incident involving an African American nurse who was denied service while traveling with her white mistress and the woman's child in July 1864, and the black community planned a meeting to discuss a collective resistance strategy in August. "A Conductor on the Pendleton line of cars," *Cincinnati Daily Gazette*, July 19, 1864, 2; "Colored People and the Street Cars," August 8, 1964, *Cincinnati Daily Gazette*, 2.

79 Of course, both might very well have been true. Hudson, *"Mammy Pleasant,"* 11.

80 Wearing a veil became a contested right in the streets of the postwar South. A September 1865 article in the *Liberator* described incidences in Georgia and South Carolina when white women tore veils off of African American women; others refused "to wear veils themselves as long as colored women wear them." "The Unconquered Class," *Liberator* 35, no. 36, September 8, 1865, 14, quoted in Frank, *Women in the Civil War*, 2:625–26.

81 Speech of Senator Charles Sumner, 39th Congress, 2nd Session, *Congressional Globe*, February 20, 1865, 915–16.

82 Scott, *Arts of Resistance*, 203.

83 Higginbotham, *Righteous Discontent*, 191.

Chapter 5

1 Donald, *Lincoln*, 520–45.

2 Lincoln approved the use of a government steamer to collect the ballots of sailors on federal gunboats. Federal employees in Washington were furloughed on election day in order to go home and vote. Ibid., 544.

3 Wilson, *Business of Civil War*, 107–47.

4 An 1863 *Harper's Weekly* cartoon, for example, lambasted contractors as parasites living off poor soldiers' wives. Among other images, the cartoon portrays the contractor's wife—who is rotund in comparison to the soldier's wife—shopping for fineries. The criticism is aimed simultaneously at the contractor for his exploitative business practices and at his wife—and by extension other middle-class women—who ought to show more restraint. "Service and Shoddy—A Picture of the Times," *Harper's Weekly*, October 24, 1863, 677.

5 Seidman, "Beyond Sacrifice," 133.

6 "The Schuylkill Arsenal," *North American and U.S. Gazette*, September 5, 1861, 1. The paper referred to one of the women who spoke at the meeting against contracting as "Yeaker," but a Martha Yeager is listed on the 1861 and 1863 petitions. Martha Yeager was in the group of women who met with Lincoln in 1865. See below.

7 "Twenty-Thousand Working Women" to Brigadier General Meigs, June 6, 1864, Old Military Records, NARA, Box 439, NM 81, e. 225. Emphasis in the original.

8 "The Wages of Sewing Women—A Letter from Secretary Stanton, 18 August 1864," *New York Times*, August 26, 1864, 1.

9 Faust, *Mothers of Invention*, 196.

10 Butler was forced to rescind Order #28 threatening to treat the disloyal of New Orleans like prostitutes in the wake of a torrent of criticism. Ibid., 212–13.

11 Occupying soldiers often required women and other civilians to take loyalty oaths to receive supplies. McPherson, *Battle Cry of Freedom*, 425. For a complete discussion of oaths, see Hyman, *Era of the Oath*.

See the discussion of rape in contraband camps in Berlin et al, *Wartime Genesis of Free Labor*, 3:674–76. Two essays in an upcoming collection consider the incidence of sexual violence in the occupied South. Schwalm, "Between Slavery and Freedom" and Barber and Ritter, "'physical abuse . . . and rough handling'" in Whites and Long, *Occupied Women*.

12 Giesberg, "'A Little Starvation is Good.'"

13 "Bread Riot in Richmond. Three Thousand Hungry Women Raging in the Streets," *New York Times*, April 8, 1863, 1. "Bread Riot in Richmond. Three Thousand Women in Revolt," *New York Tribune*, April 8, 1863, 1.

14 "Copperheads in Council," *New York Times*, April 8, 1863, 8. "Rally of the Democracy. Copperheads in Council," *New York Tribune*, April 8, 1863, 8. "Democratic Meeting in New York. Peace Platform," *New York Herald*, April 8, 1863, 1.

15 Whites, *Gender Matters*, 25–27.

16 "Women and the War," *New York Daily Tribune*, May 15, 1863, 8.

17 Whites, *Gender Matters*, 25–27.

18 Kirkland, "A Few Words."

19 Ibid., 9, 12, 22–23.

20 "Copperheads in Council," *New York Times*, April 8, 1863, 8. "Democratic Meeting in New York: The Peace Platform," *New York Herald*, April 8, 1863, 1.

21 "Copperheads in Council," *New York Times*, April 8, 1863, 8.

22 Bernstein, *New York City Draft Riots*, 259–61.

23 "The Females on the Attack," *New York Herald*, July 14, 1863, 1.

24 Ryan, *Women in Public*, 151.

25 "A Horrible Occurrence: A Woman and Child Killed," *New York Herald*, July 15, 1863, 5. Bernstein also remarks on the dominance of women in the crowd that

killed O'Brien and who beat any bystander who came to the colonel's rescue. Bernstein, *New York City Draft Riots*, 36–37.

26 "Fifth Ward," *New York Herald*, July 17, 1863, 1.

27 Ibid.

28 Leslie Harris has shown that the riots accelerated an exodus from the city, as black families left to escape racist violence and declining economic opportunities. Harris, *In the Shadow of Slavery*, 278–88.

29 Ryan, *Women in Public*, 148–49. Adrian Cook lists the riot's victims and perpetrators in the appendices to Cook, *Armies of the Streets*.

30 "The Draft in Pennsylvania: A Mob of Women in Lancaster," *Chicago Tribune*, July 23, 1863.

31 Ryan, *New York City Draft Riots*, 148.

32 Giesberg, "'Lawless and Unprincipled.'"

33 *Boston Daily Journal*, July 15, 1863.

34 "The War in Blakely: The Women in Arms against the Draft," *Luzerne Union*, October 1, 1862, 3.

35 "Resistance to the Enrollment in Archbald," *Pittston Gazette*, October 2, 1862.

36 "The War in Blakely: The Women in Arms against the Draft," *Luzerne Union*, October 1, 1862, 3.

37 "A Row in Mauch Chunk," *Luzerne Union*, September 10, 1862, 1.

38 Ibid.; "The War in Blakely: The Women in Arms Against the Draft," *Luzerne Union*, October 1, 1862, 3.

39 "Resistance to the Enrollment in Archbald," *Pittston Gazette*, October 2, 1862, 1; "A Row in Mauch Chunk," *Luzerne Union*, September 10, 1862, 1.

40 Bernstein, *New York City Draft Riots*, 28–31.

41 "A Row in Mauch Chunk," *Luzerne Union*, September 10, 1862, 1.

42 "The War in Blakely: The Women in Arms against the Draft," *Luzerne Union*, October 1, 1862, 3.

43 Michael Kelly Diary, Connecticut Historical Society, <http://www.chs.org/kcwmp/exams/KellyM.html> (accessed 05/07/08).

44 "Pittston Township," *Pittston Gazette*, September 4, 1862.

45 Adams, "Remembrance of the Boston Draft Riot," 39.

46 "Pittston Township," *Pittston Gazette*, September 4, 1862.

47 Palladino, *Another Civil War*, 102.

48 Ibid.

49 Board of Alderman Records, vol. 41, July 27, 1863, BCA.

50 Bernstein, *New York City Draft Riots*, 52–53.

51 A note in the *Pittston Gazette* reported on a Philadelphia company selling draft insurance but warned readers against buying it. "Insurance Against the Draft," *Pittston Gazette*, September 4, 1862.

52 Chessen, "Harlots or Heroines?"

53 See discussion of "Brany Patch," where the residents "took their abode, for the

time being, in the streets, in order to avoid being located." "Pittston Township," *Pittston Gazette*, September 4, 1862.

54 Bernstein, *New York City Draft Riots*, 55.

55 Ibid., 56–57.

56 "Commendable Movement," *North American and U.S. Gazette*, July 27, 1863, 1.

The original order came from Pennsylvania congressman William D. Kelly to Colonel G. H. Crosman, Assistant Quartermaster, in charge of the Schuylkill Arsenal. In the end, this was largely irrelevant to the seamstresses, as they held Crosman responsible. Colonel G. H. Crosman to Captain George Martine [*sic?*], July 20, 1863, NARA, RG 92, Box 1004.

57 "Petition," Anna Long et al. to Edwin Stanton, July 29, 1863, NARA, RG 92, Box 798 (old), e. 225.

For background on labor relations in Civil War–era Philadelphia, see Gallman, *Mastering Wartime*, 217–50. Gallman briefly mentions the seamstress' petition campaign. Gallman, *Mastering Wartime*, 247.

58 Elizabeth Steinmeyer and Maggie Murphy, et al., to E. M. Stanton, August 4, 1863, NARA, RG 92, Box 1004, No. 104, 2. "Philadelphia Seamstresses: Meeting of Women Employed in the U.S. Arsenal," *Fincher's Trades' Review*, August 8, 1863, 38.

59 "Ann Sweeney," M.Y. to Captain Martin, n.d., Schuylkill Arsenal Letters, NARA-MA, RG 92, Box 7.

There are approximately four hundred letters from women and their recommenders in this collection.

60 Sara Fries to Captain Martin, October 23, 1863, Schuylkill Arsenal Letters, NARA-MA, RG 92, Box 4. Matilda Kennedy to Mr. Irwin, November 7, 1863, Schuylkill Arsenal Letters, NARA-MA, RG 92, Box 3.

In addition to informal negotiations between seamstresses, women often requested to transfer their work to others. Sarah Hedley to unknown, n.d., Schuylkill Arsenal Letters, NARA-MA, RG 92, Box 4. Letter in re: Lucinda Boyle, September 4, 1863, Schuylkill Arsenal Letters, NARA-MA, RG 92, Box 3. Letter in re: Margaret Thompson, n.d., Schuylkill Arsenal Letters, NARA-MA, RG 92, Box 3.

61 "Mary King," Robert Carns [*sic*], n.d., Schuylkill Arsenal Letters, NARA-MA, RG 92, Box 5.

62 "Sarah Cosgrove," Joseph A. Librand [*sic*] to "Dear Father," April 23, 1865, Schuylkill Arsenal Letters, NARA-MA, RG 92, Box 6.

63 "Mary Burns," "A Soilders Wive M.G." to "Friend," December 4, 1863, Schuylkill Arsenal Letters, NARA-MA, RG 92, Box 8.

64 G. H. Crosman to George H. Boker, November 30, 1863, *Chronicle of the Union League of Philadelphia*, 113–14.

65 "A Word for Our Starving Seamstresses," *Fincher's Trades's Review*, December 12, 1863, 6.

66 For Brooklyn, see "The Sewing Women," *Finchers' Trades' Review*, December 12, 1863, 7. For New York, see "Spasmodic Sympathy for Working Women" *Fincher's Trades' Review*, April 2, 1864, 70. For Detroit, see "The Sewing Women," (Reprinted from the *Mechanic and Workingmen's Advocate*), *Fincher's Trades' Review*, March 18, 1865, 62. For Cincinnati, see "Wrongs of Sewing Women," *Fincher's Trades' Review*, March 18, 1865, 62.

Yeager seems to have gotten her job back, for her name appears again on the June 13, 1864, roster of 800 "female employees" of the arsenal. Anna Brooks et al. to Colonel G. H. Crosman, June 13, 1864, Schuylkill Arsenal Petitions, NARA, RG 92, Box 1004.

67 Sewing women in Brooklyn formed a similar organization. Philip Foner, *Women and the American Labor Movement*, 114. Early in 1864, Moses Beach, editor of the *New York Sun*, called a meeting of the Working Women's Protective Union. Ibid., 119–20. "Another Meeting of the Sewing Women," *Philadelphia Inquirer*, April 27, 1864, 8. A "Mrs. Miller" led the May 18, 1864, unionization meeting, with help from local male labor leaders, including William Sylvis, leader of the Iron Molder's Union, and Jonathan Fincher, editor of *Fincher's Trades' Review*, who were also in attendance. "The Sewing Women Again," *North American and U.S. Gazette*, May 19, 1864, 1. "Working-Women's Meeting," *Fincher's Trades' Review*, May 28, 1864, 108. For New York seamstresses' Working Women's Protective Union, see "Spasmodic Sympathy for Workingwomen," *Fincher's Trades' Review*, April 2, 1864, 70. Seidman, "Beyond Sacrifice," 152.

68 "Twenty-Thousand Working Women" to Brigadier General Meigs, June 6, 1864, Schuylkill Arsenal Petitions, NARA, RG 92, Box 439, NM 81, e. 225.

Colonel Crosman forwarded the petition of "Twenty-thousand" to Quartermaster General Montgomery Meigs with his endorsement. Meigs inquired about the piece rates paid at clothing arsenals in Cincinnati and St. Louis and surveyed those paid by private contractors in several cities. In their responses to Meigs, the heads of the major clothing depots agreed with the Philadelphia petitioners—as a result of private contracting, seamstresses throughout the north received wages that were "quite inadequate," as one put it. Lt. Col. Vinton (New York) to Meigs, June 20, 1864, Schuylkill Arsenal Petitions, NARA, RG 92, Box 439, e. 225.

69 "The Wages of Sewing Women—A Letter from Secretary Stanton, 18 August 1864," *New York Times*, August 26, 1864, 1.

Pennsylvania congressman William Kelley accompanied the delegation. The sewing women might have noted the irony of Kelley's late interest in their welfare, as he had signed the order in 1863 laying off seamstresses who could not prove their loyalty and jumpstarting their organizational efforts.

70 The New York petition was reprinted in *Fincher's Trades' Review* on September 17, 1864. Philip Foner, *Women and the American Labor Movement*, 115.

71 "Indignation Meeting of Working Women," *Philadelphia Inquirer*, January 20,

1865, 8. The women who accompanied Yeager were Mrs. Brooks, Mrs. Davison, and Mrs. Alexander.

72 "The Sewing Women on Arsenal Work," *Fincher's Trades' Review*, February 11, 1865, 42.

73 "Sewing Women of Cincinnati to Abraham Lincoln," February 20, 1865, reprinted in *Fincher's Trades' Review*, March 18, 1865, 2.

74 Wilson, *Business of Civil War*, 107–47.

Chapter 6

1 Her son had served two terms in the U.S. Army—enlisting in Maine and then reenlisting in Massachusetts—before he died.

2 Maurice O'Connell to Governor Andrew, May 4, 1863, Ninth Massachusetts Regiment Records, MSA, vol. 25, no. 90. Unfortunately, the letter does not mention Mrs. McCormack's first name, that of her son, or the circumstances of his death.

3 For a discussion of how the circumstances of Civil War death complicated the process and rituals of mourning, see Faust, *This Republic of Suffering*, 144–70.

4 Kirkland, "A Few Words," 5, 19.

5 Faust. *This Republic of Suffering*, 149.

6 Livermore, *My Story of the War*, 614.

7 Popular songs reinforced this notion of surrogacy. See "Let Me Kiss Him for His Mother," "Bless the Lips that Kissed Our Darling," and "Be My Mother Till I Die," n.d., Song Sheet Collection, LibCo.

8 Livermore, *My Story of the War*, 614.

9 Simon Cameron, General Order 71, September 11, 1861, *Official Records of the War of the Rebellion* [*OR*], series 3, 1: 498. On finding plots adjacent to battlefields, see Lorenzo Thomas, General Order No. 33, April 3, 1862, *OR*, ser. 3, 2: 2–3

10 The War Department estimated that 25,000 soldiers were never buried at all. Long, *Rehabilitating Bodies*, 65–69

11 For an excellent discussion of condolence letters and their role in helping soldiers and families recreate the "good death," see Faust, "Civil War Soldiers," 3–40.

Faust suggests that these "letters may have served as a way of moving symbolically out of the meaningless slaughter back into the reassuring mid-nineteenth-century assumptions about life's meaning and purpose." Ibid., 26.

12 Neff, *Honoring the Civil War Dead*, 51.

13 Faust, "Civil War Soldiers," 5–12.

14 Laderman, *Sacred Remains*, 30–35.

15 Ibid., 117–20.

16 To make matters worse, the undertaker refused to refund the $25 Raivley gave

him at the beginning of his trip. It was not uncommon for correspondents to leave out information that might have expedited their requests for aid, as when Raivley fails to give any specific details about her son, including his name, regiment, or where he died. Mrs. Mary Raivley to H. H. Gregg, October 30, 1865, PHMC, RG 19.29, Box 26.

17 Welke, *Recasting American Liberty*, 57.

18 Cohen, "Safety and Danger," 122.

19 Mary L. Hall to H. H. Gregg, May 8, 1865, PHMC, RG 19.29, Box 25.

20 Neff, *Honoring the Civil War Dead*, 39–40.

21 Many of these photographs were staged, with photographers moving bodies around for effect. Sweet, *Traces of War*, 107–37.

22 "Brady's Photographs," *New York Times*, October 20, 1862, 5.

23 Neff, *Honoring the Civil War Dead*, 41–42.

24 "Brady's Photographs," *New York Times*, October 20, 1862, 5.

25 Ibid.

26 Parentheses in the original. Mrs. M. Walters to "The Honorable Gov. Curtain of PA," October 6, 1865, PHMC, RG 19.29, Box 26.

27 Barbara A. Burger to Mr. Bergner, December 23, 1865, PHMC, RG 19.29, Box 27.

28 Asst Adj. Gen Seth Williams, *OR*, ser. 1, 36, pt. 3:28.

29 Margaret Bissell, quoted in Neff, *Honoring the Civil War Dead*, 55.

30 Mary Young to "Sir," November 6, 1865, PHMC, RG 19.29, Box 27. Young and others were waiting for the list of the Andersonville dead to be published in the papers, after Captain Moore and Clara Barton went to Andersonville in July 1865 to place names at the numbered graves. Oates, *A Woman of Valor*, 310–54.

31 Curtin's order no longer exists, but there is a collection of letters from family members seeking reimbursement at the Adjutant General's Correspondence, Pennsylvania Historical and Museum Commission Archives (PHMC), Harrisburg, Pennsylvania, RG 19.29, Box 24–27. Information about this program was gleaned from these letters of application, such as Mrs. William Brazer's, who referred to the reimbursement amount, and Barbara Burger's, which mentions a notice in the local paper. Mrs. William Brazer to Col. H. H. Gregg, Chief of Transportation and Telegraph, December 4, 1865, PHMC, RG 19.29, Box 27. Barbara Burger to Mr. Bergner, December 23, 1865, PHMC, RG 19.29, Box 27.

32 Williams suggested that someone at the Philadelphia office of the United States Christian Commission gave her this information. Eliza Williams to Col. S. M. Lucy, April 20, 1865, PHMC, RG 19.29, Box 25.

33 S. J. Kline to Col Gregg, September 28, 1865, PHMC, RG 19.29, Box 26.

34 Carrie Chamberlain to Andrew Curtin, November 4, 1865, PHMC, RG 19.29, Box 27.

35 Jane Deans wrote to Colonel Gregg in November and again in December 1865

to inquire about her reimbursement. Jane Deans to Colonel Gregg, November 28, 1865, and December 18, 1865, PHMC, RG 19.29, Box 27. Thomas Graham on behalf of Mrs. Ann Baird, November 23, 1865, PHMC, RG 19.29, Box 27. Graham went to retrieve Baird's husband's body outside of Fredericksburg, Virginia.

36 Jane Deans to Colonel Gregg, November 28, 1865, PHMC, RG 19.29, Box 27.

37 Laura Hull to Andrew Curtin, March 28, 1865, PHMC, RG 19.29, Box 24.

38 Mary Irwin to Colonel H. H. Gregg, October 26, 1865, PHMC, RG 19.29, Box 26.

39 Mary Dresser to O. W. Sees, April 9, 1863, PHMC, RG 19.29, Box 18. The note inscribed on the outside of the letter reads "Replied April 10, saying Act of Assembly provides only for the relief of *Penna* soldiers." [Emphasis in the original.]

40 M. L. Kean to Colonel Gregg, October 9, 1865, PHMC, RG 19.29, Box 26. M. L. Kean to Colonel Gregg, December 11, 1865, PHMC, RG 19.29, Box 27.

41 Women who sent others to get the bodies did not pay them until they received money from the state. See, for example, Matilda Moore to Colonel H. H. Gregg, December 30, 1865, PHMC, RG 19.29, Box 27.

42 Jane Deans to Andrew Curtin, November 28, 1865, PHMC, RG 19.29, Box 27. Jane Deans to Andrew Curtin, December 18, 1865, PHMC, RG 19.29, Box 27. For other women who traveled with small children — or contemplated doing so — see Elizabeth Dyson to Colonel L. M. Lucy, October 27, 1865, PHMC, RG 19.29, Box 25; and Margaret Arbuckle to A. L. Russel, Adjutant General of Pennsylvania, November 23, 1865, PHMC, RG 19.29, Box 27.

43 No details are given about James's death, nor is it clear where Nancy lived. The letter suggests that her final destination was near Pittsburgh. Affidavit of Nancy Jane Cotton, October 26, 1865, taken by Boyd Crammine, PHMC RG 19.29, Box 26.

44 *Gettysburg Compiler*, August 17, 1863. United States Christian Commission agent Andrew Cross appears to report on the same woman in his history of the battle. Cross, *War, Battle of Gettysburg*, 26.

45 *Adams County Sentinel*, September 15, 1863.

46 Mary McKenna to Colonel H. H. Gregg, November 26, 1865, PHMC, RG 19.29, Box 27.

47 R. M McMartin [?] to Harry, September 30, 1865, PHMC, RG 19.29, Box 26.

48 In her study of female nurses, Jane Schultz found that northern women expressed much less reticence about traveling alone than did southern women. Schultz, *Women at the Front*, 66.

See also Cohen, "Safety and Danger," 109–22.

49 Ryan, *Women in Public*, 64–76

50 Douglas, *Purity and Danger*, 5.

51 Ibid.

52 Davis, "Bits of Gossip," 78.

53 Turner, *Victory Rode the Rails*, 376.

54 Wightman, "'A Father's Journey,'" 230–37.

55 Ibid., 244.

56 Mrs. A. M. Hesser to Colonel Gregg, November 20, 1865, PHMC, RG 19.29, Box 27.

57 According to the National Park Service, the Mine Run Battlefield is about twenty miles west of Fredericksburg. See <http://www.nps.gov/frsp/mine.htm> [accessed 02/08/07].

58 The 107th Pennsylvania Infantry and the 87th Pennsylvania Infantry were both engaged at Robertson's Tavern. Valley of the Shadow Archives, <http://valley.vcdh.virginia.edu/OR/paynesfarmminesrun/87thpa/carr.html> and <http://valley.vcdh.virginia.edu/OR/paynesfarmminesrun/107thpa/newton.html> (accessed 01/30/07).

59 Wightman, "'A Father's Journey,'" 243.

60 Reid and Patrick to Colonel Gregg, n.d., PHMC, RG 19.29, Box 27. The enclosed unused pass that Loomis returned with this letter is dated November 23, 1865, and a notation on the back of the letter indicates that the forms were sent in January 1866.

61 Cohen, "Safety and Danger," 121.

62 On government regulations about transporting bodies, Henry Clay Trumbull in his *War Memories of an Army Chaplain* explained that "transportation of bodies on government transports was forbidden during the hotter months, or at any season unless embalmed." Trumbull, *War Memories of an Army Chaplain*, 215.

63 Raivley to Gregg, October 30, 1865, PHMC, RG 19.29, Box 26.

64 Burger to Gregg, December 23, 1865, PHMC, RG 19.29, Box 27. Perhaps Burger's grief was more palpable as Christmas approached. See also Amanda Potter to "Dear Sir," October 9, 1865, PHMC, RG 19.29, Box 26. Potter refers to the numbered graves at Andersonville.

65 Raivley to Gregg, October 30, 1865, PHMC, RG 19.29, Box 26.

66 Potter to "Dear Sir," October 4, 1865, PHMC, RG 19.29, Box 26.

67 Mary Myers to "Curnil Curtin," Oct 30, 1865, PHMC, RG 19.29, Box 26.

68 Jane Deans to Andrew Curtin, November 28, 1865, PHMC, RG 19.29, Box 26, 4.

69 Captain A. Conner of *U.S.S. Switzerland* quoted in Basler, "And For His Widow and His Orphan," 292.

70 Basler, "And For His Widow," 292–94.

71 Laderman, *Sacred Remains*, 101–2

72 Clara Barton received thousands of letters, mostly from women, searching for missing soldiers and information about graves. In 1865, Barton opened the Office of Correspondence with the Friends of the Missing Men of the United States Army to help relatives locate men who had been taken prisoner of war.

Later she expanded this work to include all missing men. Largely at her own expense, Barton compiled and circulated lists of missing soldiers—7,500 names were on her master list—in an effort to gather information for families from July to October 1865, when she had to give the work up because she ran out of money. Oates, *Woman of Valor,* 310–54.

73 Kirkland, "A Few Words," 5, 19.

74 "Mother's Waiting for her Soldier Boy," n.d., Song Sheet Collection, LibCo.

Conclusion

1 Cashin, "Deserters, Civilians, and Draft Resistance," 276.

2 "The Toll of Dead at the Eddystone Ammunition Plant Has Reached 103, 80 Per Cent of Them Women and Girls, the Number May Reach 130," *Chester (Pa.) Times,* April 10, 1917, 5 P.M. Edition, 1. Headlines on the second edition of the *Chester Times* printed earlier in the day noted: "Flying Bullets Cause of Many Deaths and Injuries" and "Women and Girls Victims."

3 "German or Austrian Plotters are Responsible for Munition Disaster, is Opinion of Many," *Chester (Pa.) Times,* April 12, 1917, 1; "Government Agents Working on Many Reported Plots in Connection With Ammunition Disaster," *Chester (Pa.) Times,* April 13, 1917, 4; "Arrest of Russian Socialists May Solve Eddystone Explosion," *Chester (Pa.) Times,* October 3, 1917, 1; "Russian Girl in Explosion Plot," *Chester (Pa.) Times,* October 4, 1917, 1.

4 "Believed that Master Mind Plotted Explosion," *Chester (Pa.) Times,* April 16, 1917, 1; "Federal and State Agents Continue Search for Cause of Munition Plant Disaster," *Chester (Pa.) Times,* April 14, 1917, 1.

5 As Mary Douglas suggests, acts of separation can be read as "symbols of the relation between parts of society, as mirroring designs of hierarchy or symmetry which apply in the larger social system." Douglas, *Purity and Danger,* 5.

6 "More Than One Hundred Men and Women Lost Their Lives in the Explosion this Morning at the Eddystone Ammunition Works," *Chester (Pa.) Times,* April 10, 1917, Second Edition, 1.

7 "Wilson's Call to Patriots," *Chester (Pa.) Times,* April 16, 1917, 1. For announcements of funerals, see, for instance, "Burial to-Day of Explosion Victims," *Chester (Pa.) Times,* April 14, 1917.

8 "Arsenal Blowup Recalled by Survivor of Big Blast," *Pittsburgh Gazette Times,* April 22, 1917, 2.

9 Wudarczyk, *Pittsburgh's Forgotten Allegheny Arsenal,* 70–72.

10 Arsenal Middle School website, <http://www.pps.k12.pa.us/14311012791719437/blank/browse.asp?a=383&BMDRN=2000&BCOB=0&c=57163> [accessed 12/5/08].

11 For a discussion of the debate about whether the Civil War was a modern war, see Introduction, note 13.

12 Anonymous, "History of Allegheny Arsenal Explosion," HSWP, MFF 309.

In his 1985 article for *Blue and Gray*, John Carnprobst defends Lieutenants Jasper Myers and John Edie, two of the officers condemned by the civilian commission. Girls were the problem, according to Carnprobst, for Myers and Edie were "two youngsters fresh from the Point," who "were responsible for a largely civilian operation — women and young girls at that, who might serve as distractions for young officers — under extremely dangerous conditions." Carnprobst, "'Ye Know Not What Hour,'" 39.

13 It is difficult to pinpoint the origin of this version of the events. The undated "History of Lawrenceville," written in part by Ruth Behringer, explains the women's deaths in this way. This document must date from the 1930s, for it refers to the new Arsenal Middle School. This pamphlet insists that the women were in no danger from the blast and that they lost their lives when they jumped from the windows. This account is still used today at Arsenal Middle School. "History of Lawrenceville," HSWP, MFF 309, 3.

14 Interestingly, a 1967 *Philadelphia Inquirer* article about the (1917) Eddystone explosion did the same thing. The reporter claimed that "many of the girls in the plant fainted, and had to be dragged out by others." Emphasizing women's weakness and fear, the author of the 1967 account does not overlook the opportunity to titillate his readers, closing his account: "Fear gave the screams of the girls and women a tinny timbre. Some of the women when they ran out were hurriedly covering partial nakedness." Orrin C. Evans, "Ammo Blast Killed 128," *Philadelphia Inquirer*, undated 1967 article in Eddystone Explosion File, Delaware County Historical Society, Media, Penn.

15 "Arsenal Blowup Recalled," *Pittsburgh Gazette Times*, April 22, 1917.

16 Reference is from Watertown Arsenal women's 1864 petition complaining of bad working conditions. See discussion in Chapter 3. Abby J. Eldridge et al. to Hon. D. W. Gooch, November 17, 1864, Watertown Investigation, NARA, 15–16.

17 "History of Lawrenceville," HSWP, MFF, 3.

18 Brown, *Public Art of Civil War Commemoration*, 69.

19 Mrs. George Tichenor quoted in Brown, 71. Laura Martin Rose, *Address on Dedication of Mississippi Monument to Confederate Women*, June 3, 1912 quoted in Brown, *Public Art*, 76–77.

20 The campaign for a national headquarters of the American Red Cross in Washington, D.C., was originally intended to memorialize the wartime work of Union women, but, as Thomas Brown shows, the structure dedicated in 1917 did not serve that purpose. In fact, at the opening ceremonies, more was said about southern white women than Clara Barton, the founder of the American Red Cross. Brown, *Public Art*, 61.

21 Ibid., 58.

22 Scott, *Arts of Resistance*, 183.

23 For a discussion of nativist sentiments and the experiences of German American and Irish soldiers, see Creighton, *Colors of Courage*.

Draft rioting in Boston, for example, was an expression of Irish women's political differences with the Republican administration of the city and came on the heels of major battlefield losses in the city's Irish regiments. Giesberg, "'Lawless and Unprincipled.'"

24 Confederate army private quoted in Ramsdell, *Behind the Lines*, 30.

25 Furguson, *Freedom Rising*, 203–5.

26 Jacqueline Glass Campbell explores the complex ways that black and white women in the Carolinas responded to Sherman's army as soldiers wreaked havoc on the southern home front. Stephanie Camp uncovers the culture of opposition that slave women created by violating the spacial and temporal prohibitions of antebellum slave society and fostering an active culture of resistance. Campbell, *When Sherman Marched North*; Camp, *Closer to Freedom*.

27 Gary Gallagher found, late in the war, women who continued to enthusiastically support the Confederate army, despite considerable wartime deprivation. Even among the nonslaveholding yeomanry, Gallagher describes "a complex mood of deepening gloom punctuated by desperate bursts of hope." Gallagher, *Confederate War*, 44.

Although Gallagher provides an important corrective to studies that have overstated the disintegration of southern morale and how much it contributed to Confederate defeat, he makes the same mistake in reverse. He concludes that because "northern soldiers contended with fewer worries about the safety and material well-being of their families," it is unlikely "that many Federals left the army because they believed their families were starving." Gallagher, *Confederate War*, 33.

BIBLIOGRAPHY

Manuscript Collections

CALIFORNIA

California Historical Society, San Francisco
    Charlotte L. Brown Papers
    Wellington C. Burnett Papers
California State Archives, Sacramento
    John J. Pleasants [sic] and Mary E. v. North Beach and Mission
        Railroad, Appeal, 1868
    Emma Jane Turner v. North Beach and Mission Railroad, Appeal, 1868

ILLINOIS

Chicago Historical Society, Chicago
    William Hertzog Papers

MASSACHUSETTS

Boston City Archives, Hyde Park
    A Manual for the Use of Overseers of the Poor in the City of Boston,
        Boston: J. E. Farwell and Co., 1866.
    Records of the Mayor and the Board of Alderman of the City of Boston
    Reports of the Committee of Relief for Soldiers' Families
Boston Police Department Central Supply (and Archives), Hyde Park
    Watch House Records
Massachusetts Historical Society, Boston
    Daily Admissions Records, City Temporary Home, 1862–64
Massachusetts Judicial Archives, Worcester
    Municipality of Boston, Lower Court Records
Massachusetts State Archives, Dorchester
    9th Regiment Records
    Massachusetts State Almshouse Records, Tewksbury State Hospital
Massachusetts Statehouse Archives
    Massachusetts State Laws
National Archives and Records Administration, New England, Waltham
    Watertown Arsenal Records

A History of Watertown Arsenal, 1816–1967, Army Materials and Mechanics Research Center, 1977.

NEW YORK

New York State Archives, Albany
Governors' Papers
Records of the Adjutant General

PENNSYLVANIA

Delaware County Historical Society, Media
Eddystone Explosion File
Historical Society of Pennsylvania, Philadelphia
George Cadwalader Papers, Civilian Letters Folder
Ladies' Union Association Papers
Philadelphia Female Anti-Slavery Society Minutes
Historical Society of Western Pennsylvania, Pittsburgh
Allegheny Arsenal Records
Library Company of Philadelphia
Song Sheet Collection
Luzerne County Historical Society, Wilkes-Barre
National Archives and Records Administration, Mid-Atlantic, Philadelphia
Allegheny Arsenal Collection (RG 92)
Schuylkill Arsenal Letters Received (RG 92)
Pennsylvania Historical and Museum Commission, Harrisburg
Papers of Governor Andrew Curtin
Records of the Adjutant General (RG 19.29)
Damage Claim Applications (RG 2.69)
Bucks County Board of County Commissioners (MG 4)
Mifflin County Relief to Families of Civil War Soldiers (MG 4)
Philadelphia County Archives, Philadelphia
"Prostitutes Register in the Female Register of the Almshouse," 1861–63,
Records of the Guardians of the Poor

WASHINGTON, D.C.

National Archives and Records Administration
Investigation into the Mismanagement of the Watertown Arsenal (RG 92)
Schuylkill Arsenal Petitions (RG 92)

Newspapers

Adams County (Pa.) Sentinel
Baltimore Sun

Chicago Tribune
Christian Recorder (Philadelphia)

Cincinnati Daily Gazette

Congressional Globe

Daily Columbus (Ga.) Enquirer

Elevator (San Francisco)

Fincher's Trades' Review
   (Philadelphia)

Frank Leslie's Illustrated Newspaper

Gettysburg Compiler

Harper's Weekly

Indianapolis Daily Sentinel

Lowell (Mass.) Daily Courier

Luzerne (Pa.) Union

National Antislavery Standard

New Orleans Tribune

New York Herald

New York Times

New York Tribune

North American and
   U.S. Gazette (Philadelphia)

Pacific Appeal (San Francisco)

Philadelphia Inquirer

Philadelphia Sunday Dispatch

Pittsburgh Gazette

Pittsburgh Gazette Times

Pittsburgh Post

Pittston (Pa.) Gazette

United States Sanitary
   Commission Bulletin

Washington (D.C.) Star

Official Documents

Laws of the General Assembly of the State of Pennsylvania. Harrisburg, Pa.: Singerly and Myers State Printers, 1867.

U.S. War Department. The War of the Rebellion: A Compilation of the Official Records of the Union and Confederate Armies. 128 vols. Washington: Government Printing Office, 1880-1901.

Wallace, Henry E., ed. Philadelphia Reports. Vol. 6: 1865–1868. Philadelphia: J. B. Hunter, 1870.

Databases and Web-based Collections

African American Newspapers: The Nineteenth Century, Accessible Archives, <http://www.accessible.com/accessible/>

America's Historical Newspapers, 1960–1922 (Readex)

Civil War Manuscripts Project, Connecticut Historical Society, <http://www.chs.org/kcwmp/cwc.htm>

1860 and 1870 U.S. Federal Census, Census and Voter Lists, Ancestry.com, <http://www.ancestry.com/>

Newspaper Clips (1860–69), Congressional Cemetery (Washington, D.C.), <http://www.congressionalcemetery.org>

U.S. Federal Census, 1790–1930, HeritageQuest, <http://www.heritagequestonline/hqoweb/library/do/index>

Valley of the Shadow Archives, <http://valley.vcdh.virginia.edu/>

Published Primary Sources

Adams, Emma Sellew. "A Remembrance of the Boston Draft Riot." *Magazine of History.* 10 (July 1909): 37–40.

Controllers of the Public Schools. *Annual Report of the Controllers of the Public Schools of the City and County of Philadelphia, By First School District of the State of Pennsylvania.* Vol. 49. Philadelphia: Board of Controllers, 1868.

Cross, Andrew B. *The War, Battle of Gettysburg, and the Christian Commission.* Baltimore: n.p., 1865.

Davis, Rebecca Harding. "Bits of Gossip [1904]." In *Rebecca Harding Davis: Writing Cultural Autobiography,* edited by Janice Milner Lasseter and Sharon M. Harris, 23–130. Nashville, Tenn.: Vanderbilt University Press, 2001.

Johannes Schwalm Historical Association. *Johannes Schwalm, the Hessian.* Lyndhurst, Ohio: Johannes Schwalm Historical Association, 1976.

Kirkland, Caroline. "A Few Words in Behalf of the Loyal Women of the United States, by One of Themselves." New York: William C. Bryant, Loyal Publication Society, no. 10, 1863.

Livermore, Mary. *My Story of the War.* 1889. Reprint, New York: Arno Press, 1972.

———. "Western Scenes, No. 2: Women in the Harvest Fields." *United States Sanitary Commission Bulletin* 1, no. 12 (April 15, 1864): 368–70.

Newton, Isaac. "Report of the Commissioner of Agriculture." Washington: Government Printing Office, 1863.

Parsons, Emily Elizabeth. *Memoir of Emily Elizabeth Parsons.* Boston: Little, Brown, 1880.

Sanborn, Frank. *Massachusetts Board of State Charities' Special Report on Prison and Prison Discipline.* Boston: Wright and Potter, 1865.

Sanger, William. *The History of Prostitution: Its Extent, Causes, and Effects Throughout the World.* New York: Harper and Brothers, 1858.

Schouler, William. *History of Massachusetts in the Civil War.* Vol. 1. Boston: E. P. Dutton, 1868–71.

Speirs, Frederic W. *The Street Railway System of Philadelphia: Its History and Present Condition.* Baltimore: Johns Hopkins Press, 1897.

Stanton, Elizabeth Cady, Susan B. Anthony, and Matilda Joslyn Gage. *A History of Woman Suffrage.* New York: Fowler and Wells, 1881.

Still, William. *A Brief Narrative of the Struggle for the Rights of the Colored People of Philadelphia.* Philadelphia: Merrihew and Sons, 1867.

———. *Underground Railroad, a Record of Facts, Authentic Narratives, Letters, &C., Narrating the Hardships, Hair-Breadth Escapes, and Death Struggles of the Slaves in Their Efforts for Freedom.* Philadelphia: Porter & Coates, 1872.

Trumbull, Henry Clay. *War Memories of an Army Chaplain.* New York: Charles Scribner's Sons, 1898.

Union League of Philadelphia. *Chronicle of the Union League.* Philadelphia: Union League of Philadelphia, 1902.

Wightman, Stillman K. "'A Father's Journey,' March 1865." In *From Antietam to Fort Fisher: The Civil War Letters of Edward King Wightman,* edited by Edward G. Longacre, 230–46. Cranbury, N.J.: Fairleigh Dickinson University Press, 1985.

Secondary Sources

Abbott, Edith. "The Civil War and the Crime Wave of 1865–1870." *Social Service Review* 1 (1927): 219–22.

Allport, Gordon W., and Leo Joseph Postman. *The Psychology of Rumor.* New York: Henry Holt, 1947.

Attie, Jeannie. *Patriotic Toil: Northern Women and the American Civil War.* Ithaca: Cornell University Press, 1998.

Bacon, Margaret Hope. *But One Race: The Life of Robert Purvis.* Albany: State University of New York Press, 2007.

Barber, E. Susan, and Charles Ritter. "'physical abuse . . . and rough handling:' Race, Gender, and Sexual Justice in the Occupied South." In *Occupied Women: Re-envisioning the Field of Battle in the American Civil War,* edited by LeeAnn Whites and Alecia Long, n.p. Baton Rouge: Louisiana State University Press, 2009.

Barton, William. *A Beautiful Blunder: The True Story of Lincoln's Letter to Mrs. Lydia A. Bixby.* Indianapolis: Bobbs-Merrill, 1926.

Basler, Roy P. "And for His Widow and His Orphan." *The Quarterly Journal of the Library of Congress* 27, no. 4 (1970): 291–94.

Bercaw, Nancy. *Gendered Freedoms: Race, Rights, and the Politics of Household in the Delta, 1861–1875.* Gainesville: University of Florida Press, 2003.

Berlin, Ira, Thavolia Glymph, Steven F. Miller, Joseph P. Reidy, Leslie S. Rowland, and Julie Saville, eds. *The Wartime Genesis of Free Labor: The Lower South.* Vol. 3 of *Freedom: A Documentary History of Emancipation, 1861–1867.* Cambridge, U.K.: Cambridge University Press, 1991.

Bernstein, Iver. *The New York City Draft Riots: Their Significance for American Society and Politics in the Age of the Civil War.* New York: Oxford University Press, 1997.

Biddle, Daniel, and Murray Dubin. "Octavius v. Catto." *Philadelphia Inquirer Magazine,* July 6, 2003, 8–20.

Boritt, Gabor. *The Gettysburg Gospel: The Lincoln Speech That Nobody Knows.* New York: Simon & Schuster, 2006.

Brands, H. W. *Masters of Enterprises: Giants of American Business from John Jacob Astor and J. P. Morgan to Bill Gates and Oprah Winfrey.* New York: Free Press, 1999.

Braukman, Stacy Lorraine, and Michael Ross. "Married Women's Property and Male Coercion: United States Courts and the Privy Examination, 1864–1887." *Journal of Women's History* 12, no. 2 (Summer 2000): 57–80.

Bremner, Robert. *The Public Good: Philanthropy and Welfare in the Civil War Era.* New York: Knopf, 1980.

Broussard, Albert. *Black San Francisco: The Struggle for Racial Equality.* Lawrence: University Press of Kansas, 1993.

Brown, Thomas. *The Public Art of Civil War Commemoration: A Brief History with Documents.* Boston: Bedford/St. Martin's Press, 2004.

Bullard, F. Lauriston. *Abraham Lincoln and the Widow Bixby.* New Brunswick, N.J.: Rutgers University Press, 1946.

Butler, Judith. *Gender Trouble: Feminism and the Subversion of Identity.* New York: Routledge, 1990.

Bynum, Victoria E. *Unruly Women: The Politics of Social and Sexual Control in the Old South.* Chapel Hill: University of North Carolina Press, 1992.

Camp, Stephanie. *Closer to Freedom: Enslaved Women and Everyday Resistance in the Plantation South.* Chapel Hill: University of North Carolina Press, 2004.

Campbell, Jacqueline Glass. *When Sherman Marched North from the Sea: Resistance on the Confederate Home Front.* Chapel Hill: University of North Carolina Press, 2003.

Carnprobst, John. "'Ye Know Not What Hour Your Lord Doth Come:' Tragedy at the U.S. Allegheny Arsenal." *Blue and Gray*, August–September 1985, 28–43.

Cashin, Joan E. "Deserters, Civilians, and Draft Resistance in the North." In *The War Was You and Me: Civilians in the American Civil War*, edited by Joan Cashin, 262–85. Princeton, N.J.: Princeton University Press, 2002.

Chessen, Michael. "Harlots or Heroines? A New Look at the Richmond Bread Riot." *Virginia Magazine of History and Biography* 92, no. 2 (April 1984): 131–75.

Clinton, Catherine. *Tara Revisited: Women, War, and the Plantation Legend.* New York: Abbeville Press, 1995.

Clinton, Catherine, and Nina Silber, eds. *Divided Houses: Gender and the Civil War.* New York: Oxford University Press, 1992.

Cohen, Patricia Cline. "Safety and Danger: Women in American Public Transport, 1750–1850." In *Gendered Domains: Rethinking Public and Private in Women's History*, edited by Dorothy O. Helly and Susan Reverby, 109–22. Ithaca, N.Y.: Cornell University Press, 1987.

Collins, Patricia Hill. *Black Feminist Thought: Knowledge, Consciousness, and the Politics of Empowerment.* New York: Routledge, 1991.

Cook, Adrian. *The Armies of the Streets: The New York City Draft Riots of 1863.* Lexington: University Press of Kentucky, 1974.

Creighton, Margaret. *Colors of Courage: Gettysburg's Forgotten History, Immigrants, Women, and African Americans in the Civil War's Defining Battle.* New York: Basic Books, 2005.

Dabney, Wendell P. *Cincinnati's Colored Citizens: Historical, Sociological and Biographical*. New York: Negro Universities Press, 1970.

Daniels, Douglas Henry. *Pioneer Urbanites: A Social and Cultural History of Black San Francisco*. Philadelphia: Temple University Press, 1980.

Domosh, Mona, and Joni Seager. *Putting Women in Place: Feminist Geographers Make Sense of the World*. New York: Guilford Press, 2001.

Donald, David Herbert. *Lincoln*. New York: Touchstone, 1996.

Dorsey, Bruce. *Reforming Men and Women: Gender in the Antebellum City*. Ithaca, N.Y.: Cornell University Press, 2002.

Douglas, Mary. *Purity and Danger: An Analysis of Concepts of Pollution and Taboo*. New York: Frederick A. Praeger, 1966.

Dublin, Thomas. *Women at Work: The Transformation of Work and Community in Lowell, Massachusetts, 1826–1860*. New York: Columbia University Press, 1979.

Edwards, Laura. *Scarlett Doesn't Live Here Anymore: Southern Women in the Civil War Era*. Urbana: University of Illinois Press, 2000.

Emerson, Jason. "America's Most Famous Letter." *American Heritage*, February/March 2006, 41–47.

Engerman, Stanley. "The Economic Impact of the Civil War." *Explorations in Entrepreneurial History* 3, no. 3 (1966): 176–99.

Engerman, Stanley, and J. Matthew Gallman. "The Civil War Economy: A Modern View." In *On the Road to Total War: The American Civil War and the German Wars of Unification, 1861–1871*, edited by Förster Stig and Jörg Nagler, 217–48. New York: Cambridge University Press, 1997.

Ericson, Christina. "'The World Will Little Note nor Long Remember:' Gender Analysis of Civilian Responses to the Battle of Gettysburg." In *Making and Remaking Pennsylvania's Civil War*, edited by William Blair and William Pencak, 81–101. University Park: Pennsylvania State University Press, 2001.

Faust, Drew. *This Republic of Suffering: Death and the American Civil War*. New York: Alfred A. Knopf, 2008.

———. "The Civil War Soldier and the Art of Dying." *Journal of Southern History* 67, no. 1 (2001): 3–40.

———. *Mothers of Invention: Women of the Slaveholding South in the American Civil War New York*. 1996. Reprint, New York: Vintage, 1996.

Foner, Eric. *Free Soil, Free Labor, Free Men: The Ideology of the Republican Party before the Civil War*. New York: Oxford University Press, 1970.

Foner, Philip S. *Women and the American Labor Movement, from Colonial Times to the Eve of World War I*. New York: Free Press, 1979.

———. "The Battle to End Discrimination against Negroes on Philadelphia Street Cars: (Part I) Background and Beginning of the Battle." *Pennsylvania History* 40, no. 3 (1973): 261–92.

———. "The Battle to End Discrimination against Negroes on Philadelphia Street Cars: (Part II) The Victory." *Pennsylvania History* 40, no. 4 (1973): 368–72.

Forbes, Ella. *African-American Women During the Civil War.* New York: Garland Publishing, 1998.

Frank, Lisa Tendrich, ed. *Women in the Civil War.* 2 vols. Santa Barbara, Calif.: ABC-CLIO, 2008.

Furguson, Ernest. *Freedom Rising: Washington in the Civil War.* New York: Alfred A. Knopf, 2004.

Gallagher, Gary. *The Confederate War.* Cambridge: Harvard University Press, 1997.

Gallman, J. Matthew. *America's Joan of Arc: The Life of Anna Elizabeth Dickinson.* New York: Oxford University Press, 2006.

———. *Mastering Wartime: A Social History of Philadelphia During the Civil War.* Philadelphia: University of Pennsylvania Press, 1990.

Giesberg, Judith Ann. "'A Little Starvation is Good:' The 40th Congress and the Post-War Occupied South." In *Occupied Women: Re-envisioning the Field of Battle in the American Civil War,* edited by LeeAnn Whites and Alecia Long, n.p. Baton Rouge: Louisiana State University Press, 2009.

———. "'Lawless and Unprincipled': Women in Boston's Civil War Draft Riot." In *Boston's Histories: Essays in Honor of Thomas O'Connor,* edited by David Quigley and James O'Toole, 71–91. Boston: Northeastern University Press, 2004.

———. *Civil War Sisterhood: The United States Sanitary Commission and Women's Reform in Transition.* Boston: Northeastern University Press, 2000.

Ginzberg, Lori. *Women and the Work of Benevolence: Morality, Politics, and Class in the Nineteenth-Century United States.* New Haven: Yale University Press, 1990.

Glymph, Thavolia. "The Civil War Era." In *A Companion to American Women's History,* edited by Nancy A. Hewitt, 167–92. Oxford, U.K.: Blackwell Publishers, 2002.

Greene, Lorenzo, Gary Kremer, and Anthony Holland. *Missouri's Black Heritage.* Columbia: University of Missouri Press, 1993.

Hahn, Steven. *A Nation Under Our Feet: Black Political Struggles in the Rural South from Slavery to the Great Migration.* Cambridge: Harvard University Press, 2003.

Harris, Leslie. *In the Shadow of Slavery: African Americans in New York City, 1626–1863.* Chicago: University of Chicago Press, 2003.

Headley, Joel Tyler. *The Great Riots of New York, 1712–1873.* Indianapolis: Bobbs-Merrill, 1970.

Higginbotham, Evelyn Brooks. *Righteous Discontent: The Women's Movement in the Black Baptist Church.* Cambridge: Harvard University Press, 1993.

Holmes, Amy E. "Widows and the Civil War Pension System." In *Toward a Social History of the Civil War,* edited by Maris Vinovskis, 171–95. New York: Cambridge University Press, 1990.

Holzer, Harold. "As Bad as She Could Be: Who Was the Widow Bixby?" *American Heritage,* February/March 2006, 44–45.

Hoogenboom, Ari, and Philip S. Klein. *A History of Pennsylvania.* New York: McGraw-Hill, 1973.

Hudson, Lynn. *"Mammy Pleasant": A Black Entrepreneur in Nineteenth-Century San Francisco.* Urbana: University of Illinois Press, 2003.

Humez, Jean. *Harriet Tubman: The Life and the Life Stories.* Madison: University of Wisconsin Press, 2003.

Hyman, Harold. *Era of the Oath: Loyalty Tests During the Civil War and Reconstruction.* Philadelphia: University of Pennsylvania Press, 1954.

Jeffrey, Julie Roy. *Frontier Women: The Trans-Mississippi West, 1840–1880.* New York: Hill and Wang, 1979.

Jensen, Joan. *Loosening the Bonds: Mid-Atlantic Farm Women, 1750–1850.* New Haven: Yale University Press, 1986.

Jones, James Boyd. "A Tale of Two Cities: The Hidden Battle against Venereal Disease among Union Soldiers in the Far West, 1861–1865." *Civil War History* 31, no. 3 (1985): 257–69.

Kelley, Robin D. G. "'We Are Not What We Seem': Rethinking Black Working-Class Opposition in the Jim Crow South." *Journal of American History* 80, no. 1 (1993): 75–112.

Kerber, Linda. *No Constitutional Right to Be Ladies: Women and the Obligations of Citizenship.* New York: Hill and Wang, 1998.

Laderman, Gary. *Sacred Remains: American Attitudes toward Death, 1799–1883.* New Haven: Yale University Press, 1996.

Lebsock, Suzanne. *The Free Women of Petersburg: Status and Culture in a Southern Town, 1784–1860.* New York: W. W. Norton, 1985.

———. "Radical Reconstruction and the Property Rights of Southern Women." *Journal of Southern History* 43, no. 2 (1977): 195–216.

Lefebvre, Henri. *The Production of Space.* Translated by Donald Nicholson-Smith. Cambridge: Blackwell, 1991.

Leonard, Elizabeth. *All the Daring of the Soldier: Women of the Civil War Armies.* New York: W. W. Norton, 1999.

———. *Yankee Women: Gender Battles in the Civil War.* New York: W. W. Norton, 1994.

Long, Lisa. *Rehabilitating Bodies: Health, History, and the American Civil War.* Philadelphia: University of Pennsylvania Press, 2005.

McClelland, Keith. "Time to Work, Time to Live: Some Aspects of Work and Re-Formation of Class in Britain, 1850–1880." In *The Historical Meanings of Work,* edited by Patrick Joyce, 180–209. New York: Cambridge University Press, 1987.

McClintock, Megan. "Civil War Pensions and the Reconstruction of Union Families." *Journal of American History* 83, no. 2 (1996): 471–79.

McCurry, Sally Ann. *Transforming Rural Life: Dairying Families and Agricultural Change, 1820–1885.* Baltimore: Johns Hopkins University Press, 1995.

McCurry, Stephanie. "Citizens, Soldiers' Wives, and 'Hiley Hope up' Slaves: The Problem of Political Obligation in the Civil War South." In *Gender and the Southern Body Politic*, edited by Nancy Bercaw, 95–124. Jackson: University of Mississippi Press, 2000.

McPherson, James. *For Cause and Comrades: Why Men Fought in the Civil War.* New York: Oxford University Press, 1997.

———. *Battle Cry of Freedom: The Civil War Era.* New York: Oxford University Press, 1988.

Miller, Richard F. "For His Wife, His Widow, and His Orphan: Massachusetts and Family Aid During the Civil War." *Massachusetts Historical Review* 6 (2004): 71–106.

Mitchell, Reid. *The Vacant Chair: The Northern Soldier Leaves Home.* New York: Oxford University Press, 1992.

Montgomery, David. *Beyond Equality: Labor and the Radical Republicans, 1862–1872.* New York: Knopf, 1967.

Neely, Mark. "Was the Civil War a Total War?" In *On the Road to Total War: The American Civil War and the German Wars of Unification, 1861–1871*, edited by Stig Förster and Jörg Nagler, 29–51. New York: Cambridge University Press, 1997.

Neff, John R. *Honoring the Civil War Dead: Commemoration and the Problem of Reconciliation.* Lawrence: University of Kansas Press, 2005.

Nevins, Allan. *The Emergence of Modern America, 1865–1878.* New York: Macmillan, 1927.

Oates, Stephen B. *A Woman of Valor: Clara Barton and the Civil War.* New York: Free Press, 1994.

Osterud, Mary Gray. *Bonds of Community: The Lives of Farm Women in Nineteenth-Century New York.* Ithaca, N.Y.: Cornell University Press, 1991.

Palladino, Grace. *Another Civil War: Labor, Capital, and the State in the Anthracite Regions of Pennsylvania, 1840–68.* Chicago: University of Illinois Press, 1990.

Paludan, Philip Shaw. *"A People's Contest:" The Union and the Civil War, 1861–1865.* New York: Harper and Row, 1988.

Ramsdell, Charles W. *Behind the Lines in the Southern Confederacy.* New York: Greenwood Press, 1969.

Ransom, Roger L. *Conflict and Compromise: The Political Economy of Slavery, Emancipation, and the American Civil War.* New York: Cambridge University Press, 1989.

Riley, Glenda. *Women and Indians on the Frontier, 1825–1915.* Albuquerque: University of New Mexico Press, 1984.

Rose, Sonya. *Limited Livelihoods: Gender and Class in Nineteenth-Century England.* Berkeley: University of California Press, 1992.

Ross, Ellen. "'Not the Sort That Would Sit on the Doorstep:' Respectability in

Pre–World War I London Neighborhoods." *International Labor and Working Class History* 27 (Spring 1985): 39–59.

Ryan, Mary P. *Women in Public: Between Banners and Ballots, 1825–1880.* Baltimore: Johns Hopkins University Press, 1990.

Sanders, Charles W., Jr. *While in the Hands of the Enemy: Military Prisons of the Civil War.* Baton Rouge: Louisiana State University, 2005.

Schultz, Jane. *Women at the Front: Hospital Workers.* Chapel Hill: University of North Carolina Press, 2004.

Schwalm, Leslie. "Between Slavery and Freedom: African-American Women in the Slave South." In *Occupied Women: Re-envisioning the Field of Battle in the American Civil War*, edited by LeeAnn Whites and Alecia Long, n.p. Baton Rouge: Louisiana State University Press, 2009.

———. *A Hard Fight for We: Women's Transition from Slavery to Freedom.* Champaign: University of Illinois Press, 1997.

Scott, James C. *Domination and the Arts of Resistance: Hidden Transcripts.* New Haven: Yale University Press, 1990.

Silber, Nina. *Daughters of the Union: Northern Women Fight the Civil War.* Cambridge: Harvard University Press, 2005.

Silber, Nina, and Mary Beth Sievens, eds. *Yankee Correspondence: Civil War Letters between New England Soldiers and the Home Front.* Charlottesville: University Press of Virginia, 1996.

Sklar, Kathryn Kish, ed. *Women's Rights Emerges within the Antislavery Movement, 1830–1870.* Boston: Bedford/St. Martin's Press, 2000.

Skocpol, Theda. *Protecting Soldiers and Mothers: The Political Origins of Social Policy in the United States.* Cambridge: Belknap Press of Harvard University Press, 1992.

Stanley, Amy Dru. *From Bondage to Contract: Wage Labor, Marriage, and the Market in the Age of Slave Emancipation.* Cambridge, U.K.: Cambridge University Press, 1998.

Stanley, Gerald. "Civil War Politics in California." *Southern California Quarterly* 64, no. 2 (1982): 115–28.

Stansell, Christine. "The Origins of the Sweatshop: Women and Early Industrialization in New York City." In *Working-Class America: Essays on Labor, Community, and American Society*, edited by Michael H. Frisch and Daniel J. Walkowitz, 78–103. Urbana: University of Illinois Press, 1983.

Sweet, Timothy. *Traces of War: Poetry, Photography, and the Crisis of the Union.* Baltimore: Johns Hopkins University Press, 1990.

Tap, Bruce. *Over Lincoln's Shoulder: The Committee on the Conduct of the War.* Lawrence: University Press of Kansas, 1998.

Turner, George Edgar. *Victory Rode the Rails: The Strategic Place of the Railroads in the Civil War.* Lincoln: University of Nebraska Press, 1992.

Venet, Wendy Hamand. *A Strong-Minded Woman: The Life of Mary Livermore.* Amherst: University of Massachusetts Press, 2005.

———. *Neither Ballots nor Bullets: Women Abolitionists and the Civil War.* Charlottesville: University Press of Virginia, 1991.

Vinovskis, Maris. "Have Social Historians Lost the Civil War?" In *Toward a Social History of the American Civil War,* edited by Maris Vinovskis, 1–30. New York: Cambridge University Press, 1990.

Weigley, Russell F. *A Great Civil War: A Military and Political History, 1861–1865.* Bloomington: Indiana University Press, 2000.

———. *Philadelphia: A 300-Year History.* New York: W. W. Norton, 1982.

Weiner, Marli. "Rural Women." In *A Companion to American Women's History,* edited by Nancy A. Hewitt, 150–66. Oxford, U.K.: Blackwell Publishers, 2002.

Welke, Barbara. *Recasting American Liberty: Gender, Race, Law, and the Railroad Revolution, 1865–1920.* New York: Cambridge University Press, 2001.

Whites, LeeAnn. *Gender Matters: Civil War, Reconstruction, and the Making of the New South.* New York: Palgrave Macmillan, 2005.

Wiebe, Robert. *The Search for Order, 1877–1920.* New York: Hill and Wang, 1967.

Wilson, Mark R. *The Business of Civil War: Military Mobilization and the State, 1861–1865.* Baltimore: Johns Hopkins University Press, 2006.

Woodworth, Steven E. *Beneath a Northern Sky: A Short History of the Gettysburg Campaign.* Wilmington, Del.: Scholarly Resources, 2003.

Woollacott, Angela. *On Her Their Lives Depend: Munitions Workers in the Great War.* Berkeley: University of California Press, 1994.

Wudarczyk, James. *Pittsburgh's Forgotten Allegheny Arsenal.* Apollo, Pa.: Closson Press, 1999.

———. *Notes and Documents Relating to Pittsburgh's Allegheny Arsenal.* Pittsburgh, 1997.

Yellin, Jean Fagan. *The Abolitionist Sisterhood: Women's Political Culture in Antebellum America.* Ithaca, N.Y.: Cornell University Press, 1994.

———. *Women and Sisters: The Antislavery Feminists in American Culture.* New Haven: Yale University Press, 1989.

Zaeske, Susan. *Signatures of Citizenship: Petitioning, Antislavery, and Women's Political Identity.* Chapel Hill: University of North Carolina Press, 2003.

Unpublished Theses

Carlisle, Marcia Roberta. "Prostitutes and Their Reformers in Nineteenth-Century Philadelphia." Ph.D. diss., Rutgers University, 1982.

Mantilla, Jeanette Davis. "'Hush, Hush, Miss Charlotte': A Quarter-Century of Civil Rights Activism by the Black Community of San Francisco, 1850–1875." Ph.D. diss, Ohio State University, 2000.

Seidman, Rachel Filene. "Beyond Sacrifice: Women and Politics on the Pennsylvania Homefront During the Civil War." Ph.D. diss, Yale University, 1995.

Wilson, Russell Mark. "The Business of the Civil War: Military Enterprise, the State, and Political Economy in the United States, 1850–1880." Ph.D. diss, University of Chicago, 2002.

INDEX

Abolitionism, 105–6, 115–16; and petitions, 79–80

Adams, Anna, 107–8, 199–200 (n. 63)

Adams County, Pa., 29–30, 37

African American women: disguises of, 6; in history, 11; streetcar battles of, 16, 92–118 passim; visiting USCT in camp, 65; and loyalty, 122; and draft riots, 128; and sewing work, 138–39; and freedom of movement, 164; politics of, 175; as cartridge formers at the Allegheny Arsenal, 189 (n. 6). *See also* Veils

Aid to soldiers' wives/families: from state, 2, 5, 6, 9–10, 31–33, 36, 42, 45–67 passim, 185 (n. 5); from soldiers' aid societies, 3–4, 40; and relief money, 22, 30, 36, 45, 120, 122, 172, 177; and local relief boards, 31–33; middle-class attitudes toward, 144

Allison, Joseph, 95, 111

Almshouses, 32, 44, 47, 51, 57–67, 59 (ill.), 60 (ill.), 188 (n. 47)

Anderson, Ellen, 109–10

Andrew, Governor John: and the letter to Bixby, 2–3; and requests for aid, 45, 49, 67, 143; and response to draft riot, 134; and state aid, 185 (n. 5)

Arsenals, U.S. Army: women at, 6, 9, 67, 76–78, 145, 163; Schuylkill, 65, 119–23, 137–41; and Allegheny explosion, 68–72, 71 (ill.), 73–75, 78, 86–87, 166–71, 167 (ill.), 176; and Washington explosion, 72, 78, 89–91, 90 (ill.), 176, 192 (n. 34), 193 (n. 47), 194 (n. 58), 194–95 (n. 64), 195 (nn. 65–70); Watertown, 75–89, 77 (ill.), 176, 191–92 (n. 32); and Eddystone Explosion, 164–66, 190 (n. 16), 211 (n. 14); African American women at, 189 (n. 6), 190 (n. 16), 193 (nn. 47–48), 211 (n. 13)

Barton, Clara, 11, 173, 209–10 (n. 72), 211 (n. 20)

Battlefield burials, 146, 153–54, 159

Bixby, Lydia, 1–7, 10, 16, 171–73, 175, 180 (n. 8)

Blackwell, Elizabeth, 11

Bodies: retrieval of dead soldiers, 5, 6, 16, 143–62 passim, 209 (n. 62); women's, 68–91 passim; Mary Douglas on, 14, 71–72, 210 (n. 5); as sites of resistance, 92–118 passim, 145; working class bodies, 97–98; African American women's bodily integrity, 101, 111, 116–17; black men's bodies, 132; women's bodies at Eddystone explosion, 164–65

Booth, Mary, 159–60, 175

Boston, 1–5, 49, 53, 54–56, 61, 65, 143; and lack of monuments, 173

Bounties, 21, 31, 35, 45, 49–50, 177

Brown, Charlotte, 6, 92–94, 98–105, 104 (ill.), 108–11, 113, 115–18, 119, 195–96 (n. 2), 197 (n. 32)

Butler, Benjamin, 123, 135, 136, 202 (n. 10)

Confederate invasion of Gettysburg, 183 (n. 35); lampooned, 201 (n. 4)

Miles, Mary Ann, 107, 199–200 (n. 63)

Mills, Amelia, 107–8, 114

Modern war, 13, 165, 177, 180–81 (n. 13)

Monuments to women: Lydia Bixby's grave, 3 (ill.), 164–75, 211 (n. 20); monument gap, 16, 173–75; Allegheny plaques, 69, 168–71, 170 (ill.), 174; to southern mothers, 171, 172 (ill.)

Mothers of soldiers: in poetry and song, 8–9, 161 (ill.), 162; and displacement, 57–63; and confinement, 58; and retrieval of bodies, 143–62 passim; viewing photographs, 149; southern, 171, 172 (ill.) *See also* Bixby, Lydia; Children; McCormack, Mrs.

Mott, Lucretia, 105

Movement of women: Lydia Bixby, 2, 171–73; and everyday politics, 6–7, 9–10; rural, 22, 44; as wartime refugees, 49; and confinement in childbirth, 58; enlistment and women's displacement, 60–63; freedom of, 92–118 passim; and pollution fears, 97, 154; traveling to retrieve bodies, 143–62 passim; and monuments, 171

National Women's Loyal League, 124–27

Newton, Isaac, 17–18, 40–41

New York, 15, 49, 54, 155; and streetcar segregation, 95, 96, 100, 106, 108, 109; wartime arsenal, 120; National Women's Loyal League, 124; Rally of the Democracy, 126–27; draft riots, 127–30, 132–36; union of seamstresses, 140; Alexander Gardner's Antietam exhibit in, 149

New York Times, 149, 160

Nursing/nurses, 6, 10, 20, 40, 53; and soldier death, 145–46, 161–62; monuments to, 173; African American,

200–201 (n. 78); and traveling, 208 (n. 48)

O'Brien, Henry, 128, 129 (ill.)

O'Connell, Maurice, 143–44, 153, 160

Pacific Appeal: and black activism, 99; and streetcar ejections, 100, 105

Palmer, Mrs., 107

Pensions, 37, 151, 185–86 (n. 11), 186 (n. 18); pension applications, 1

Petitions, 14, 192 (nn. 37–38); of cartridge formers, 70, 79–81, 83–84; Philadelphia streetcar, 97–98, 106, 198 (n. 43); of seamstresses, 119–20, 122–23, 137–40, 205 (n. 68)

Philadelphia, 22, 49, 51, 57, 63, 65; and streetcar segregation, 6, 16, 92–118 passim, 145; and women's wartime travel, 147, 151, 152, 153, 156. *See also* Arsenals, U.S. Army: Schuylkill

Photography, battlefield, 148–50

Pittsburgh, 51, 68–70, 73, 87–88; and Chester explosion, 164–65; and remembering Allegheny blast, 164–71

Pittsburgh Gazette, 68–69, 87

Pittsburgh Gazette Times, 166

Pittston Gazette, 133–34

Pleasant, Mammy, 94, 114–15, 116 (ill.), 175

Police officers: and streetcar segregation, 93, 109–10, 113; and draft riots, 129, 135–36

Politics of the street/everyday life, 5, 6, 9–10, 12, 16, 43–44, 175–77; and James Scott on infrapolitics, 14, 175, 177, 186 (n. 16); public grieving as, 16, 145; rural women's, 34, 36; and streetcar segregation, 94–96, 107, 112–13, 116–17; draft riots as, 127–36; widows and, 160, 175

Potter, Amanda, 159, 160

CPSIA information can be obtained
at www.ICGtesting.com
Printed in the USA
LVOW04s1044220817
545935LV00010B/137/P